MARKET SEGMENTATION

D0496218

MARKET
SEGMENTATION

HOW TO DO IT
HOW TO PROFIT FROM IT

Second edition

Malcolm McDonald and Ian Dunbar

© Malcolm McDonald and Ian Dunbar 1998
Foreword © Sir Colin Marshall 1998

All rights reserved. No reproduction, copy or transmission of
this publication may be made without written permission.

No paragraph of this publication may be reproduced, copied
or transmitted save with written permission or in accordance
with the provisions of the Copyright, Designs and Patents
Act 1988, or under the terms of any licence permitting limited
copying issued by the Copyright Licensing Agency, 90 Tottenham
Court Road, London W1P 9HE.

Any person who does any unauthorised act in relation to
this publication may be liable to criminal prosecution and
civil claims for damages.

The authors have asserted their right to be identified
as the authors of this work in accordance with
the Copyright, Designs and Patents Act 1988.

First edition 1995
Second edition 1998
Published by
MACMILLAN PRESS LTD
Houndmills, Basingstoke, Hampshire RG21 6XS
and London
Companies and representatives
throughout the world

ISBN 0–333–733703 hardcover
ISBN 0–333–73369X paperback

A catalogue record for this book is available
from the British Library.

This book is printed on paper suitable for recycling and
made from fully managed and sustained forest sources.

10 9   8   7   6   5   4   3   2   1
07 06 05 04 03 02 01 00 99 98

Editing and origination by
Aardvark Editorial, Mendham, Suffolk

Printed in Great Britain by
Antony Rowe Ltd
Chippenham, Wiltshire

Contents

List of Figures

List of Tables

Please note:

1

Successful segmentation is the product of a detailed understanding of your market and will therefore take time.

2

Segmentation is appropriate for those markets where it is essential to combine individual customers or consumers into larger buying 'units' to ensure your marketing activity is both cost effective and manageable.

3

The process as presented in this book is aimed primarily at defining segments in terms of the particular marketing mix each requires. Segmentation at higher levels of aggregation is, of course, possible and many of the principles contained in this book would apply, although in a less detailed form.

Foreword

One of the abiding principles of sound business practice is: 'Know your customer; know your market.'

The objective, of course, is to gain competitive advantage by building sustained customer loyalty, with products and services meeting, quite precisely, the demands of closely defined markets.

As markets have become more complex, so has this essentially basic process of market segmentation. It is the view of many that, in both the manufacturing and service sectors, the art of defining target markets rarely progresses beyond the assembly of somewhat dull demographics. The logical conclusion is that, if everybody is doing the same, differential advantage is difficult to attain.

Now, Professor Malcolm McDonald and Ian Dunbar have peeled away the layers of complexity and confusion to produce a step-by-step guide through the difficult terrain of market segmentation. The value of their book to business people everywhere, is that it offers the kind of practical applications needed in today's intensely competitive marketplace.

SIR COLIN MARSHALL
Chairman, British Airways
January 1998

Preface

This book is the result of a painstaking process of research into the practical difficulties that organisations experience in segmenting their markets.

We discovered that most of the academic work in this domain is prescriptive, with virtually no pragmatic guidelines provided to enable managers to make sense of the confusing array of data and information available to them.

So we developed a process, which we tested on some of the best known companies in the world, amending the process until it was sufficiently robust for us to be able to share it with a wider audience. The result was the first edition of this book, then titled *Market Segmentation: A step-by-step approach to creating profitable market segments*.

Since its launch in 1995, the extensive adoption of our market segmentation process has broadened our knowledge base substantially and enabled us to refine the process and identify where more detailed explanations are required. The result is this second edition of the book which, in addition to containing more examples and extended guidelines, also contains a worked-through case study and a series of worksheets for use by the practitioner.

Although the process as presented in this book enables the segmentation practitioner to follow each step manually, the range of information they may need to consider for some markets can become a distraction. Therefore, to enable practitioners to concentrate on the marketing issues they need to address, rather than be diverted by concerns over the amount of information they need to manage, a PC-based package was developed to support the segmentation process. This package, called *Market Segment Master*, the registered trade mark for this process, has also been refined to reflect the process as it now appears in this book. If readers feel that they would like the help of information technology in segmenting their markets, they can obtain details from Professor Malcolm McDonald, at Cranfield University School of Management, Cranfield, Bedford, MK43 0AL, United Kingdom (fax +44 (0)1234 751806), or from Ian Dunbar at *the* Market Segmentation Company, Chandos House, 26 North Street, Brighton, BN1 1EB, United Kingdom (tel +44 (0)1273 746747, fax +44 (0)1273 737981, e-mail *t*MSC@BTinternet.com).

Returning to this book, we would like to stress that it is most definitely a practical book which, if used properly, will result in actionable market segments. To achieve this result will require time and resources. It is not a book just for reading. It is for reading and *doing*, and is best used by a team, rather than by an individual.

We both wish you happy and profitable segmentation!

MALCOLM MCDONALD
IAN DUNBAR
January 1998

USEFUL DEFINITIONS

Benefit

A perceived or stated relationship between a product feature and what a customer gets that they explicitly need (or want). *See also* Differential advantage *and* Feature.

Demographics

Measurable descriptions of a 'population' (consumer and business-to-business).

Differential advantage

A benefit or cluster of benefits offered to a sizeable group of customers which they value (and are willing to pay for) and which they cannot obtain elsewhere. *See also* Benefit *and* Feature.

Experience effect

It is a proven fact that most value-added cost components of a product decline steadily with experience and can be reduced significantly as the scale of operation increases. In turn this cost (and therefore price advantage) is a significant factor in increasing the company's market share.

Feature

A characteristic or property of a product or service such as reliability, price convenience, safety and quality. These features may or may not satisfy customer needs. To the extent that they do, they can be translated into benefits. *See also* Benefit *and* Differential advantage.

Gap

In marketing terms, the difference between a product's present or projected performance and the level sought. Typically, the gaps in marketing management are those relating to return on investment, cash generation or use, return on sales, and market share.

Gap analysis

The process of determining gaps between a product's present or projected performance and the level of performance sought. *See also* Gap.

Geodemographics

Attaching a demographic profile to a specified geographic area. *See* Demographics.

Growth/share matrix

A term synonymous with 'product portfolio' which in essence is a means of displaying graphically the amount of 'experience' or market share a product has and comparing this share with the rate of growth of the relevant market segment. With the matrix, a manager can decide, for example, whether he or she should invest in getting more 'experience' – that is, fighting for bigger market share – or perhaps getting out of the market altogether. These choices are among a number of strategic alternatives available to the manager (strategic in the sense that they not only affect marketing strategy but determine use of capital within the organisation). *See also* Experience effect.

Market   A customer need that can be satisfied by the products or services seen as alternatives.

Market segment   A group of actual or potential customers who can be expected to respond in approximately the same way to a given offer; a finer more detailed breakdown of a market.

Market segmentation   The process of splitting customers, or potential customers, within a market into different groups, or segments, within which customers have the same or similar requirements satisfied by a distinct marketing mix. *See also* Marketing mix. A critical aspect of marketing and one designed to convert product differences into a cost differential that can be maintained over the product's life cycle. *See also* Product life cycle.

Market share   The percentage of the market represented by a firm's sales in relation to total sales. Some marketing theorists argue that the term is misleading since it suggests that the dimensions of the market are known and assumes that the size of the market is represented by the amount of goods sold in it. All that is known, these theorists point out, and correctly, is the volume sold; in actuality, the market may be considerably larger.

Marketing audit   A situational analysis of the company's current marketing capability. *See also* Situational analysis.

Marketing mix   The 'tools' or means available to an organisation to improve the match between benefits sought by customers and those offered by the organisation so as to obtain a differential advantage. Among these tools are product, price, promotion and distribution service. *See also* Differential advantage.

Marketing objectives A statement of the targets or goals to be pursued and achieved within the period covered in the marketing plan. Depending on the scope and orientation of the plan – whether, for example, the plan is designed primarily to spell out short-term marketing intentions or to identify broad business directions and needs – the objectives stated may encompass such important measures of business performance as profit, growth and market share.

Marketing objectives with respect to profit, market share, sales volume, market development or penetration and other broader considerations are sometimes referred to as 'primary' marketing objectives. More commonly, they are referred to as 'strategic' or 'business' objectives since they pertain to the operation of the business as a whole. In turn, objectives set for specific marketing sub-functions or activities are referred to as 'programme' objectives to distinguish them from the broader business or strategic objectives they are meant to serve.

Marketing plan   Contains a mission statement, SWOT (strengths, weaknesses, opportunities and threats) analysis, assumptions, marketing objectives, marketing strategies and programmes. Note that the objectives, strategies and policies are established for each level of the business.

Mission   The chief function of an institution or organisation. In essence it is a vision of what the company is or is striving to become. The basic issue is: 'What is our business and what should it be?' In marketing planning, the mission statement is the starting point in the planning process, since it sets the broad parameters within which marketing objectives are established, strategies developed, and programmes implemented. Some companies, usually those with several operating units or divisions, make a distinction between 'mission' and 'charter'. In these instances, the term 'mission' is used to denote the broader purpose of the organisation as reflected in corporate policies or assigned by the senior management of the company; the term 'charter', in comparison, is used to denote the purpose or reason for being of individual units with prime responsibility for a specific functional or product-marketing area.

Objective   A statement or description of a desired future result that cannot be predicted in advance but which is believed, by those setting the objective, to be achievable through their efforts within a given time period; a quantitative target or goal to be achieved in the future through one's efforts, which can also be used to measure performance. To be of value, objectives should be specific in time and scope and attainable given the financial, technical and human resources available. According to this definition, general statements of hopes or desire are not true 'objectives'. *See also* Marketing objectives.

Planning   The process of predetermining a course or courses of action based on assumptions about future conditions or trends which can be imagined but not predicted with any certainty.

Positioning   The process of selecting, delineating and matching the segment of the market with which a product will be most compatible.

Product   A term used in marketing to denote not only the product itself (its inherent properties and characteristics) but also service, availability, price, and other factors which may be as important in differentiating the product from those of competitors as the inherent characteristics of the product itself. *See also* Marketing mix.

Product life cycle   A term used in marketing to refer to the pattern of growth and decline in sales revenue of a product over time. This pattern is typically divided into stages: introduction, growth, maturity, saturation and decline. With time, competition among firms tends to reduce all products in the market to commodities – products which can only be marginally differentiated from each other – with the result that pioneering companies (those first to enter the market) face the choice of becoming limited volume, high-priced, high-cost speciality producers or high-volume, low-cost producers of standard products.

Product portfolio A theory about the alternative uses of capital by business organisations formulated originally by Bruce Henderson of the Boston Consulting Group, a leading firm in the area of corporate strategy consulting. This theory or approach to marketing strategy formulation has gained wide acceptance among managers of diversified companies, who were first attracted by the intuitively appealing notion that long-run corporate performance is more than the sum of the contributions of individual profit centres or product strategies. Other factors which account for the theory's appeal are: (1) its usefulness in developing specific marketing strategies designed to achieve a balanced mix of products that will produce maximum return from scarce cash and managerial resources; and (2) the fact that the theory employs a simple matrix representation useful in portraying and communicating a product's position in the market place. *See also* Growth/share matrix.

Programme A term used in marketing planning to denote the steps or tasks to be undertaken by marketing, field sales and other functions within an organisation to implement the chosen strategies and to accomplish the objectives set forth in the marketing plan. Typically, descriptions of programmes include a statement of objectives as well as a definition of the persons or units responsible and a schedule for completion of the steps or tasks for which the person or unit is responsible. *See also* Marketing objectives.

Psychographics A consumer's inner feelings and predisposition to behave in certain ways.

Relative market share A firm's share of the market relative to its largest competitor. *See also* Market share.

Resources Broadly speaking, anyone or anything through which something is produced or accomplished; in marketing planning, a term used to denote the unique capabilities or skills that an organisation brings to a market or business problem or opportunity.

Situational analysis The second phase in the marketing planning process (the first consisting of defining the mission and corporate objectives), which reviews the business environment at large (with particular attention to economic, market and competitive aspects) as well as the company's own internal operation. The purpose of the situational analysis is to identify marketing problems and opportunities, both those stemming from the organisation's internal strengths and limitations, and those external to the organisation and caused by changes in economic conditions and trends, competition, customer expectations, industry relations, government regulations and, increasingly, social perceptions and trends. The output of the full analysis is summarised in key point form under the heading SWOT analysis; this summary then becomes part of the marketing plan. The outcome of the situational analysis includes a set of assumptions about future conditions as well as an estimate or forecast of potential market demand during the period covered by the marketing plan. Based on these estimates and assumptions, marketing objectives are established and strategies and a programme formulated.

Socio-economic classification
A classification of individuals according to their level of income and occupation (or that of the head of household).

1 *Preparing for Segmentation*

In this chapter, we discuss how to arrive at a definition of the *market* to be segmented and look at some examples which demonstrate the importance of successful segmentation. The chapter also presents a definition of segmentation before moving on to discuss a framework for looking at how companies currently define and segment their markets, some views on who should be in the segmentation team, the rules and advantages of segmentation, and then provides a summary of the segmentation process contained in this book.

Objective of this book

Market segmentation seems comparatively simple as a concept, yet it is a fact that, particularly in business-to-business marketing as opposed to consumer goods marketing, companies still organise their marketing effort principally around the *products* they make, thereby missing many opportunities for creating competitive advantage. The reason is that segmentation is viewed as being extremely difficult to implement in practice, requiring, as it does, a *market-based* approach.

The problem with segmenting markets according only to the products offered, or the technology type, is that, in most markets, many *different* types of customers buy or use the same products. These different customer types, therefore, often get subsumed under one category. For example, if a mail company organises itself around express packages, or around mail sorting, it is unlikely that the company will ever get to understand fully the real and different needs of, say, universities, banks, advertising agencies, direct mail houses, manufacturing companies, retailers and so on.

However, before jumping to any early segmentation conclusions, reorganising your marketing effort along business classification lines is not necessarily the most creative segmentation structure for your market. The business classification approach could well be ignoring one or more of the following:

- different divisions existing behind the business descriptor, which may have different applications for the product/service you supply. For example, does the advertising and promotions department have the same requirements and specifications for mail services as the sales ledger department?
- the requirements of, say, advertising and promotions departments may well be the same regardless of business type;
- even within a single division of a company, there may well be different applications for the product/service you supply which, in turn, may have different specifications attached to them. This could be associated with differences amongst their own customer base. For example, a decorating contractor buying gloss paint could vary their buying criteria according to:

  - whether it is to be applied to the external or internal woodwork, to a public or private room
  - the different requirements expressed by their own customers;

- segmentation along business classification lines assumes all the companies within the classification employ identical people with identical values. Businesses don't buy anything; it's their employees you have to sell to!

The objective of this book is to provide a logical process by which managers can explore whether there is any potential for new business opportunities as a result of re-examining the way in which they define their market segments. It then moves on to identifying the appropriate objectives and strategies for these segments and how segmentation fits into the marketing plan.

No computer program, let alone a book, however advanced, could ever cover all possible market segmentation outcomes. This particular book does not claim to provide the definitive answer to any organisation's segmentation problems. What it will do is to provide a logical process for you to follow. Above all else, however, it requires you to be creative and flexible in your thinking and asks you not to be hidebound by your current market segmentation definitions.

Defining markets

Market segmentation is easy to understand once an organisation has done it successfully! Examples such as BMW, Castrol GTX, Marks & Spencer, Mars and so on are legendary in the history of marketing. *The problem is how to get there!*

Most business people already understand that there is a direct relationship between relatively high share of any market and high returns on investment, as shown in Figure 1.1.

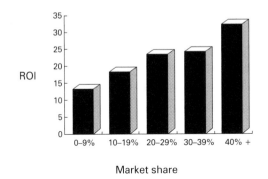

ROI

0–9%   10–19%   20–29%   30–39%   40% +

Market share

Source: PIMS database.

Figure 1.1   The relationship between market share and return on investment (ROI)

Clearly, however, since BMW are not in the same market as Ford, it is important to be most careful about how 'market' is defined. Correct 'market' definition is crucial for:

● measuring 'market' share and 'market' growth;
● the specification of target customers;
● recognition of relevant competitors; and, most important of all
● the formulation of marketing strategy, for it is this, above all else, that delivers differential advantage.

Developing the market definition

The general rule for 'market' definition is that it should be described in terms of a *customer need* in a way which covers the aggregation of all the alternative products or services *customers* regard as being capable of satisfying that need. For example, lunch-time hunger can be satisfied not only by the in-company caterer, but also by external restaurants, public houses, fast food specialists and sandwich bars. The emphasis for 'market' definition, therefore, is clearly on the word '*need*'.

A market is a customer need that can be satisfied by the products or services seen as alternatives.

Aggregating currently available products/services regarded by users as alternatives is, however, simply an aid to arriving at the definition, as it is important we recognise that new products, yet to be developed, could better satisfy the users' need. For example, the button manufacturer who believed its 'market' was the 'button market' would have been very disappointed when zips and Velcro began to satisfy the need for garment fastenings! A needs-based definition for such a company would have enabled the management to recognise the fickleness of current products, and to accept that one of their principal tasks is to seek out better ways of satisfying their market's needs and to evolve their product offer accordingly. It is for this reason that the definition should avoid the inclusion within it of specific products or services, as this can lead to a narrow and blinkered understanding of the real market. Table 1.1 contrasts some product-specific definitions with their possible needs-based definitions.

Table 1.1   Defining markets

Definition based on the product	Definition based on the need
Car insurance (personal)	Protect the individual from unexpected financial exposure associated with accidents and losses linked to a motor vehicle
X-ray equipment (medical)	To provide visual images of the inside of a body
Business books	Convey information about business
Fertilisers	Nutrients for plants
Potato crisps	Savoury snacks
Lubrication oil	To extend the working life of mechanical parts by reducing the negative impact of friction

In addition to avoiding a market definition that is too narrow, it is also important you avoid arriving at a market definition that is too broad. For example, 'financial services' embraces a vast range of very different products and services, far too many to be regarded as a single market. Despite this, a company in the financial services sector has attempted to segment 'financial services' as a whole. The outcome for a project which is attempting to segment a 'market' which is too broadly defined is usually one of the following:

(a) the segmentation project becomes unmanageable because of the broad range of products and services being looked at and because of the very diverse needs the different ranges of products and services are actually satisfying; or,

(b) the concluding segments (markets usually divide into between five and eight segments) can only be described in vague terms, making it very difficult, if not impossible, to define clearly the specific marketing mix (product/service, price, promotion and place) each segment requires, therefore defeating the whole object of segmentation.

For the company in question, the project was abandoned because it became unmanageable.

For companies with a range of products or services looking to define the market(s) they should be segmenting, the following sequence may help:

1. Allocate your company's products into their product ranges as defined by your company or, preferably, as viewed by the customer. Please note, it is possible to have the same product appearing in more than one list if it can be put to more than one use. For example, pensions can be used to provide retirement income or to finance a loan for a house purchase.

2. Add to each product range the appropriate competitor's products along with any additional products the customers are known to use as alternatives. Once again, a single product can appear in more than one list.

3. For each resulting product range, describe the use the customer puts the products to, in other words, the *need* customers are seeking to satisfy. Avoid using any of the product names in this description. If necessary, split product groups if this is the only way you are able to arrive at a meaningful description of their use.

4. Merge those product lists which appear to be put to the same use and therefore meet the same or similar customer need. For each concluding list, refine the words describing the use the competing products are put to, such that the description conveys the need they are meeting. These are now possible 'market' definitions.

5. For each 'market', assess the total value (or volume) of business the competing products represent for the geographic area being looked at. In deciding on the geographic area, take into account any known geographic limits customers impose on the location of suppliers they will consider. For example, suppliers of office equipment may need to be within a certain drive time.

6. As markets tend to divide into five to eight segments, divide the value (or volume) figure for each 'market' by five:

   If the resulting figure represents sufficient value (or volume) to justify a distinct marketing mix, your market definitions are probably correct. However, if the resulting figure can be divided by five again and still justify a distinct marketing mix, the 'market' definition is probably too broad and requires more focus.

If the resulting figure is too small to justify a distinct marketing mix, re-divide the 'market' figure by four (to allow for some segments being small and others being an acceptable size) and if this figure is still too small your 'market' definition is probably too narrow and needs to be merged with another.

The following is a further example of a business striking a meaningful balance between a broad market definition and a manageable market definition:

> Television broadcasting companies could be described as being in the 'entertainment' market, which also consists of theatres, cinemas and theme parks, to name but a few. This is a fairly broad definition. It may, therefore, be more manageable and productive for the television broadcasters when looking at segmenting their market, to define their market as being the 'home entertainment' market. This could then be further refined into the pre-school, child, teenager, family, or adult home entertainment market.

Similarly, companies supplying, for example, industrial lubricants may find segmentation more manageable and productive if their market is defined in terms of the particular application of the product, such as heavy industrial use or precision engineering.

Whose needs are being defined?

A question that sometimes occurs when developing a market definition, particularly in complex markets, concerns the use of the word 'customer'. Specifically, who is the customer and, therefore, whose needs are being defined?

For some practitioners of marketing the term 'customer' refers to the distribution channel while the term 'consumer' refers to the final user of the product or service, usually the one who has to find the money which pays everyone else along the distribution chain. As a general rule, the definition for a market should focus around the needs of the final user, the consumer. However, given the association of 'consumers' with particular types of markets, that segmentation is applicable to both consumer and business-to-business markets, and that there is not a general consensus on the distinction between customers and consumers, this book will subsume both under the title of 'customer'. As a general rule, therefore, the definition for a market should focus around the needs of the final customer, in other words, the final user.

The exception to this general rule is when the product or service in question has little, if any, value to the final user. For example, the manufacturer of small electronic components for cars is unlikely to find that the drivers of cars have a great deal of interest in their particular product. Defining the market in terms which describe the needs of drivers with respect to this product is therefore unlikely to be very useful. In such circumstances the 'customer' for market definition purposes would be the final individual or department which attributes value to the product/service in question.

Refining the definition

In some instances the sequences discussed in this chapter so far still result in a market definition that is not as meaningful as it could be to your company, particularly if you are a company focused into a particular part of an overall market. The following example may therefore provide further help in defining the market your business is in.

EXAMPLE 1.1   Defining a Market

A company manufacturing nylon carpet for the commercial sector wanted to check that it had a realistic definition of the 'market' it was in. The first step was to sketch out the total available market for all floor covering. This is summarised in Figure 1.2.

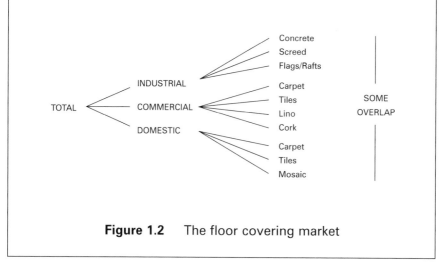

Figure 1.2   The floor covering market

EXAMPLE 1.1   Defining a Market (cont'd)

Clearly, it would be wrong to include the first group, namely those used in the industrial sector, in the company's market definition. The qualities required from such flooring cannot hope to be matched in a carpet made from any currently known type of fibre; they are, therefore, not seen as alternative products to the industrial sector. Similarly, in both the commercial and domestic sectors, nylon carpet is not a competitor for the luxury end of the market. This luxury part of the market buys carpet made from natural fibres, particularly wool.

This leaves the non-luxury commercial and domestic sectors which, in total, represented the company's potential available market. It was potentially available because the company could, for example, produce nylon carpet for the domestic sector and extend its market this way. Similarly, the company could move into manufacturing nylon carpet tiles and extend its operation into this product for both the domestic and commercial sectors. There was also no reason why the company should not look at replacing lino, cork or mosaic flooring with nylon carpet.

Many of the opportunities in the potentially available market, however, represent possible strategies for the future. They would be considered during the marketing planning process when the future plans for the current business activity did not achieve the required financial targets. (See Malcolm McDonald, *Marketing Plans – How to Prepare Them: How to Use Them*, 4th edn, Oxford: Heineman, 1998, Chapter 6, particularly 'Gap Analysis' and the 'Ansoff Matrix'.) The question now, therefore, is, what is the company's realistically available market?

To assist the company in this final stage of arriving at a market definition, the 'needs' being met by the current products, as highlighted by the current customers, were first listed. This revealed that the company's nylon carpet was bought because:

- it fell into a particular price range;
- it was quiet underfoot;
- it had a life expectancy of 15 years;
- it was available in pleasant colours and textures;
- the manufacturing plant was within a 60 mile radius.

In addition to the obvious, this list removed lino, cork and mosaic from the company's available market.

Finally, the company looked at the applicability of its current distribution and selling methods to the potentially available market, ruling out those sections of the market which required different selling and distribution approaches. This meant that it was unrealistic to include the domestic sector in the market definition.

EXAMPLE 1.1   Defining a Market (cont'd)

Products and manufacturers which met all the criteria were then listed, along with their end users. The company had now arrived at both a market definition and a current market size.

This example once again illustrates the need to arrive at a meaningful balance between a broad market definition and a manageable market definition. Too narrow a definition has the pitfall of restricting the range of new opportunities segmentation could open up for your business, while too broad a definition has the potential of overwhelming the segmentation exercise.

The market definition sequence highlighted in the example of the nylon carpet manufacturer can be summarised as follows:

1. First, define the totally available market (TAM) by expressing it as 'a need that can be satisfied by *all* the alternative products or services'. For the carpet manufacturer this meant *all* floor coverings. To take another example, for the canner of dog food this would include *all* dog food. This would ensure that the canner had an overview of what was happening in the market as a whole as some of the trends may be of great interest (including trends in buying meat from the butcher). However, to segment the whole market when it includes alternatives your company could not hope to offer is not very helpful.
2. Now define the potentially available market (PAM) by taking into account what your company's products or services and their directly competitive products or services *could* be used for within the TAM. For the carpet manufacturer this excluded industrial floor coverings but included, for example, the domestic sector, a sector they did not currently sell into but could serve with the products they had. For the canner, this would exclude meat from the butcher and dried dog food. For the button manufacturer it would exclude zips and velcro. These exclusions, however, represent possible strategies for the future. PAM is therefore expressed as 'the need that could be satisfied by products and services supplied by your company along with their competing products or services'. However, to segment a 'possible' market before segmenting your current market could result in your company missing growth opportunities which offered quick rewards and carried very little risk.
3. Finally, therefore, define the realistically available market (RAM) as this will become the market to be segmented. This refines the market further

by taking into account the requirements of the company's customers and prospects and the current distribution channels used by the company, along with any realistic alternatives. This really focused the carpet manufacturer on to a particular fibre, texture and geographic selling area; would focus the dog food canner to any similar requirements associated with their customers; and would focus the button manufacturer on to buttons. RAM is therefore expressed as 'the need that is currently satisfied by the products and services supplied by your company along with all their competing products or services'.

Whatever definition you finally arrive at, ensure it can be directly related to the products or services in question. General 'motherhood' statements, such as defining the customer need as 'maximising profit', tend to lose sight of their origins. Only a specialist area of financial services would be able to obtain meaningful benefits from a market defined as 'maximising profit'.

Whenever in doubt about customers and their needs, ask them! To help arrive at a market definition, it may be necessary to undertake some qualitative research either as one-to-one discussions, or with groups of customers. Understanding the alternative products and services as the customers see them, listening to how they discuss their needs along with their likes and frustrations with the alternatives on offer today can save hours of hypothetical discussions and lead you to a truly market-focused definition.

To conclude this section on defining markets, it is worth reflecting on the comments made by the founder of Revlon, Charles Revlon, as he is credited with one of the more famous needs-based definitions of a market. When he drew the distinction between products and needs for his company, he captured it by describing the factory as being the place where the company made chemicals, 'but in the store', he sold 'hope'. Clearly, this is not a suitable market definition, but it does illustrate a needs-based approach to the process described in this chapter.

Segmentation case histories

This chapter continues with three case histories to illustrate how superior profitability results from successful market segmentation. The book itself goes on to take you through a logical process which will enable you to create differential advantage from market segmentation.

CASE 1.1   A National Off-licence Chain

In the mid-1980s, a national off-licence chain, with retail units in major shopping centres and local shopping parades, was experiencing both a decline in customer numbers and a decline in average spend. The original formula for success of design, product range and merchandising, meticulously copied in each outlet, no longer appeared to be working.

The chain had become a classic example of a business comfortably sat in the middle ground, attempting to be all things to all men, but managing to satisfy very few of them.

Rather than sit back in the belief that the business was just passing through a difficult patch, and what worked yesterday was bound to work again, the company embarked on a project designed to understand both their actual and potential customer base.

The first stage of this study turned to one of the more sophisticated geodemographic packages (CCN's MOSAIC) in order to understand the residential profiles of each shop's catchment area. Not unexpectedly, many geodemographic differences were found, and the business quickly accepted it was unlikely that the same retail formula would appeal to the different target markets found in them.

Rather than look at each shop separately, the catchment area profiles for each shop were subject to a clustering routine in order to place similar catchment areas together. This resulted in 21 different groupings, each of which were then profiled in terms of their potential to buy different off-licence products using purchasing data from national surveys. (The company's own in-house retailing data would, of course, only reflect the purchasing pattern of their existing customers, or, at worst, only a proportion of their requirements if this was limited by the company's current product range.)

However, stocking the requisite range of products in their correct geographical location would not necessarily attract their respective target markets. The chain was already associated with one type of offer which, in addition to including a particular range of drinks, also included the basic design of the shops and overall merchandising.

The project, therefore, moved into a second stage, in which the market's attitudes and motivations to drinking were explored and relative values attached to the various dimensions uncovered. This was achieved through an independently commissioned piece of market research and resulted in the market being categorised into a number of psychographic groups. This included, amongst others, 'happy and impulsive' shoppers, 'anxious and muddled' shoppers, 'reluctant but organised' shoppers, and the 'disorganised, extravagant' shoppers.

CASE 1.1   **A National Off-licence Chain (cont'd)**

By ensuring this stage of the project linked the attitude and motivational findings to demographic data, the two stages could be brought together. This enabled the original 21 clusters to be reduced to five distinct segments, each of which required a different offer.

The company now had to decide between two alternative strategies:

(a) to focus into one segment using one brand and re-locate its retail outlets accordingly through a closure and opening programme; or,

(b) to develop a manageable portfolio of retailing brands, leave the estate relatively intact, and re-brand, re-fit and re-stock as necessary.

They decided to pursue the second.

Realising that demographic profiles in geographic areas can change over time, and that customer needs and attitudes can also evolve, the company now monitors its market quite carefully and is quite prepared to modify its brand portfolio to suit changing circumstances. For the time being, however, the five retail brands of 'Bottoms Up', 'Wine Rack', 'Threshers Wine Shop', 'Drinks Store from Threshers' and 'Food and Drinks Store' sit comfortably within the five segments. They also sit comfortably together in the same shopping centre, enabling the group to meet effectively the different requirements of the segments found within that centre's catchment area.

Perhaps more importantly, this strategy sits comfortably alongside the financial targets for the business.

Source: J. Thornton, 'Market segmentation from Bottoms Up', *Research Plus – The magazine of the Market Research Society,* December 1993.

CASE 1.2   **Sodium Tri-poly Phosphate**

Sodium tri-poly phosphate (STPP) was once a simple, unexciting, white chemical cleaning agent. Today, one of its uses is as the major ingredient of a sophisticated and profitable operation, appearing under many different brand names, all competing for a share of what has become a cleverly segmented market.

Have you ever wondered how the toothpaste marketers classify you in their segmentation of the market? Much simplified and for illustrative purposes only, Table 1.2, based on R. Haley's 'Benefit segmentation: a decision-oriented research tool', *Journal of Marketing*, **32**, July 1968, which presents an overview of the main segments, may assist you.

CASE 1.2   Sodium Tri-poly Phosphate (cont'd)

Table 1.2   Segments in the market for toothpaste

		Segment name			
		Worrier	*Sociable*	*Sensory*	*Independent*
Who buys	*Socio-economic*	C1 C2	B C1 C2	C1 C2 D	A B
	Demographic	Large families 25–40	Teens Young smokers	Children	Males 35–50
	Psychographic	Conserv-ative: hypochon-driosis	High sociability: active	High self-involve-ment: hedonists	High autonomy: value orientated
What is bought, Where, When and How	*Product examples*	Crest	McLeans Ultrabrite	Colgate (stripe)	Own label
	Product physics	large canisters	large tubes	medium tubes	small tubes
	Outlet	super-market	super-market	super-market	independent
	Purchase frequency	weekly	monthly	monthly	quarterly
Why it is bought	*Benefits sought*	stop decay	attract attention	flavour	functionality
Price paid		low	high	medium	low
Percentage of market		50%	30%	15%	5%
Potential for growth		nil	high	medium	nil

CASE 1.3   Amber Nectar

A privately owned brewery in the UK was enjoying exceptional profitability for its industrial sector. In terms of output, it was by no means the largest brewery in the UK, and in terms of geographic cover, it only operated within a particular metropolitan area.

At one of the regular meetings of the board, it was agreed that the company had clearly developed a very successful range of beers and it was time to expand into new geographic areas.

CASE 1.3   **Amber Nectar (cont'd)**

The expansion programme met with aggressive opposition from other brewers, particularly the very large brewers. This came as no great surprise to the board who, before setting on the expansion path, had built up a large 'war chest', largely made up of past profits, to finance the plan. The board knew the competition would react in this way, because they were being challenged by a very successful range of beers, a 'success' that would ensure product trial, then customer loyalty, in the new areas.

As with all good marketing-focused companies, the progress of the marketing plan was regularly monitored against its target by a specially appointed task force headed by the chief executive. In addition, the sales and marketing director, a key member of the task force, held regular meetings with his own key staff to ensure continuous evaluation of the sales and marketing strategies being followed.

The plan badly under-performed and was eventually abandoned.

In the post-mortem that followed, the brewery discovered why it had been so successful in the past, and why this success could not be extended to other areas of the UK. To its loyal customers, a key attraction of the beers manufactured by this brewery was the 'local' flavour. The 'market' for this company was the metropolitan area it already operated in, its competitors being other local brewers in the same area. Exporting this success was clearly, therefore, not going to work. Expansion could only be achieved by setting up new local breweries in other areas, or by acquiring already established local breweries.

Without this brewery realising it, the customers for beer in the UK had already segmented themselves. This brewer's segment was the 'regional chauvinist', and in the particular region it operated in, the company already had an overwhelming market share: hence its profitability.

With an earlier understanding of this segmentation structure, the company would have spent its war chest more effectively and achieved its growth objectives.

Case history conclusion

These three case histories illustrate the importance of intelligent segmentation in guiding companies towards successful marketing strategies. However, it is easy to understand this success *after* the event, as occurred in one of the cases! The problem, for most of us, is how to arrive at a definition of 'market segmentation' that will enable us to create differential advantage. That is the purpose of this book.

Definition of market segmentation

Not all customers have the same requirements and a marketing strategy which does not recognise this fact will result in a scatter gun approach and dilute the marketing effort.

> Market segmentation is the process of splitting customers, or potential customers, within a market into different groups, or segments, within which customers have the same, or similar requirements satisfied by a distinct marketing mix.

While a 'market' describes a customer need in a way which covers the aggregation of *all* the alternative products or services customers regard as being capable of satisfying that need, 'segments' focus on specific products or services, along with other elements of the marketing mix, that the different customer groups are looking for within a market in order to satisfy their particular requirements. A key difference, therefore, between a 'market' and a 'segment' is that a specific marketing strategy can be defined for a segment, whereas for a market we can only list the alternative products or services. It is simply a different level of aggregation of customer needs.

Segmentation is a creative and iterative process, the purpose of which is to satisfy customer needs more closely and, in so doing, create competitive advantage for the company. It is defined by the *customers'* needs and requirements, not the company's, and should be revisited periodically.

The process of segmentation also helps identify new opportunities, for both products and markets.

The importance of segmentation to any business should not be underestimated: segmentation is the basic building block for effective marketing planning, as illustrated in Figure 1.3, and should reflect a market/customer orientation rather than a product orientation.

Most organisations will need to use more than one level of segmentation criteria to identify the customer types and to categorise their specific requirements. Organisations are also likely to find that the process of segmentation needs to be carried out at more than one stage in the overall distribution and value added chain, different stages having distinct customer types with their own specific requirements.

Market segments offering the greatest opportunities will be those that are growing and profitable, in which companies can effectively meet their customers' needs of today, or for which companies can develop their products/services to meet the needs of tomorrow.

Following the selection of market segments to be targeted, companies can then develop focused marketing strategies. This planned approach to meeting the needs of the customers helps companies to be proactive instead of reactive, enabling them to take advantage of market opportunities and gain competitive advantage.

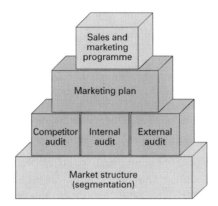

Figure 1.3 The building blocks of effective marketing planning

It should be noted, however, that, whilst the segmentation process itself is externally focused in its consideration of the market 'out there', companies looking to 'meet their customer's needs effectively', should also consider how the company's own departmental structure and staff relate to the chosen target segments. For example, when a customer from a particular segment contacts your company in the course of doing business with you, it could well negate the company's segmented approach in its external marketing activity if, in dealing with this customer's requirements, the applicable internal department subsumes the customer under one, all-embracing procedure, and fails to match up to the external activity.

Segmentation archetypes in companies

The 'internal' and 'external' matching required for effective segmentation provides a convenient framework for looking at how companies currently define and segment their markets.

In their paper, 'Strategic and operational market segmentation: a managerial analysis', *Journal of Strategic Marketing*, **1**(1), 1993, pp 123–40, N. F. Piercy and N. A. Morgan provide a conceptual framework for viewing market segmentation which acknowledges the distinction between 'explicit' and 'implicit' aspects of the market. An 'explicit' perspective refers to the view that markets are 'out there' and are essentially groups of customers. The 'implicit' perspective relates to the role of a company's perceptions, culture, processes and structure in determining the company's view of the market. Although this framework was not developed from empirical sources, it does provide an intuitive basis for understanding how markets may be defined and segmented in practice.

By assessing a number of companies on the basis of the framework suggested by Piercy and Morgan, a series of archetypes which represent differing approaches and emphasis in segmenting the marketplace have been developed by Mark Jenkins and Malcolm McDonald (Cranfield University School of Management, 1995). These archetypes help demonstrate how companies actually relate to their target markets and the potential implications of these differing positions.

Company archetypes

In order to develop a clearer picture as to how different approaches to explicit and implicit segmentation may appear in companies, four case studies are described. It should be stressed that the role of case studies is not empirical but illustrative. It is intended to clarify some of the ideas which have been raised in conceptual terms within the marketing literature.

These case studies summarise a wider series of marketing-based projects undertaken with a number of large companies. The sample frame was, therefore, driven by convenience and opportunity. The process followed was to record observations and commentaries on particular company situations and then bring the data together to provide an account of the different approaches to segmentation. Interpretation of the data is necessarily subjective, its presentation anecdotal and is brought together in a loose, but considered framework. The concluding four archetypes which represent how companies segment their markets are each exemplified by an actual organisation.

CASE 1.4　　**The International Airline**

Many commentators agree that the major international airlines of today have achieved their current size primarily through one of the following three routes:

* the sheer size and wealth of their home market, such as United Airlines of the USA for example;
* dogged determination by their home country to have a major carrier operating in the industry, Singapore Airlines being a prime example;

| **CASE 1.4** | The International Airline (cont'd) |

- they are the national airline of a former colonial power, such as British Airways for example.

However, regardless of their origin, all these airlines, on the whole, have segmented their global market on the basis of geographic territories.

Before the development of products and brands in British Airways, the airline's marketing was driven by powerful territorial line managers. Country managers reported to regional managers who, in turn, reported through their route general managers based at the company's headquarters in London. The only exception was the country manager for the UK who, primarily because of the size of revenue generated in the UK, was equivalent in status to a route general manager. These individuals were responsible for generating the bulk of the airline's revenue, other revenue coming from the sale of in-house tour operations and third party activities.

The word 'Market' could be found on individual office doors in route head offices, regional offices and in many of the country offices, and the route general managers, along with the general manager UK sales, reported to a marketing director. The focus of marketing was territorial, and although the airline discussed its markets in terms of 'business', 'leisure' and 'visiting friends and relatives' (VFR), even, at times, having campaigns focused into these travel sectors, marketing expenditure budgets were set by territory and were often judged in terms of the revenue generated by that territory. Revenue performance for the route general managers, however, was judged both by territory and by route, with route revenue coming from all over the world. A prime function for the routes, therefore, was the allocation of seats and cargo space to the different territorial markets around the world. Revenue per seat, however, was the major determinant by which a territory was given capacity to sell on any flight, although, in some instances, it was accepted that a minimum number of seats or amount of cargo space had to be made available for sale in certain territories in order to retain a 'presence' in that area. Obtaining such capacity, however, was particularly difficult on services operated by a route division other than the one in which a territory manager was geographically located, an exception being a situation where the territory manager had capacity which the route manager wanted, which could then be used for leverage in negotiations.

With an aircraft fleet and crew traversing all geographic boundaries, product design was primarily a corporate task and was kept fairly simple by looking at the world in terms of first class travel and economy class travel, later supplemented by business class travel. Schedules were rarely designed around customer requirements and were governed by:

CASE 1.4   The International Airline (cont'd)

- the drive to keep aircraft in the air for as much time as possible, as this was when they were earning revenue;
- night time restrictions at airports;
- agreements between governments and airlines themselves.

Tweaking of the in-flight offer was, however, available to the route offices. They could request menus to suit the palates of the geographical areas through which the aircraft flew, and they could employ extra cabin crew members from their overseas territories to bring a 'local flavour' to their services for the indigenous traveller. Essentially, however, the company was sales orientated, the emphasis being to fill capacity and thereby requiring seats to be sold. Customers were those who happened to sit in the seats. There was no strategic perspective as to how particular groups of customers should be managed.

CASE 1.5   The Chemical Company

In 1917, the British Government bought a site in Billingham on the north bank of the River Tees for a factory to make synthetic ammonia, 'Synthonia', as a first stage for producing the chemicals for munitions. After the First World War, in 1919, Brunner Mond and Company took over the site to make fertilisers from ammonia using the same process as originally intended in the government plan.

It was not until 1923 that the first ammonia plant started production and by the following year the first nitrogen product, sulphate of ammonia, was manufactured. This was followed five years later by another nitrogen fertiliser product, 'Nitrochalk', which was particularly suited to grassland. Nitrogen, however, is not the only element likely to be depleted in the soil on commercial farms. Phosphate and potash are two further important soil nutrients that need topping up on these farms, and by 1930 the company was producing 'complete' fertilisers containing nitrogen, phosphate and potash in compound form. This extension of the product range suited the company, as it meant its nitrogen was being used in a greater number of products.

Usage of fertilisers tends to fall into three distinct product groups; nitrogen on its own; nitrogen with phosphate and potash; and a third group consisting of just phosphate and potash. To ensure the company had a complete range, the third group of products, those just containing phosphate and potash, were also sold, primarily because it was believed that

---

CASE 1.5   **The Chemical Company (cont'd)**

offering the full range pulled through sales of the separate product lines (later proved to be largely a myth). The principal focus of the business, however, was around the ammonia production technology. This was the most complex chemical process for the fertiliser business, and the company's greatest margins came from products containing the most nitrogen. The production of compounds was fairly simple in comparison (once the nitrogen had been produced) and was carried out in a separate plant on the site.

Given the origin of the business, the source of its margins and distinct manufacturing plants, it could only appear logical to structure the management of the business and its information flows around the three product lines. This is exactly what happened and the three product lines were represented in the marketing function by product managers. The product management teams not only liaised with the manufacturing plant on product specifications and production volumes, they also drove the promotional campaigns of the business and set the sales targets, though only for their products. This was perfectly acceptable, of course, because the market, on the whole, bought these three product types largely at different times of the year.

It was readily accepted in the company that, broadly speaking, the market was split between fertilisers for growing grass and fertilisers for the growing of arable crops. There were even products specifically manufactured for each of these two sectors, distinct services offered to each of them, and dedicated specialist advisers based at headquarters. Despite this, the thrust of the business was based around product lines, each of which eventually fell under the control of its own business team. Lying over this split was the salesforce, divided, for management purposes, into geographical territories. Their sales targets were, as already mentioned, presented to them along product lines, and any sales support literature was similarly divided, as all the budgets were allocated along product lines. This organisational structure had been in place for over 60 years.

CASE 1.6 **The Bank**

Some years ago, the senior customer services representative of one of the big five UK banks was being interviewed on the radio. The main area of discussion centred around opening times (usually 10.00 a.m. to 3.30 p.m. at that time) and the limited number of cashiers (tellers) on duty during the peak, lunchtime period. The reason given for the opening times was that the public forgot that the transactions which the bank undertook on their behalf took time, and if they were open to their customers from 9.00 a.m. to 5.30 p.m. during the week, never mind at weekends, the staff at the bank would probably need to work from 8.00 a.m. to 7.00 p.m. The bank's public hours were the most it could offer when its staff worked from 9.00 a.m. to 5.30 p.m., which seemed fair, of course, because these were the hours worked by most of their customers! With regard to the lunchtime queues, the reasons for these were equally straightforward and reasonable: the bank's cashiers also had to have lunch breaks.

These issues, rather than humbling the customer into acceptance, fuelled the growth of the building societies. Marketing arrived in the financial world in a big way during the 1980s and attractive salaries and extra financial benefits attracted some of the best. They had found a gold mine waiting to be developed. Unlike many businesses, banks clearly know who their customers are. The switching costs for these customers are high when compared to other industries. This means the banks have traditionally enjoyed a high level of customer retention. Here, therefore, was a great opportunity for developing financial products and selling the variety of services available from the bank into a known customer base. Here, also, was the opportunity to develop products suited to the different stages of life and put them in front of the customer progressively as they travelled along life's highway.

The large, in-house database could also be profiled by matching them up against externally held databases containing psychographic information. This would help in the better targeting of new product offers into the bank's own customer base, and enable the banks to specify target customer profiles from externally held lists when prospecting for new customers. Inevitably complex segmentation structures were devised and numerous new products developed, and the banks became portrayed more as centres for financial services.

However, the purpose of these segments was to find ways of selling internally or competitively defined products, these segments being variable according to the different projects for which they were devised. The majority of banks still opened at the times the customers were in work and the cashiers still went to lunch during the peak period. If anyone wanted to talk about any of the new services, the unmanned enquiry desk always had a welcome for them, once someone had responded to the bell!

CASE 1.7   **The Retailing Group**

There is a very large retailing group in the UK which is a prime example of an organisation which has structured itself around its chosen segments.

The different high street brands of the group are targeted into specific segments and are not just fronts. Behind each lies a complete infrastructure with its own marketing group, buyers, financial controllers, administration and so on, all focused into the survival of the brand in its segment. Some brands eventually tire, but this is due, in part, to 'time out' being called on the segment. At the same time, however, the company has introduced new brands to exploit the opportunities available in newly emerging segments.

Case study conclusion

These cases are presented as illustrations of the potential alignment of the organisation to market segments. They are subjective accounts drawn from contact with, and knowledge of, the organisations in question. The purpose of presenting these mini-cases is to determine how they may clarify and extend our understanding of segmentation processes. In the international airline, segmentation is driven by internal structures and processes. The power of the territory manager defines the way the organisation aligns itself to the market. This perspective does not begin with the customer, but with the structure of the sales organisation. This view of the market is also limited to particular functions and activities within the organisation and does not appear to operate across functions or at a strategic level.

In contrast, the chemical company represents an organisation whose entire structure and mode of operation represents a particular view of the market. This view is clearly process- or product-led and is not a customer driven view of the marketplace. Unlike the international airline, it is a view which is embedded throughout the organisation.

The bank presents a different type of situation. Here, the organisation has a customer-based approach as to how it segments the marketplace. This view, however, is restricted to the functional marketing activities of the organisation. It does not permeate the way in which the organisation, as a whole, sees the external world and does not appear to influence many of the processes and procedures which do impact on the customer.

The retailing group provides an organisational view which is centred on customer groups. This form of segmentation is deeply embedded in the operations and perspective of the employees as it forms the basis for the organisational structure.

All of the above examples reflect different approaches as to how an organisation may align itself to the segments within the marketplace. The purpose of the case studies has been to illustrate potential divergence which differentiate these examples. The explanation for this divergence may provide further insights into the process aspects of how different organisations may segment their markets. It appears that there are two principal dimensions which differentiate between these examples:

- *Customer driven*
  The example of the bank and the retailing group are both approaches which are clearly centred on the customer. In these situations, a market and its segments are customer groups as defined by, amongst others, Philip Kotler, *Marketing Management: Analysis Planning and Control*, 7th edn, Englewood Cliffs, NJ: Prentice-Hall, 1991. In the case of the bank, the customer focus is limited to particular initiatives which are task- and function-specific. In the case of the retailing group, customer focus permeates and defines the separate business units. In contrast, the approach taken by the international airline and the chemical company is not centred on the customer. This is not to imply that at some point they were not customer driven. The issue is that these approaches for defining and segmenting the market no longer begin with the customer. They have become internalised and are thereby driven by internal factors such as salesforce territories, budgets and organisational structures. These are implicit views of the marketplace which have become part of the organisation's culture and perspective on its environment.

- *Organisational integration*
  The international airline and the bank both exhibit low levels of organisational integration. The way in which the market is segmented is the domain of particular groups, or functions within the organisation. In these situations, segmentation is very much an operational, as opposed to a strategic, process. It is concerned with a particular media campaign or for establishing particular sales objectives. Outside these particular groups, these segments are not understood or recognised. In contrast, the chemical company and the retailing group both illustrate a high level of organisational integration. In these situations, segmentation is not just a way of targeting potential customers, but an intrinsic part of the structure and culture of the organisation. All parts of the organisation recognise that the market is segmented in this particular way, these segments providing a strategic basis for how the organisation understands its interaction with the business environment.

Classifying market segmentation in organisations

These two dimensions for considering the organisational aspects of segmentation, customer driven and organisational integration, can be incorporated into a matrix as shown in Figure 1.4.

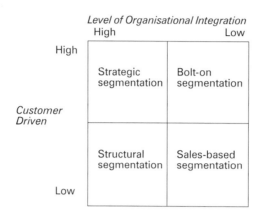

Figure 1.4   Segmentation archetypes in companies

- *Sales-based segmentation*
  The first cell, sales-based segmentation, describes an organisational archetype where the market is segmented on the basis of how the sales function is organised, which does not necessarily reflect clusters of particular customer characteristics or needs. In addition, these approaches are relatively superficial, and they are not embedded in the way the organisation, as a whole, is structured, or the way it operates. This archetype represents segmentation which is driven by, and is largely exclusive to, the sales operations of an organisation. The international airline is an example of this particular archetype. Here, the approach to segmentation operates at a territory level where some adjustment of the offer is permitted (use of local menus and cabin staff). However, this view of the market is not embedded in the way the organisation as a whole is driven. The organisational priorities are represented by the need to maximise the capacity of the fleet of aircraft and the fact that this capacity resource is allocated through the management of routes rather than particular territories. The international airline, therefore, provides an example of an approach to segmentation which is internally (sales territories), as opposed to being externally (customer) driven and which does not reflect the priorities and focus of the organisation as a whole.

- *Structural segmentation*

  The second cell, structural segmentation, represents a further archetype where there is little emphasis on segments as groups of customers. Segments are defined by how the organisation is structured. However, in contrast to the sales-based archetype, this approach to the market is deeply embedded in the organisation as a whole. The chemical company is an example of this situation. The organisation described in this case uses product management teams, who are responsible for marketing activity at both the strategic and operational levels. These groups are also working with sales territories which are allocated on a geographical basis. At this level, therefore, the segmentation is not explicitly customer driven, although the sales territories may reflect differing patterns of agriculture, and the differing product types may be applied at different times of the year. However, the product divisions which are fronted by the product management teams are embedded in the structure and nature of the organisation. The requirements of a complex and capital-intensive process (producing ammonium nitrate) have meant that the product divisions which represent different aspects of this process are highly integrated into the fabric of the organisation. This cell, therefore, presents an approach which is both production and sales driven and which is embedded in all the structures and processes of the organisation.

- *Bolt-on segmentation*

  The third cell, bolt-on segmentation, presents an archetype where a high level of customer focus is brought into the defining of market segments. In this case, the organisation applies customer data which are often available within the organisation, such as location, purchase patterns and product preference. These data are combined with external classification systems which align the customer base to particular socio-economic profiles. In contrast to the previous archetypes, this segmentation approach is driven by the information held on the customer base as opposed to the structure of sales operations. However, this archetype is close to sales-based segmentation, as it is limited to a number of functional areas within the organisation and is not integrated into the organisation as a whole. In this case, the purpose of the segmentation exercise is to assist in selling existing products and targeting promotional campaigns, which are essentially operational, as opposed to strategic issues. In this archetype the segmentation framework does not guide new product development, nor does it affect the core processes and power base of business. The bank is presented as an example of this particular archetype. In this example, a high level of customer information already exists within the business. In many situations this is applied simply to target mail shots or other promotions, aimed at selling existing products.

These segments do not provide a focus for redefining the business processes, a basis for new service concepts or the removal of existing products. A customer focus exists, but this does not permeate the whole operation of the business, as it is not considered at a strategic level.

- *Strategic segmentation*
  The fourth cell, strategic segmentation, combines both a customer focus and a high level of organisational integration. In this cell, the organisation is able to apply customer-based data in order to develop a set of defined segments. In contrast to the bolt-on segmentation approach, the organisation has integrated these segments across the key functional activities. They provide a basis, not only for the promotional activity, but also for strategic decision-making and internal marketing; in the case of the latter, this clarity of particular market segments provide a powerful basis for bringing the customer into the organisation; see Theodore Levitt, 'Marketing myopia', *Harvard Business Review*, July–August 1960, pp 45–56. They also provide a focus for the entire processes and operations of the organisation on these market segments. The large retailing group is suggested as an example for this cell. This group has a set of retailing concepts which are driven by clearly defined market segments. These segments have been defined around customer groups, but are also deeply embedded in the organisation through their own operations and processes, which are tailored to the needs of their respective segments. In this case, all those in the organisation can picture the target segment and have a basic appreciation of how the segment can be served most effectively.

The four case studies indicate that it must surely be better to be more customer focused and organisationally committed to a particular form of segmentation. The airline concerned made massive losses for a sustained period and only survived through this period because of its state-owned status. The international chemical company sustained enormous losses during the 1980s and only escaped closure by the narrowest of margins. Likewise, banks made substantial losses. The aim of this framework is, therefore, to provide a basis for beginning to asses segmentation, not only as an external clustering of customers, but also in terms of the strategic and internal implications for an organisation.

Segmentation team

Before embarking on a segmentation project, a key question to answer concerns who should be involved in the segmentation team.

Whilst it is not unusual for short-term sales and profit pressures to prevent the allocation of time and resources to carry out market segmentation, it should be the primary responsibility of the general manager to ensure that it is done.

Ideally, a mixed team of representatives from the main functions of the company is required, because segmentation is central to corporate strategy and affects all areas of the business, and because each function has different contributions to make to the process. Within the team, a core group consisting of two to three individuals should be established. The function of this core group is to carry out all the detailed work required in the segmentation process, the core group reporting back to the full team for consultation, comment and guidance.

Team members from the functional disciplines should have had customer contact and have a good knowledge of the products, markets, customers and the company.

In some circumstances, there should also be an outsider, who knows nothing about the products and markets, to act as a facilitator for the process and to offer an objective and alternative viewpoint to the discussion. Segmentation, however, is not a project to be contracted out to an external consultancy from whom you eventually receive a report and presentation. Complete ownership of the project and its conclusions is essential if the company intends to commit itself to implementing the findings.

Segmentation can be carried out at all levels of the organisation. Strategically, there needs to be a corporate segmentation which will fit within, or help companies develop, their mission statement. At lower levels within the organisation, there will be segmentation within the strategic business units (SBUs), and, finally, segmentation at a lower level, such as customer group, product, or geographic. This book principally concerns segmentation at SBU and lower levels.

Segmentation is also a subject that should be periodically revisited, as markets are dynamic, and changes in the macro-economy and the markets can alter the attractiveness of different market segments, especially in fast-changing markets. Also, there are benefits in being creative and innovative and developing new alternative approaches in order to gain competitive advantage.

As your selected team progresses through the process, you will need to answer the following questions:

- How should you segment the market?
- How detailed should your segmentation be?
- How do you define segments in the best possible way?
- Which segments offer the greatest opportunities?

Data for segmentation

Segmentation, when carried out thoroughly, usually requires a great deal of data. The segmentation team will therefore require access to sales and financial data and market research findings in order to provide extra information to help the decision-making process. Inevitably, the quality of the input will have a large impact on the quality of the output.

The data required for segmentation can be summarised as follows:

- an understanding of how the market works;
- the size of the market and how this divides between the competing products and services (approximations at least);
- descriptors for the different customers found within the market (customer profiling);
- the key product and service requirements, from the customer's point of view;
- the benefits delivered by these requirements;
- the relative importance of these benefits to the different customers found within the market.

It is because of these data requirements that many segmentation projects benefit from the support of specifically designed computer-based packages, as briefly mentioned in the Preface. Having such a resource enables the segmentation team to concentrate on the marketing issues they are addressing.

Rules for segmentation

The criteria used for segmentation must have the following characteristics:

- the ability to distinguish between segments, such that each segment has a unique set of characteristics and can be served by an equally unique marketing strategy;
- each identified segment should have sufficient potential size to justify the time and effort involved in planning specifically for this business opportunity;
- each identified segment should be capable of being described or measured by a set of descriptors, such that the customers in that segment can be communicated with by means of a distinctive promotion, selling and advertising strategy;
- each identified segment should have relevance to its purchase situation (in other words it is a decision-making factor or affects the process of buying behaviour);

- the company must be capable of making the necessary changes to its structure, information and decision-making systems so that they become focused on to the new segments.

The advantages of segmentation

These can be summarised as follows:

- recognising customers' differences is the key to successful marketing, as it can lead to a closer matching of customers' needs with the company's products or services;
- segmentation can lead to niche marketing, where appropriate, where the company can meet most or all of the needs of customers in that niche segment. This can result in segment dominance, something which is often not possible in the total market;
- segmentation can lead to concentration of resources in markets where competitive advantage is greatest and returns are high;
- segmentation can be used to gain competitive advantage by considering the market in different ways from your competitors;
- by means of segmentation, you can market your company as a specialist in your chosen market segments, with a better understanding of customers' needs, thus giving your products/services advantages over competitors' products.

The additional benefits of the approach to segmentation outlined in this book are:

- it checks your logic and your basic assumptions about your market;
- it helps with your team-building approach;
- it goes across vertical structures, often uncovering hitherto undiscovered customer needs.

Segmentation process summary

The segmentation process consists of two phases:

Phase 1   Developing segments for your market.

Phase 2   Prioritising and selecting segments.

The first phase of the process, which covers the essential steps you should follow to develop a segmented structure for your market, is applied to the whole market your business is operating in, not just to that bit of the market you are currently successful in. *It therefore looks at your competitor's products and/or services as well as your own.* A clear definition of your market is, therefore, essential. A guide for arriving at that definition was provided earlier in this chapter, namely, a 'market' describes a *customer need* which covers the aggregation of *all* the alternative products or services *customers* regard as being capable of satisfying that need.

The second phase of the process then looks at how to select those segments your business should be operating in.

Developing segments

This first phase of the process contains three stages, broken down into seven steps and is summarised in Figure 1.5.

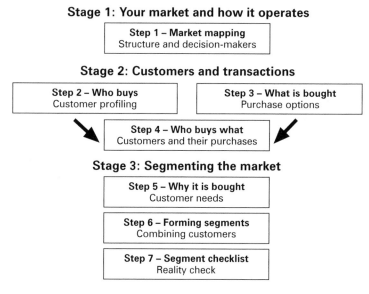

Stage 1: Your market and how it operates

> **Step 1 – Market mapping**
> Structure and decision-makers

Stage 2: Customers and transactions

> **Step 2 – Who buys**
> Customer profiling

> **Step 3 – What is bought**
> Purchase options

> **Step 4 – Who buys what**
> Customers and their purchases

Stage 3: Segmenting the market

> **Step 5 – Why it is bought**
> Customer needs

> **Step 6 – Forming segments**
> Combining customers

> **Step 7 – Segment checklist**
> Reality check

Figure 1.5   The process of segmentation:
Phase 1 – developing segments

Stage 1: Your market and how it operates

The first step, market mapping, requires you to present the market you are operating in as a diagram. It's rather like a flow chart along which your products and services, and those of your competitors, flow to the final users and their cash flows back to you, the supplier. In many markets, however, a flow chart simply tracking the physical delivery of products/services is inadequate in covering the role played by 'influencers' on the purchase decision, and/or the purchase decision routines encountered by businesses in the market.

The market map, in truth, is probably better described as depicting the obstacle course suppliers have to get through in order to reach the final user.

Once the market map is complete, you are then required to determine at which points along it decisions are made about competing products and services, as it is at these points segmentation should occur.

Stage 2: Customers and transactions

The three steps in Stage 2 progressively enable you to look at any of the decision-making points on the market map and construct a model of the market based on the different customers found there and the transactions they make.

Step 2 presents an early opportunity to start recording information about customers which can be used to identify them in the market. This step also enables you to introduce into the process any current segmentation structure you may have for the market being segmented and to test its validity.

Step 3 records the key features sought by the market when deciding between alternative offers. These are selected from the actual products and services on offer (what is bought) and from the options presented by where it can be bought, when it is bought and how.

This second stage concludes with the fourth step developing a model of the market based on the different customers found within it (Step 2) and the choices they make between the alternative features on offer (Step 3).

Stage 3: Segmenting the market

Step 5 moves on from the somewhat mechanistic look at the market covered in the previous four steps to looking at the reasons why the features sought by the market when deciding between alternative offers are actually bought. Once the real needs, the real benefits, have been understood, their relative importance to each 'cell' in the model generated by Step 4 is assessed. The importance of price in each purchase is also recorded.

Step 6 then describes a technique of grouping these cells together in order to obtain the best fit. Similar cells in terms of the relative importance of the needs they are looking to have satisfied are therefore combined to form 'segments'.

In most markets the number of concluding segments lies between five and eight.

The final step then subjects each 'segment' to a reality check based on the size of each segment, the differentiation between the offers they require, your ability to identify the different customers found in each segment, and the compatibility of these segments with your company.

The process is presented primarily in a format designed to utilise information already held by your company. As you progress through the various steps, the process may, however, reveal information shortfalls which you will need to address. In many instances, the most appropriate method of addressing these shortfalls will be by commissioning market research. Guidelines on how to incorporate market research findings can be found in the text.

To help explain the process of developing segments, a case study is used. This not only helps illustrate each step in turn, it also demonstrates how each step relates to the other steps. Further examples are also included where appropriate, both alongside the case study and throughout the text.

Prioritising and selecting segments

The second phase of the process looks at how to select those segments in which your company should be operating and for which it should be developing marketing strategies. There are two stages in this second phase broken down into five steps. These are summarised in Figure 1.6.

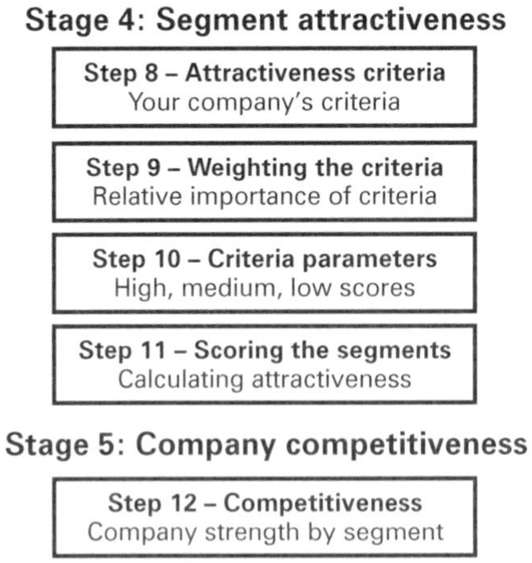

Stage 4: Segment attractiveness

Step 8 – Attractiveness criteria Your company's criteria

Step 9 – Weighting the criteria Relative importance of criteria

Step 10 – Criteria parameters High, medium, low scores

Step 11 – Scoring the segments Calculating attractiveness

Stage 5: Company competitiveness

Step 12 – Competitiveness Company strength by segment

Figure 1.6   The process of segmentation:
Phase 2 – prioritising and selecting segments

Stage 4: Segment attractiveness

The first step in Stage 4, being Step 8 in the overall process of segmentation, defines the criteria your company would use in order to determine the attractiveness to the company of any segment.

Step 9 then establishes the relative importance of these criteria to each other.

Means of quantifying each criterion are then established in Step 10 and high, medium and low scores are set for each of them.

Step 11 finally arrives at an overall attractiveness score for each concluding segment based on how well each of them satisfies your company's requirements.

Stage 5: Company competitiveness

The final stage of the segmentation process then establishes your company's ability to meet the requirements of each concluding segment, compared with the ability of the competition to meet these requirements, from the *segment's* point of view.

By combining segment attractiveness and relative company competitiveness, you can construct a strategic picture of your market which can be used to select those segments which will enable your company to achieve its corporate objectives.

Marketing objectives and strategies

Segmentation is not an end in itself. Only by developing and implementing the appropriate strategies for each of your chosen segments will your company be able to reap the benefits of segmentation. It is because of this that a chapter has been set aside in this book to discuss the setting of marketing objectives and strategies for segments (Chapter 11).

PART I

The Segmentation Process

2 *Market Mapping (Step 1)*

Stage 1: Your market and how it operates

Step 1 – Market mapping
Structure and decision-makers

Figure 2.1   Kicking off the segmentation process

This first step in developing a segmentation structure for your market consists of two parts. The first requires you to draw a map of the market your business is segmenting and the second determines at which points on this map you should be developing segments.

Market mapping is usually simpler in consumer markets than in business-to-business markets.

With the suggested starting point for your segmentation project being to use information already held by your company, information for market mapping should initially be sought from departments such as sales, customer services, customer enquiries, customer ordering and from distribution. Past market surveys and industry statistics could also be useful sources of information, assuming you are fortunate enough to have any. If verification is required, this can be included in the specification for any follow-up activity required for your segmentation project as a whole.

Although in structurally very simple markets it may be possible to move immediately to Step 2 in the process of segmentation, it is strongly recommended that you read this chapter and give it most careful thought before deciding that market mapping is not relevant. In our experience, market mapping is relevant to all organisations.

Markets and SBUs

The 'boundary' for your market map is usually outlined by the definition of the market being segmented, a market being defined in terms of a customer need that can be satisfied by the products or services seen as alternatives. This is therefore a useful point at which to capture your market definition.

Market definition:

It might help if you also listed under the market definition the competing products or services used by the market to satisfy the defined need.

If, in arriving at this definition, you have used the sequence in the first chapter which takes you from the totally available market (TAM), through the potentially available market (PAM) to the realistically available market (RAM), your market definition and map normally would be for that part of the market in which you can realistically compete, in other words, the RAM. However, bearing in mind that the financial goals you have been given may not be met from what you can realistically be expected to achieve from this part of the market, it may be helpful if you took this opportunity to map the market at the next level, in other words, the PAM. The rest of the segmentation project would, however, continue to focus on your realistically available market, only returning to the potential market if required. This extension of the map should be straightforward if the channels to market are the same. If, however, the channels are different and to include them overcomplicates the market map, keep the map within the limits of your market definition.

Returning to the button manufacturer (in the garment fastenings market), the decision for this company would fall between including or excluding zips and Velcro on the market map. Whatever the decision, the first segmentation project would focus on buttons, their current realistic available market (given the difference in equipment required to manufacture the competing products).

Another issue you may need to address is associated with corporate structure.

In many companies the market being segmented will fall within the responsibilities of one SBU. Progressing the project is therefore quite straightforward.

An SBU will:

- have common customers and competitors for most of its products;
- be a competitor in an external market;
- be a discrete, separate identifiable unit;
- have a manager who has control over most of the areas critical to success.

As a general rule, therefore, one composite market map can be drawn for the SBU. If, however, some products or services go through totally different channels and/or to totally different final users and/or meet the needs of totally different markets, there will be a need for more than one market map. For example, the domestic users may well be reached in an entirely different way from the business-to-business users.

For some companies, the market being segmented doesn't sit so neatly within their current structure and straddles two or more divisions. This can occur when a business is structured along product lines and these products are seen to compete with each other in one, or more, of their markets. For example, in a market defined in terms of 'being able to afford a particular standard of living from a planned date of retirement' both pension plans and investment plans are used, yet these two lines are often found within two different business units.

Although the preferred solution is to segment the market as defined and therefore include the competing product lines, it may be that in the first instance it is more pragmatic to segment that part of the market currently satisfied by your product line.

Great care is needed in making the decision to exclude products or services from a market map. If in doubt, include them in your first pass.

A good point at which to start is to use your *current* SBU structure.

Such structures usually exist because the volume or value of business justifies such a specific focus. For example, in the case of a farming co-operative supplying seeds, fertilisers, crop protection, insurance and banking to farmers, it would be sensible to start, initially, by drawing a separate market map for each of these product groups, even though they all appear to go through similar channels to the same end users. In the organisation concerned, each one is treated as a separate SBU.

In other words, *it is recommended that you start the mapping (and subsequent segmentation) process at the lowest level of disaggregation within the organisation's current structure.*

Later on, it should be possible to use the same process for higher and higher levels of aggregation to check whether it may be possible to merge any of your current SBUs. Indeed, it may even be possible, eventually, to reorganise the whole company around 'new' groupings of either customers or products. This is covered at the end of Step 5 in Chapter 6.

Constructing your market map

Draw a market map for the market you plan to segment that defines the distribution and value added chain between the suppliers and final users. This should take into account the various buying mechanisms found in your market, including the part played by 'influencers'. Before you draw the map, however, it is suggested that you read the whole of this chapter.

This is a key step in the market segmentation process and you should spend as much time as necessary to complete the details.

The series of figures which follow progressively incorporate various points made in the text about market maps. Although the diagrams in these figures are a useful first stage in constructing market maps, it should be noted that, unless your business operates in a market with a very simple structure, this method of market mapping will only be an illustrative aid. For most businesses, you will find your market is too complex to be clearly presented in a diagram. The alternative is to construct your market map in a tabular format. This chapter contains guidelines designed to assist you in constructing your market map this way.

It is, therefore, recommended that you first read all of Step 1, using diagrams as a means of observing how the various steps in market mapping help develop a detailed picture of your market. Then, if you wish, you can change to the tabular format and construct your market map this way.

Getting started

It is useful to start your market map by plotting the various stages that occur along the distribution and value added chain between you, and *your competitors*, and the final users. At the same time, indicate the particular routes to market the products go down as not all of them will necessarily pass through all of these stages. An example of this starting point for market mapping is shown in Figure 2.2.

These transaction stages (represented by the cubes in Figure 2.2) are referred to as *'junctions'*, with each junction on a market map positioned hierarchically, according to how close it is to the final user. The last junction along the market map would, therefore, be the final user.

It is not essential to draw the map starting from the supplier. In fact, it may even be easier to draw the map starting with the final user, backtracking to the supplier. Do whatever you feel most comfortable doing.

Although the suppliers in Figure 2.2 are represented by a single junction, it may be appropriate for your market to identify the field salesforce employed by you and/or your competitors as a separate junction. This is particularly useful in markets where business can either be conducted through a field salesforce or 'direct' with an office-based sales team without reference to field sales. This situation is captured in Figure 2.3.

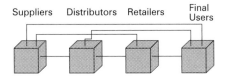

Figure 2.2   Starting a market map

Note: This market map consists of four stages, one each for suppliers, distributors, retailers and final users. This map illustrates that products are also acquired by the final users direct from the suppliers and the distributors, as well as from retailers. Some retailers also bypass distributors and acquire their stocks direct from the suppliers.

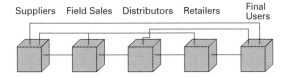

Figure 2.3   Market map with field sales identified separately

Note: In this market map, field sales do not contact any of the final users and only some of the retailers. All the distributors have their business conducted through field sales.

The junction which represents your own company need not always be at the extreme of the map. For example, if you were a distributor in the above market it would be important when mapping the dynamics of this particular market to capture the fact that some product was sourced direct from the suppliers. Your market map in these circumstances would therefore include a junction for suppliers. If this particular route to market was growing at your expense, it would be important to capture that fact and to understand why it was taking place.

It is very important that your market map tracks your products/services, along with those of your competitors, all the way through to the final user, even though you may not actually sell to them direct.

In some markets, the direct customer/purchaser will not always be the final user, as is illustrated in the following set of circumstances.

A company (or household) may commission a third party contractor to carry out some redecoration, or an advertising agency to develop and conduct a promotional campaign, or a bank/accountant/financial adviser to produce and implement a financial programme. For all of us, the doctor we visit when seeking treatment is, in many respects, a contractor when it comes to prescribing medicine.

Although the contractor is strictly the direct buyer, they are not the final user. The distinction is important because, to win the commission, the contractor would have needed to understand the requirements of their customer and, in carrying out the commission, would have carried out those requirements on behalf of their customer. To miss out the final user from the market map would, therefore, have ignored an array of different needs which the supplier would benefit from being aware of (and have included in their product offer) if the supplier were to ensure their company name appeared on the contractor's 'preferred supplier list'. The inclusion of a contractor on a market map is illustrated in Figure 2.4.

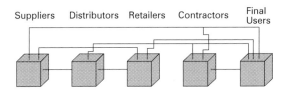

Figure 2.4   Market map with contractor

If you would prefer to present your market map in tabular form, Table 2.1 presents the same information contained in Figure 2.4 in this format.

Table 2.1   Market map with contractor presented in tabular form

A	B	C	D	E
Suppliers	*Distributor*	*Retailers*	*Contractors*	*Final Users*
	From A	From A	From A	From A
		From B	From B	From B
				From C
				From D

Note: For ease of reference each junction is given an alpha code.

Ensuring your market map continues right the way through to the final user is also appropriate in those situations where final users have their products/services purchased for them, for example, by their company's purchasing department. In such instances, the market map would track your products/services down the corridors of your business clients and continue beyond the purchasing department to the department(s) in which the final user(s) were found. This is illustrated in Figure 2.5.

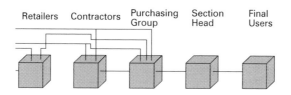

Figure 2.5   Market map with final users 'hidden' from the suppliers

In many markets the final user is often represented by the last individual in the chain who has to dig into their pocket, or budget, to pay everyone else in the chain. There are, inevitably, some exceptions, such as, for example, food and clothes for children, most office staff, workers on the shop floor, nurses and radiographers, and so on.

A further refinement to your market map, particularly in business-to-business markets, could be the inclusion of purchasing procedures as a distinct junction to capture the fact that there is yet another hurdle to be surmounted between you and the final user. In Figure 2.5 this would most likely be located between the purchasing group and the section heads, the purchasing group simply carrying out instructions, though they may, of course, be involved in the purchasing procedure.

For some businesses, it will also be important when drawing the market map to go beyond that stage in the value added chain where their particular product becomes incorporated into another (and even becomes unrecognisable). For example, many chemical companies are switching to more environmentally friendly processes in the manufacturing of their products. However, few chemicals are seen in their raw state by their final user. As well as being good environmentalists, these companies need to be alert to the environmentally aware consumers. These consumers are clearly a key target market for their products. It may, therefore, be in the interest of the chemical company to spend resources in this segment to ensure they buy products which incorporate the chemicals produced in an environmentally friendly way.

One of the more recent, and apparently successful, examples of a company spending resources beyond the stage in their market map where their product becomes incorporated into another is Intel Corporation. Intel promote their microprocessors to the final user under the 'intel inside' logo (a registered trademark of Intel Corporation).

If it is not obvious, mark on the market map the point at which your product becomes incorporated into another and begins to lose its own identity (an event which could, of course, occur in a single step).

As the figures have illustrated, most market maps will have at least two principal components:

- the channel (distribution channel, often referred to as customers);
- final users/purchasers (often referred to as consumers).

For many markets, however, it is also essential that their maps include a third component, namely the stage(s) where influence/advice/decisions occur (not necessarily a transaction) about which products to use.

For example, a co-operative may simply act as a buyer on behalf of its members (the members deciding on both the product type and specific manufacturer), and once it has sourced the product, arrange for it to be distributed direct to its members. Alternatively, the members of a co-operative may decide on the generic product type they require, leaving the co-operative to decide on which specific manufacturer's product to buy, as well as arrange delivery either to a central depot or, again, direct to its members. Although, in the first instance, the role of the co-operative is quite passive and, in the second, quite active, the co-operative has played a part in the transaction and should therefore appear on the market map for both. Similarly, in both cases, the 'members' should appear on the market map.

Exactly the same situation can occur when, for example, accountants feature in financial transactions. In some transactions, the accountant purchases or sells investments according to the instructions they receive from their client (the final user). In others, the accountant may be authorised to make, and carry out, investment decisions on behalf of the client.

Another role for the accountant in the investment market could be purely that of an adviser contributing to the final decision, with the client carrying out the actual transaction. A more detailed look at the market in which the co-operative featured may have also revealed that the members referred to an outside consultant, such as an independent technical expert, for advice on which specific product to buy. In addition, for both the consumer and business markets, it is important that you should not overlook in your market map the influence of specialist publications, or the influence of special reports in generalist publications (such as newspapers). Here, we are *not* referring to the power, or otherwise, of advertising. It is unusual for advertising to be deliberately sought out by the readers. We are referring more to the influence of well-researched articles on the buying behaviour of those final users who deliberately seek out such publications/articles as part of their buying process. For example, the range of *Which?* publications from the Consumers' Association (UK) can be a very powerful influence for some consumers on their choice of product and even on their selection of investments. The important point here is that in all three instances, we are seeing an 'influencer' not directly featuring in any transaction. These influencers should also appear on the market map, as shown in Figure 2.6, just as if they were a transaction stage.

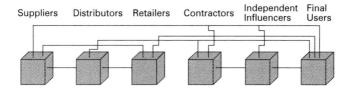

Figure 2.6   Market map with influencers

Overlooking the role of independent influencers in a market can result in lost sales opportunities. For example, the market map constructed for a company involved in supplying expensive capital goods to businesses eventually illustrated that nearly 40 per cent of their market was in fact determined by independent consultants. At that stage the company in question had no activity at all targeted at these consultants. They were therefore potentially missing out on 40 per cent of the market, a shortfall they rapidly addressed.

Independent influencers need not necessarily be consultants. For many technically sophisticated products it is crucial in any sales strategy to get the equipment installed in what may be termed 'luminary sites'. The influence generated by these sites on the choice of equipment made by other sites can be quite substantial. Such sites should therefore appear on the market map.

For most market maps, the decision on which junction a particular activity should be placed in will be very clear. However, there will be instances where the decision is not immediately apparent. Referring, again, to the co-operative example: a co-operative may simply replace a retail outlet or a wholesaler, in which case it could just as easily be placed in the same junction as the retailer or wholesaler, as appropriate. Alternatively, a co-operative may source its products from either a wholesaler, or direct from the manufacturer, in which case it is clearer to position the co-operative on the market map at a stage which is nearest to the final user. Following the same guidelines, the consultant would be placed in a junction one stage below the membership.

In implementing these directions and those which follow, you may find that you have to redraw or amend your market map a number of times. All you are doing at this stage is progressively creating a preliminary form of macro-market segmentation. Later on, you will proceed to do more detailed segmentation.

A worksheet for this first phase of market mapping appears in Table 2.2. It contains a section for a trial run before you move on to draw the final map.

It is useful to verify the routes to market and the role of influencers in any market research project you commission.

Initial quantification of the market map

With quantification playing an important part later on in the process, mark at each junction and along each route the volumes or values dealt with by each of them. In most cases the annual figures for the market would be used. Where figures are not available guesstimates should be made in order to scale the project. Also note your market share (again guesstimate if necessary). This is illustrated in Figure 2.7.

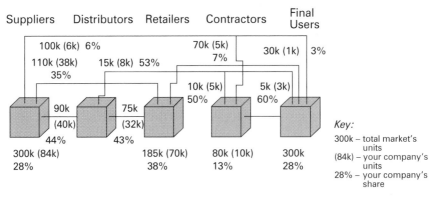

Figure 2.7   Initial quantification of a market map

Note: The number of units entering a market usually equates to the number of units 'consumed' by the final users. Please take some time to follow the lines through the chain and you will observe that, like the work of an accountant, it all 'balances'. In some markets, however, it is possible for intermediaries to both take product from suppliers and put together the product themselves. In these circumstances, the number of units in the market will increase along the distribution/value added chain.

Table 2.2   Worksheet – market map for your selected market

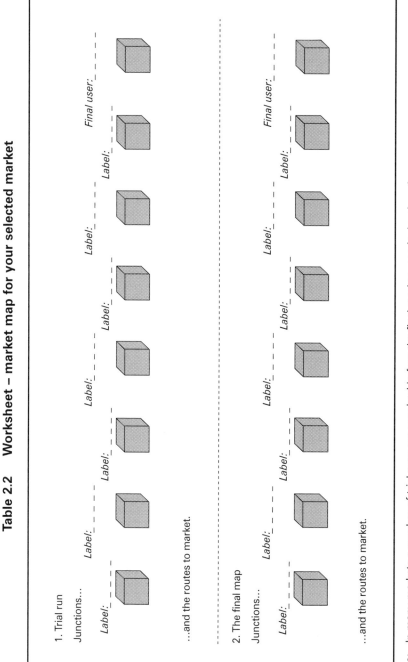

1. Trial run

Junctions...

Label: _ _ _ _   _Label:_ _ _ _ _   _Label:_ _ _ _ _   _Label:_ _ _ _ _   _Label:_ _ _ _ _   _Label:_ _ _ _ _   _Final user:_ _ _ _ _

...and the routes to market.

2. The final map

Junctions...

Label: _ _ _ _   _Label:_ _ _ _ _   _Label:_ _ _ _ _   _Label:_ _ _ _ _   _Label:_ _ _ _ _   _Label:_ _ _ _ _   _Final user:_ _ _ _ _

...and the routes to market.

Note: In many markets a number of trial runs are required before the final market map is developed.

In addition to recording the volumes/values dealt with (or influenced) by each junction, also note the number of businesses/customers that exist at each junction. Once more, guesstimate if the number is unknown.

Companies occasionally indicate a preference to quantify a market in terms of profitability. As profitability is often a reflection of the efficiency or inefficiency of individual companies, it is not an appropriate measure of market size. The ability to generate profit, however, is a consideration when looking at how to prioritise and select segments (see Chapter 9).

If you are constructing your market map in tabular form, Table 2.3 presents the same information contained in Figure 2.7 in this format, this time with the addition of the number of businesses/customers that exist at each junction.

Table 2.3   Initial quantification of a market map in tabular form

A Suppliers [17]	B Distributors [62]	C Retailers [465]	D Contractors [150]	E Final Users [5 500]
	From A 90k (40k) 44%	From A 110k (38k) 35%	From A 70k (5k) 7%	From A 30k (1k) 3%
		From B 75k (32k) 43%	From B 10k (5k) 50%	From B 5k (3k) 60%
				From C 185k (70k) 38%
				From D 80k (10k) 13%
Total: 300k (84k) 28%	90k (40k) 44%	185k (70k) 38%	80k (10k) 13%	300k (84k) 28%

Key: Using junction 'C' as an example; The total number of companies/customers located at this junction is '[465]'; the total number of units acquired from junction 'A' is '110k' and your company supplies '(38k)' of these, which is '35%'. The total number of units which pass through junction 'C' is '185k', of which your company supplies '(70k)', in other words, '38%'.

As pointed out earlier in this chapter, it isn't essential to construct the map starting from the supplier. It may be easier to construct the map starting with the final user, backtracking to the supplier. As already suggested, do whatever you feel most comfortable doing.

Expanding the detail on your market map

The next stage for your market map is to expand the detail it contains, as the 'top line' picture developed so far is probably hiding some important differences between customers. These differences could provide useful information for your segmentation project.

Note at each junction on your market map, if applicable, all the currently understood different types of companies/customers that occur there, as illustrated in Figure 2.8. If your market map even before this stage has become quite complex you may need to develop the detail by sketching out the various junctions separately, and/or sketching out the various companies/consumers separately. It may also assist you if, in this first look at the detail, you construct an outline (as opposed to the definitive picture). The definitive picture can be entered once you have determined at which junction(s) it is appropriate to develop a segmentation structure.

If you already have a segmentation structure for any of these junctions and you are following this process to test its validity, use this structure to define the respective junction types. This will be useful for Step 2 of the process. The market mapping routine may, of course, be challenging the traditional lists of company/customer types at the various junctions around which you currently conduct your marketing effort. In such instances, replace what now appears to be the out-of-date list with the new list.

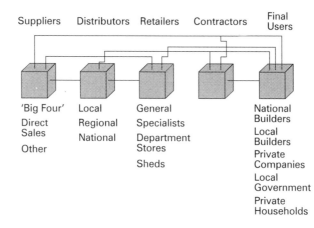

Figure 2.8   Market map listing the different company/customer types

Note: This market map combines domestic and business-to-business end users. 'Sheds' is the name sometimes used to refer to hardware superstores.

Once these lists have been put together, the next stage is to redraw the market map using these respective junction types, as illustrated in Figure 2.9.

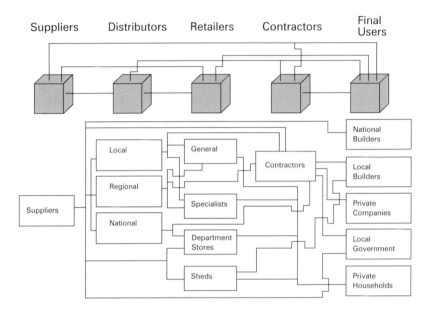

Figure 2.9   Market map with the different company/customer types

Note: This particular market map could now be showing that there is little commonality between the domestic and business-to-business end users. In developing the market map further, it may now be preferable to treat them as different markets, each with their own market map. For the time being, however, we will continue to cover them with one map.

For those of you constructing your market map in tabular form, Table 2.4 presents the same information contained in Figure 2.9 in this format.

To assist in developing your market map you could apply letters to your diagram as illustrated in the tabular format example.

Be sure to draw a total market map rather than just the part you currently deal with. The purpose of this is to ensure that you understand your market dynamics properly. For example, beware of writing in only the word 'distributor' if there are, in fact, different kinds of distributors who behave in different ways and who supply different customers. Similarly, avoid writing in only the word 'buyer' if there are buyers who have different ranges of responsibilities (some may specify as well as buy) or who carry out their responsibilities in different ways. This is explained in more detail below under the heading, 'Identifying the junction(s) where segmentation should occur (market leverage points)'.

Table 2.4   Market map with the different company/customer types presented in tabular form

A *Suppliers*	B *Distributors*	C *Retailers*	D *Contractors*	E *Final Users*
AA* Suppliers:	**BA** Local: From AA **BB** Regional: From AA **BC** National: From AA	**CA** General: From BA From BB **CB** Specialists: From BA From BB **CC** Department Stores: From AA From BC . **CD** Sheds From AA	**DA** Contractors: From AA From BA From BB From BC	**EA** National Builders: From AA **EB** Local Builders: From CD From DA **EC** Private Companies: From DA **ED** Local Govt: From AA From DA **EE** Private Households: From CA From CB From CC From CD

Note: * If you prefer, you can, of course, allocate codes to each supplier, or type of supplier (AA, AB, AC and so on), and then illustrate for each junction type dealing with the suppliers directly which supplier(s) they obtain their supplies from.

A further detail you may wish to show on your market map, if appropriate, could be a listing of the different purchasing procedures encountered by suppliers such as committees, authorisers, sealed bids and so on, as shown in Figure 2.10.

The map in Figure 2.10 also illustrates the participants in particular purchasing procedures and lists them within the appropriate junction type. This detail may be important later on in the process when you are required to identify decision-makers, as only some of those involved in the purchasing procedure may have the real power.

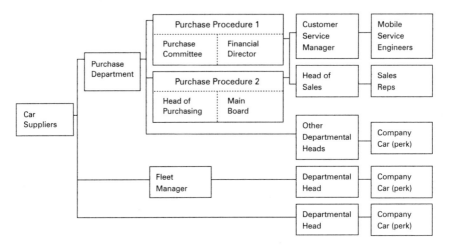

Figure 2.10   Market map with business purchasing procedures

Note: In this market map, the physical delivery of the product to the final user (car supplier to car user) is insufficient in representing the sales route and purchasing routines encountered. The market map also illustrates that not all the final users who appear beyond 'Purchase Procedure 1' are subject to the same purchasing routine, even though they are within a single company type. In some instances, of course, certain final users may purchase direct. For example, all the departments in a company may use mail, but the advertising department may 'purchase' its mail through their direct mail agency and therefore bypass the normal purchase procedures.

In addition to tracking down the corridors of business clients, Figure 2.10 has also differentiated between the departments of final users according to the different use they have for the product, namely as a vehicle for service engineers, for sales or as a pure company perk. *Separating final users according to whether they either utilised your product/service differently, or utilised it to achieve a different objective could be a useful way of taking the map forward into Step 2.* Each of these final user departments would be listed separately on your market map. (Where a *single* final user department, or individual, puts your product/service to a number of different end-use applications, it is sometimes easier if they appear on the market map only once. Different end-use applications by single final users are captured in Step 3.)

 Ensure any market research project you commission uncovers and develops an understanding of the different uses the products and/or services are put to.

Detailed quantification of the market map

The more detailed market map you have now constructed should be quantified as shown in Figure 2.11 with the volumes or values allocated to the different junction types (again, guesstimate if necessary). Also, note your market share, if known.

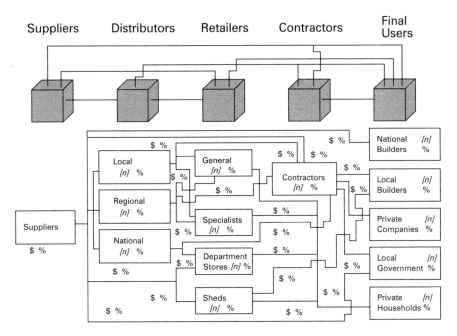

Key: *[n]* – Number of active companies/customers in this junction type
     $ – Total units (volume or value)
     % – Your share

Figure 2.11   Market map with different company/customer types, their volumes or values, number of each type and your market share

A fully quantified market map appears later in this chapter.

As already suggested earlier in this chapter, the complexity of your market map may be such that going to this level of detail is best left until you have determined at which junction(s) it is appropriate to develop a segmentation structure.

In tabular form the extra detail captured in Figure 2.11 would be recorded as shown in Table 2.5.

Table 2.5 Market map in tabular form with different company/customer types, their volumes or values, number of each type and your market share

A	B	C	D	E
Suppliers	*Distributors*	*Retailers*	*Contractors*	*Final Users*
AA* Suppliers: *[n]* $ %	**BA** Local: *[n]* $ % From AA	**CA** General: *[n]* $ % From BA From BB	**DA** Contractors: *[n]* $ % From AA From BA From BB From BC	**EA** National Builders: *[n]* $ % From AA
	BB Regional: *[n]* $ % From AA	**CB** Specialists: *[n]* $ % From BA From BB		**EB** Local Builders: *[n]* $ % From CD From DA
	BC National: *[n]* $ % From AA	**CC** Department Stores: *[n]* $ % From AA From BC		**EC** Private Companies: *[n]* $ % From DA
		CD Sheds: *[n]* $ % From AA		**ED** Local Govt: *[n]* $ % From AA From DA
				EE Private Households: *[n]* $ % From CA From CB From CC From CD

Key: *[n]* – Number of active companies/customers in this junction type; $ – Total units (volume or value) going through this junction type; % – Your share.

Note: Any or all of the non-domestic final users could be extended beyond one type if it was known that more than one purchase procedure existed in any of them. For example, if there were two different purchasing procedures known to exist with National Builders, there would be two sets of National Builders. Companies could additionally be extended further along the map if there were different departments using the product/service you supply.

A fully quantified example of a market map in tabular form appears later in this chapter.

Ensure any market research project you commission is able to provide you with useful statistics about your market in order to reduce the amount of guesswork.

It should be emphasised that the market maps used to illustrate the text are relatively simplistic, especially for business-to-business markets, both in the identification of final user departments and in tracking through the various purchasing procedures that may be encountered (see earlier parts of Step 1).

Your market map should now be complete.

Identifying the junction(s) where segmentation should occur (market leverage points)

First, *highlight* those junctions where decisions are made about which of the competing products/services should be purchased. These are known as *Market Leverage Points*. It is not necessary for *all* the various buying types (companies/customers) listed at each junction to make this decision.

The segmentation process does not concern itself with the actual decision to satisfy a particular need, only with the decision about which particular product/service to purchase in order to satisfy that need (see 'market' and 'market segmentation' definitions in Chapter 1).

Although the segmentation process detailed in Steps 2 to 7 should, ideally, occur at each junction along the market map where decisions are made (as long as the volume/value or number of customers/consumers at that junction justifies it, for example, if there are five or more) it is recommended that you first segment the junction furthest away from the supplier (manufacturer) where decisions are made. Once the segmentation process has been completed for this particular junction, the process can then be repeated for each successive junction where decisions are made, progressively backtracking along the market map away from the final user towards you, the supplier. This will be particularly important for those businesses where the salesforce is required to deal with buyers who act on behalf of final users.

 Combining junctions into a single segmentation exercise rather than looking at their requirements separately can become a major obstacle to successful segmentation. It is unlikely that the buying requirements of each junction will consist of the same criteria. Comparing requirements across junctions is therefore difficult. Comparisons are usually more meaningful when conducted across the 'members' found within a junction.

It is possible to start this stage of the segmentation process at junctions other than the one furthest away from the supplier (manufacturer), though it is suggested that starting at the furthest junction will help in segmenting the junctions closer to the supplier.

For businesses where their particular product/service becomes incorporated into another and is both unrecognisable and has little or no influence on decisions at the final user junction, a consensus will be needed to determine where along the market map the segmentation process outlined in this book should occur. For example, the circuit boards used inside a television have little, if any, influence on the decision made by a television buyer between alternative models. For the manufacturer of the television, however, the selection of which circuit boards to use may be important. The same would apply to the selection of canner used to supply the cans for baked beans; the consumer is rarely interested in the specification for the can, though it is probably an important decision for the baked bean manufacturer. The guideline in selecting which junction to segment first in these circumstances is to find the junction furthest away from the supplier where the product has leverage on a decision. In other words, where the value of the benefits derived from the product are seen to be important. This issue may have already been addressed when arriving at your market definition (see Chapter 1, 'Whose needs are being defined').

At the junction selected on the market map where you are proceeding with the segmentation process, refine your identification of market leverage points by *highlighting* the company/customer types who make decisions about which product to have, assuming you have split this junction into different types. If appropriate, this will enable you to focus your segmentation project on to clearly defined market leverage points (see Chapter 3). Note at the selected junction the volume/value that it decides upon and allocate this total figure to the junction types. Guesstimate these figures if they are not known and note this as a requirement for any follow-up work generated by this first pass at segmenting your market.

In addition to dividing the volume/value figures on your market map into leveraged and non-leveraged amounts, it is also useful to record the following two refinements at the junction level and, if applicable, at the junction type level:

- the number of customers who make the decision for themselves;
- your company's share of the volume/value decided on.

Once again, guesstimate these figures if they are not known and note these as requirements for any follow-up work generated by this segmentation project.

If the selection of which product to have at any junction is always influenced by decisions at other junctions further along the map towards the final users, the earlier junction does not contain any leverage points. To explain this, let us return to the case of the co-operative once more and use this as an example. When the co-operative just buys what it is instructed to buy by its members, the members represent the leverage point. The leverage point, however, reverts to the co-operative in those instances where the co-operative decides which manufacturer's product to buy. On some occasions, especially in business-to-business marketing, this distinction is not always so clear cut. For example, the purchasing procedure for any department (final user) wishing to acquire any 'substantial' items may require the department to obtain three quotes and submit these to the financial director, a purchasing group or committee for the final decision. The principal leverage point usually lies with the department drawing up the shortlist of the three alternative suppliers, because if your company's product is not included at this stage there is no possibility of progressing any further. However, because the department wishing to make the purchase has its freedom of action constrained by a company policy, the leverage is 'shared' with those involved in the final purchase decision. The requirements of both have to be taken into account and may even need to be regarded as two segmentation exercises. Alternatively, in drawing up the shortlist of three quotes, the department in question, being pragmatic, may base its selection on the vetting criteria used by the body which makes the final decision. The leverage now lies with the individual(s) deciding between the quotes shortlisted.

In those situations where you are having difficulty in deciding where leverage really lies, apply the 'one phone call test'. This assumes you have sufficient funds only for one final phone call in order to swing the sale in your favour. You therefore have to make this call to the most important decision-maker (or influencer). Who would you call?

If, when discussing whether a particular company/customer type (or a junction as a whole) is a leverage point or not, it appears that in some instances it is and in some instances it isn't, this could indicate one of two things.

(a) Beyond this leverage point and further along the map, the market must split in two (or more). For example, Consumer Group 1 will buy any brand of toothpaste stocked by their preferred retailer, because they trust the retailer to supply good quality products. If this retailer drops a particular brand, it makes no difference to these particular consumers. Here, the retailer is a leverage point. At the same time, however, Consumer Group 2 visit the same retailer as Group 1, but will only buy a particular brand of toothpaste. If the retailer doesn't stock it, then Group 2 will find an alternative retailer that does. Here, the *consumer* is a leverage point. Consumer Groups 1 and 2 are clearly different and the retailer is a leverage point for one but not for both groups. (Also see the 'Note' at the end of this particular explanation.)

A typical instance where this can be seen in a business-to-business stage of a product's flow from manufacturer to final user is when a junction appears on the market map for 'contractors'. Contractors normally do business with a variety of customers, and it is unlikely these customers will demonstrate the same approach to buying the services of a contractor. Take a building contractor as an example. Customers of the building contractor will include local authorities, health authorities, private hospital groups, private house builders, commercial property builders, new developments, renovations, industrial concerns and central government. Some of these customers will specify which products the contractor should use (making the 'customer' the leverage point), whilst others will leave product specification to the contractor (making the 'contractor' the leverage point). It may help you in your discussions about contractors to review the specifications they issue for different types of jobs. Contractors will reflect the different require-ments of those customers with whom the leverage point lies in the specifications issued to their suppliers. This may well, of course, have been picked up while constructing the market map. It also illustrates the importance of carrying out the first segmentation pass at the junction of the final user.

To cover these situations, split out the volume/value figure decided upon at each of the appropriate junction types, or junction as a whole, and highlight it. Alternatively, add a letter or numeric code in order to indicate that two roles are found here and highlight the one being used to identify leverage, for example, 'L' (for leverage) and 'P' (for passive), with the 'L' highlighted for clarity. Do not be put off by the fact that it is, for example, the same distributor or customer type. This merely indicates that a single operating policy to that distributor or customer is unlikely to be effective.

Note: In the example above, which refers to Consumer Groups 1 and 2 buying toothpaste through retailers, it is possible that, although Group 2 have a brand preference, if it is out of stock at their preferred retailer they will opt for one of the alternative brands in stock. This does not mean that in constructing the market map, the leverage point lies with the retailer for both consumer groups. The leverage point for Group 2 still rests with them, but it is a very weak one. This situation will be covered in Step 5, which allocates weightings of importance to the reasons for purchase.

b) There are different types of consumers/business units at this leverage point. For example, in constructing the market map for hi-fi products, a particular junction (or junction type) may have been labelled 'retailers', but this could well be too broad a description and should be split between, say, specialist retailers and department stores. If this is the case, redraw the market map to accommodate these two junction types (or list them separately if using the tabular form and give them distinct letter codes: for example, CB and CC).

Taking the toothpaste example above, if, in constructing the market map, a discussion about leverage points had not occurred at the retailer junction (and therefore hadn't identified Consumer Groups 1 and 2 at this stage), a discussion could occur at the consumer junction and identify the two consumer groups at this later stage. If this is the case the map should now show that there are two consumer types, either by using your selected code for distinguishing between leverage and non-leverage customers or by splitting out the volumes/values as suggested in (a). (In addition, to assist with segmentation of the retailer junction at a later stage, the map should now be amended to show that leverage and non-leverage are found within retailers, together with the associated volumes/values.)

Don't forget to identify clearly where leverage occurs, along with any associated figures. Finally, identify throughout your market map the approximate number of customers with leverage, assuming you have included these figures on your market map. Clearly, in those instances where the members of a single junction or junction type act as a leverage point on some but not all occasions (as for the retailer of toothpaste mentioned earlier) only a total number as a whole can be recorded.

The inclusion of leverage points is illustrated in Figure 2.12.

At this stage of the process, you may find that your discussions have revealed some differences between the products included in one of your SBUs. Later stages of the process separate out the specific products and enable you to note the reasons why each one is bought. A regrouping procedure then takes place based on similarities. This should be sufficient to overcome any problems observed at this stage. (In extreme cases, where progressing to the next stage of the process is held up because of these differences, it is, of course, possible to split the products between different market maps.)

MARKET RESEARCH NOTE	The market map provides important guidelines for any market research project commissioned to improve your understanding of the market your business is in. It identifies the different target groups to be included in the sample frame for both the qualitative and quantitative stages of the research.

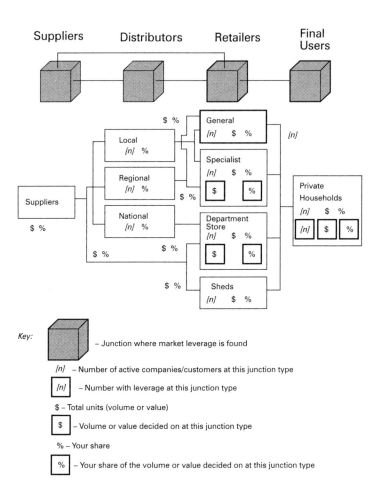

Figure 2.12   Leverage points on a market map

Note: This market map is based on the map appearing in Figure 2.11 except that it is now split between the domestic and business-to-business final users. The map shows that the distributor junction has no leverage in the domestic market and illustrates a range of possibilities at the retailer junction: sheds have no leverage, specialists and department stores have some leverage, and the general retailers have leverage over everything they sell. (This is for illustrative purposes only.)

Due to the specialists and department stores catering both for final users depending on them for a decision and for final users coming to them with a particular specification, it is not possible to divide the number of these retailers between leverage and non-leverage outlets.

Process check

So far, we have mapped out the different transaction stages (junctions) that are found in your market all the way through to the final user, and seen how these junctions relate to each other. By quantifying these various 'routes' and determining your company's share along them, we have identified the most important routes and seen your company's position along each of them.

By then looking at where decisions are made between the products/ services of competing suppliers, we have identified a number of junctions where segmentation could occur. For most organisations, it is recommended that segmentation should first take place at the junction *furthest away* from the supplier/manufacturer, *where decisions are made*.

The next step provides you with an opportunity, if you so wish, to introduce into the process a segmentation structure you may want to test for the selected junction (preliminary segments). This preliminary structure could well benefit from taking into account the existence of leverage and non-leverage customer groups, assuming both exist at the selected junction. You may also want to take into account the different purchasing 'routes' highlighted for this junction on the market map, though there is an opportunity to cover this in Steps 3 and 4. Other options are possible and these are discussed in the next chapter. The principal focus of Step 2, however, is on putting together the information you can use to identify the various customers found in the market (profiling). This will be very important at the end of the project as it will be used to distinguish between the customers found in each of the concluding segments.

Case study and further examples

As briefly mentioned in Chapter 1, a case study is used to illustrate each step in turn. The case study is based on the company featured in the last chapter of this book and picks up the story as it stood in 1988. For reasons of commercial confidentiality, however, as well as to assist in demonstrating the process in practice, the case study has been modified. Due to these changes the company in the case study is renamed 'Agrofertiliser Supplies'.

CASE 2.1   Agrofertiliser Supplies

To briefly summarise the background to the case: Agrofertiliser Supplies is an independent business within a large, international chemical company, though its sales of fertilisers are predominantly in the UK. Within the larger group there exists a company which produces seeds for the agricultural sector and an agrochemical company, both of which also operate as independent businesses. Unfortunately, Agrofertiliser Supplies are losing market share and making financial losses in a line of business which is becoming increasingly competitive, a situation not helped by a steady fall in the level of overall demand. Cost-cutting measures have helped stem the losses but more needs to be done. The board are now looking to the marketing group for some answers.

To provide a basis for these answers, a small team within the marketing group has been charged with developing a detailed understanding of the UK market in order to determine where the most profitable opportunities exist for Agrofertliser Supplies. Supporting the team is a group drawn from across the business including finance, distribution, sales and manufacturing.

A segmentation project is about to start.

But before even beginning to consider putting together a market map for Agrofertiliser Supplies, the team recognise it is essential that the project has a very clear definition of the market to be segmented.

Fertilisers represent one of the components required for growing commercial crops, the others (under the control of the farmer) being seeds and, in most cases, agrochemicals. The question to be addressed, therefore, is whether the market should be defined in terms of 'commercial crop growing' or focused around 'commercial crop nutrients'?

The arguments put forward in favour of 'commercial crop growing' could be summarised as follows:

- the three products have similar distribution channels;
- the three products are complementary to each other;
- dealing with one sales representative would appeal to farmers;
- it would offer greater cross-selling opportunities.

On the other hand, the arguments put forward in favour of focusing the definition around 'commercial crop nutrients' included:

- they have a distinct contribution to the growing of commercial crops;
- there is a practical limitation on the technical knowledge of the salesforce;

| **CASE 2.1** | **Agrofertiliser Supplies (cont'd)** |

- the realistic timescale for putting together a combined offer was too long;
- farmers appeared to regard the three products as distinct product lines.

Two particular observations became pivotal to the final decision:

1. The final users, the farmers, did consider fertilisers to be a distinct group of products and, in fact, 'compartmentalised' the products required for growing crops into their three distinct categories. The three product lines were, therefore, not seen as alternatives.

2. The realistically available market to Agrofertiliser Supplies for the foreseeable future was that of 'commercial crop nutrients'. The technology and skills required to produce and sell seeds and/or agrochemicals was outside the scope of the company.

The market to be segmented, therefore, was the 'commercial crop nutrients' market. This does not mean to say, however, that as time moves on this definition will continue to be the right one. It was just the most pragmatic definition at the time of the project.

It should be noted that 'crops' refers to both arable crops and the production of grass for feeding livestock.

The market map put together by Agrofertiliser Supplies is summarised in Figure 2.13.

To conclude this stage of the process for Agrofertiliser Supplies, it is worth noting that although the output from farms continues along a further distribution and value added chain to the point where it is consumed as food, only a very small percentage of these customers expressed any interest in how crops were grown at the time of the project. The situation has changed since then and, as a result, more and more farms have become organic, using nutrients for their crops that satisfy the requirements of this particular group of ultimate final users. UK farmers appear, however, to be lagging behind the growth in demand for organic produce, because in 1997, the latest estimate available at the time of writing this book, two-thirds of the demand was having to be met by imports.

This case study is continued in the following chapters.

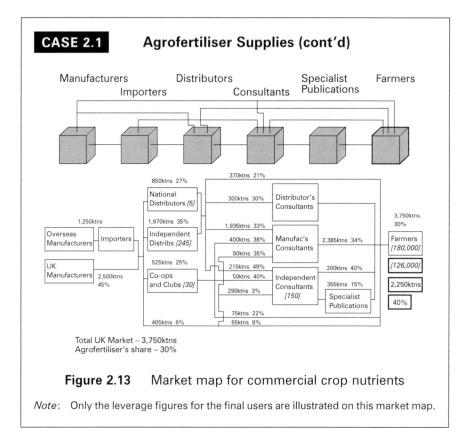

Figure 2.13   Market map for commercial crop nutrients

Note: Only the leverage figures for the final users are illustrated on this market map.

Further examples

The following series of figures presents some slightly different styles for drawing market maps. The level of information they contain is varied. All have been edited for reasons of commercial confidentiality.

Figure 2.14 is for a market whose needs are met by employing very expensive, specialised technical equipment. This equipment is found in both large companies and in specialist, smaller companies.

As can be seen in the market represented by Figure 2.14, leverage occurs in a number of junctions. This project progressed by considering each junction in turn.

The next example, Figure 2.15, is for a market whose needs are met by a particular type of internal wall covering which, although principally targeted at professional tradesmen, is also bought by home owners who wish to do it themselves (DIY). This particular map was drawn at the very early stages of the project and is included more for its presentation style than for the information it contains.

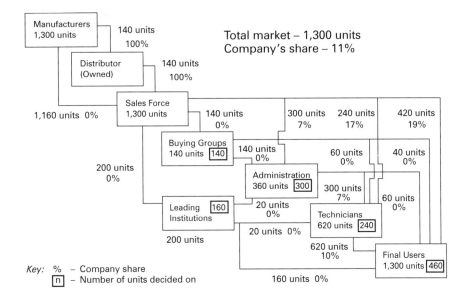

Total market – 1,300 units
Company's share – 11%

Key: % – Company share
n – Number of units decided on

Figure 2.14   Market map example – specialised technical equipment

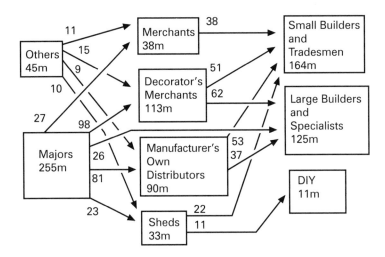

Figure 2.15   Market map example – internal wall covering

It is worth noting that the particular company undertaking the segmentation project for the market represented in Figure 2.15 was, in fact, located in the middle junction. However, because some customers were dealing direct with the major manufacturers, it was essential this was captured on their market map.

Finally, a simplified example of a completed market map in tabular form appears in Table 2.6.

Table 2.6   A completed market map for a UK manufacturing company (the units are in thousands)

Manufacturer and Brand	Distributor	Installer	Consultants	Final Users
AA The Company – brand X 1 365 units	**BA** National Distributors *[No. 16]* 1 560 units Co. share: X – 70.2% Y – 21.2% From AA: 1 095 From AB: 330 From AC: 75 From AD: 55 From AE: 5	**CA** National Fitters *[No. 3]* 280 units Co. share: X – 50.4% Y – 18.1% From BA: 175 From BB: 105	**DA** Consultants *[No. 2 000]* 330 units Co. share: X – 44.2% Y – 16.3% From CA: 17 From CB: 100 From CC: 183 From CE: 30	**EA** Residential – type A *[No. 600 000 per annum]* 1 535 units Co. share: X – 38.2% Y – 15.1% From CA: 220 From CB: 1 205 From CC: 65 From CD: 45
AB The Company – brand Y 515 units				
AC Competitor 1 – brand R 365 units		**CB** Local Independents *[No. 17 500]* 1 655 units Co. share: X – 36.9% Y – 15.0% From BA: 635 From BB: 810 From BC: 210		**EB** Residential – type B *[No. 53 000 per annum]* 480 units Co. share: X – 47.3% Y – 16.7% From CB: 30 From CC: 450
AD Competitor 1 – brand S 290 units	**BB** Large Independents *[No. 275]* 1 315 units Co. share: X – 17.5% Y – 12.9% From AA: 230 From AB: 170 From AC: 270 From AD: 160 From AE: 150 From AF: 335			
AE Competitor 2 – single brand 180 units		**CC** Contractors *[No. 3 500]* 1 145 units Co. share: X – 48.0% Y – 16.8% From BA: 680 From BB: 325 From BC: 140		**EC** Public – type A *[No. 1 800]* 660 units Co. share: X – 43.3% Y – 16.2% From CA: 30 From CB: 235 From CC: 300 From CE: 95
AF imports – 560 units	**BC** Small Independents *[No. 5 500]* 355 units Co. share: X – 11.3% Y – 4.2% From AA: 40 From AB: 15 From AC: 20	**CD** Domestic do-it-yourself *[No. 16 000 per annum]* 45 units Co. share: nil From BD: 45		

Manufacturer and Brand	Distributor	Installer	Consultants	Final Users
	From AD: 75 From AE: 25 From AF: 180 **BD** Superstores *[No. 9]* 45 units Co. share: nil From AF: 45	**CE** Organisation's own dept *[No. 1 200]* 150 units Co. share: X – 42.1% Y – 16.8% From BA: 70 From BB: 80		**ED** Public – type B *[No. 1 800]* 60 units Co. share: X – 42.1% Y – 16.8% From CE: 60 With 50% via DA
				EE Commercial *[No. 45 000]* 540 units Co. share: X – 44.4% Y – 16.3% From CA: 30 From CB: 180 From CC: 330 With 55% via DA
Total: 3 275	**Total: 3 275**	**Total: 3 275**	**Total: 330**	**Total: 3 275**

Note: The market information accessible to this company was limited. The above table was produced by using well-informed guesstimates, linked into data that were available. As in many companies, the nearer this company came to the final users, the less they actually knew about them.

In the market represented by Table 2.6, the number and proportion of units bought by final users selecting their own brand is summarised in Table 2.7.

Table 2.7   Brand specification by final users from the market map for a UK manufacturing company (thousands of units*)

Final Users	Number of units with brand specified	Proportion of total units bought %
Residential – type A	1 235	80.5
Residential – type B	nil	–
Public – type A	630	95.5
Public – type B	30	50.0
Commercial	150	27.8
Total	**2 045**	**62.4**

* See Table 2.6.

3 Who Buys (Step 2)

A key requirement for each concluding segment is the ability to identify clearly which customers are to be found in each of them. This is critical for targeting your segment-specific offers.

In the example presented in Chapter 1 of a completed segmentation project for the users of toothpaste, the typical profile of customers to be found in each of the concluding segments was clearly identified. For ease of reference, this is repeated in Table 3.1.

Table 3.1   Customer profiles for segments in the market for toothpaste

| | | Segment name | | | |
		Worrier	Sociable	Sensory	Independent
Who buys	Socio-economic	C1 C2	B C1 C2	C1 C2 D	A B
	Demographic	Large families 25–40	Teens Young smokers	Children	Males 35–50
	Psychographic	Conservative: hypo-chondriosis	High sociability: active	High self-involvement: hedonists	High autonomy: value orientated

Step 2 is, therefore, your opportunity to record the profiling information you believe will help distinguish between the concluding segments in your market. Selecting the information to record should be governed by its practical use in enabling you to identify the members of each concluding segment. It is recorded at this early stage of the process because you may be able to link it to information put together in later steps. For example, certain features identified in Step 3 and taken through to Step 4 may be associated with specific types of customers. Profiling is *particularly* important in Step 4.

Step 2 is also the opportunity to introduce into the process any current segmentation structures you may have or believe exist at the junction being segmented.

This could well be the different junction types appearing on your market map. The process you are now following will test their validity.

Step 2 therefore consists of two parts. The first, which is optional, draws up a preliminary list of segments in your market using demographic, geographic or psychographic descriptions. The second part contains examples of profiling information which you may use or add to when putting together your own profiling data bank.

The first part of the chapter also contains a discussion of whether non-leverage groups should or should not be included in your segmentation project.

A summary of where this step lies within the segmentation process can be found in Figure 3.1.

Stage 1: Your market and how it operates

> **Step 1 – Market mapping**
> Structure and decision-makers

Stage 2: Customers and transactions

Step 2 – Who buys
Customer profiling

Figure 3.1   The process of segmentation – Step 2

Introducing preliminary segments into the process (optional)

At the junction on the market map selected for this pass of the segmentation process, which, in the first instance, should be the junction *furthest away* from the supplier (manufacturer), *where leverage points occur*, draw up a preliminary segmentation structure. This could well be the different junction types appearing on your market map. If you elect not to break down this junction into a current or 'best guess' segmentation structure, the junction as a whole will become your preliminary segment.

It is important to note that preliminary segments simply form a base from which to work as the segmentation process contained in this book takes the segmentation team from the preliminary structure to a thought-through conclusion.

As a guide to the number of preliminary segments to be used here, answers to the following questions may help.

> For up to how many is it commercially sensible to offer tailored products and/or services?

Alternatively,

> at what number would we need to start grouping individual customers together in order to manage our offer to them in a viable way?

However, whatever number you arrive at in answer to these questions, it is recommended that this list is kept to between five and eight preliminary segments at most. Less than five, therefore, is perfectly acceptable.

At the other extreme, you may well be in a business which only deals with, say, 12 purchasers at a particular junction, all of whom are leverage points. *In such circumstances, a segmentation process along the lines being described here is unlikely to be required*, as a one-to-one bespoke service would be offered anyway.

Although the title of this chapter is 'Who Buys', it is important to note that in many situations, *those who buy are not necessarily those who specify, and the junction being looked at may consist of both buyers and specifiers*. For example, the employees entitled to a company car would not necessarily carry out the buying transaction, though they could specify the car model they wished to have bought on their behalf. The term, 'who buys', should therefore be seen as including specifiers in such circumstances.

Your preliminary list of segments, assuming you have split the junction out this way, could be just a simple division between leverage and non-leverage groups. It is, however, unlikely that all the members in either one of these groups have homogeneous requirements, a situation this process would progressively uncover. This lack of homogeneity could, of course, have already been established by your business, with sub-groups and their different 'requirement packages' already identified. (A detailed look at the reasons why your customers buy takes place in Step 5, which can be found in Chapter 6.) If this is the case, the preliminary segments can be those currently in use by the business.

On the other hand, it could well be that, in constructing the market map, you have already developed the basis of a new segmentation structure at the junction being looked at (beyond a simple division between leverage and non-leverage groups) which you identified as junction types and would now prefer to explore in this segmentation process. You may also have begun to question the business' real understanding of its market and feel uncertain about even the new structure developed during the market mapping routine (let alone the previous segmentation structure assumed by the business). While you may need market research to check your assumptions, you can still continue with what you have now. By proceeding as best as you can through Steps 3, 4 and 5, further areas requiring research may be identified and should be included in the research brief.

It is worth noting here that when large numbers of purchasers are involved and impersonal contact, such as advertising, is likely to be the method of communication in the promotional plan, the resulting segments could end up being quite loosely defined. However, large numbers of purchasers still warrant a sophisticated approach to segmentation. Valuable niche opportunities could be uncovered.

To include or exclude non-leverage groups

At junctions where you have already distinguished between groups who are leverage points and those who are not, you could just focus the segmentation process on to the group(s) which have been identified as having leverage. For example, the selection of sophisticated, expensive medical equipment found in hospitals is, for some hospitals, decided upon at the senior management level without reference to the users of the equipment (their only input being that they need this type of equipment). In other hospitals it may be a decision left entirely to the users. For a segmentation project looking at the user junction, it would be pointless including those who had no leverage in the market. The next stage of segmenting this particular market would then be to understand the requirements of the senior administrators at those hospitals where they had the leverage. However, you may be in a situation where your knowledge about a particular junction is, in truth, inadequate. In such circumstances, this preliminary segmentation should cover *all* the businesses/individuals who make up the market at this junction. It therefore includes those who are and those who are not leverage points. We suggest you continue down this track, because you may uncover profitable opportunities existing for the non-leverage groups, if only the right offer were put together.

For example, consumers who depend on their retailer for the selection of which brand to buy, should still be grouped as a preliminary segment, or even segments. There could be different reasons for this dependence, resulting in different 'requirement packages' to be met by the retailer, and there could be varying degrees of dependence, any of which could be a reflection of shortfalls in the products on offer. By addressing these shortfalls, the leverage point may well be moved away from the retailer to the consumer. Such a move may be very important to the business strategically and affect the distribution of power in its marketplace. This was certainly the case for the following two companies.

For both the companies below, a better understanding of customer requirements, including the requirements of customers previously regarded as having no interest in selecting between alternative offers, identified extra revenue and higher margins.

EXAMPLE 3.1

A manufacturing company, whose products were installed in domestic, industrial and commercial premises by trade professionals, conducted an analysis of the total UK market for their product line. This analysis illustrated that around half the total volume went to final purchasers who, they believed, were not leverage points. Key in this group were the domestic users who were heavily dependent on a very diverse group of installers who, in turn, were heavily dependent on the purchasing policies of powerful distributors. In looking for opportunities to develop 'pull through' for their product, this company researched both the non-leveraging domestic and non-leveraging installer groups. The findings of the research had important strategic implications, and to have ignored these two non-leverage groups in developing their segmentation structure, would have clearly been very short sighted.

EXAMPLE 3.2

For another manufacturing company, a market research project, commissioned to assist them in their market segmentation process, identified that 11 per cent of the total market went to final users, who simply bought whatever their local distributor stocked. This same research exercise, however, also identified that if a manufacturer were to put together a product range specifically targeted at this group (a group previously ignored by all the manufacturers) a pull-through effect would be generated, thereby shifting the leverage point away from powerful buyers.

Profiling preliminary segments

As your project will refer to the preliminary segments on a number of occasions, it is easier if each of them is identified by using a term which describes their dominant profiling characteristic. This should, therefore, be one you would include in your lists of demographic, geographic or psychographic descriptions appearing in your profiling data bank. For example, location (rural, urban, metropolitan), Standard Industrial Classification (SIC) or your own business classification (doctors in private general practice/group practice/partnership or in nationalised hospital/private hospital; professional/ manufacturer; arable farm/grassland farm); size of business (big/small); age; lifestyle; family life cycle and so on. Some further examples appear in Table 3.2.

Table 3.2   Preliminary segment descriptions from a range of markets

'Market'	Preliminary segments				
	Demographic-based				
Transportation power units	Automotive	Construction	Bus/coach	Marine	
High tolerance electrical connections	Telecommunications	Defence	Aerospace (civil)	Nuclear	Other
Contents insurance	Young singles and couples – no children	Singles and couples – 30+, no children	Families – children at home	Families – children left home	Retired
	Geographic-based				
Package delivery service	Metropolitan	Urban	Rural		
Floral gifts	Industrial areas	Services dominated areas	Suburbia	Other	
	Psychographic-based				
Shopping centres	Busy bees	Shopaholics	Browsers	'Day out'	
Mid-range cosmetics	Experimenters	Sophisticates	Occasionalists	Youth-seekers	

Avoid using descriptions at this stage which represent 'what' is bought, 'where' it is bought, 'when', 'how' or 'why' it is bought, as these are addressed in subsequent steps.

It will assist subsequent steps in the process if you ensure that this preliminary segmentation is based on descriptions related to 'who buys'. For example, you may have a preliminary segmentation split between 'large users' and 'small users', which is really describing the volume bought and is covered later in the process. These 'volume' descriptions could be replaced by 'large companies' and 'small companies' (or 'large families' and 'small families'), or even combined under a common SIC code (or common stage in the family life cycle), assuming any of these were the case. Splits into different usage levels are carried out during Step 3.

For some companies, the preliminary segment structure they wish to test is built up from the characteristics they believe, at this stage, to be determinants of different buying behaviour (or wish to test as determinants of different buying behaviour). For example, a company looking to develop new opportunities in the market for executive cars may believe that there is a difference in requirements between male and female users, and a further difference according to whether they are single, married without children or married with children. This would lead the company to start their process by looking at six distinct preliminary segments, as illustrated in Figure 3.2.

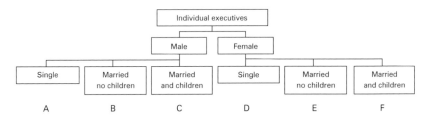

Figure 3.2   Developing preliminary segments for individual executives in the company car market

Note: The letters are used to identify the preliminary segments. Thus, preliminary segment 'A' is: individual, single, male executives, whilst preliminary segment 'F' is: individual, married, female executives with children.

The profiling descriptions allocated to each 'who' can, therefore, consist of a single characteristic or a combination, whichever is appropriate to the market being looked at.

To further help you develop a preliminary list of segments, it may be useful to review some of the standard methods of demographic, geographic and psychographic segmentation in use today. These can be found later in the second part of this chapter. A detailed breakdown of the UK/European and USA SICs and the full list of Great Britain's 124 postcode areas appear in Appendices II and III.

If your preliminary segments are based on a previous needs-based segmentation project you should, of course, have identified in that project a distinct profiling characteristic for each segment. These can now become your identifiers for your preliminary segments. The alternative, of course, is to identify each preliminary segment by their dominant reason for buying (their 'why'). The former approach is strongly recommended to the latter at this stage simply because the process will be addressing the reasons why customers buy at a later stage.

Lapsed users and prospects

If, at this stage, you know (or suspect) there are lapsed users who have completely opted out of the market (those who no longer buy your products/services or any of those on offer from the competition) and/or non-user prospects who, on the face of it, appear to have the 'need' being looked at, you could open up preliminary segments for each of them as appropriate. Although 'unmet requirements' are looked at in more detail during Chapter 6 (where these two preliminary segments re-enter the process), capturing the fact at this stage will assist you later on.

Finalising preliminary segments

All projects will have at least one preliminary segment, which will either cover all the customers found at the junction being segmented or just those who have decision-making power (leverage). For those projects running with more than one preliminary segment, it is important to emphasise that this will not prejudice the final output of the project. The process you are following will break these preliminary segments down into smaller buying units and then look across these buying units for similarities in their requirements, regardless of which preliminary segment they originated from. Preliminary segments, therefore, represent a structure you wish to test and are purely optional.

You should now finalise your list of preliminary segments and attach to each of them a distinct 'label' such as 'A', 'B', 'C' and so on, as appeared in Figure 3.2.

Sizing preliminary segments

If you have chosen to break your junction down into preliminary segments, this is a useful stage at which to allocate to each of them the volume or value they account for. This will help you in later steps of the process. If necessary, come up with your best guess.

Adding further profiling information to preliminary segments

Due to the importance of customer profiling in segmentation, it is helpful if you can build up the standard segmentation profiles of each preliminary segment by attaching to them any further descriptions you are aware of. This profiling data will be used later in the process and it is not restricted to those characteristics you believe (at this stage) to be determinants of different buying behaviour. They may be useful at a later stage for identifying the concluding target segments when deciding whether they are reachable or not. The following example illustrates the point.

EXAMPLE 3.3

You may have used 'large companies', 'medium companies' and 'small companies' as descriptions for three of your preliminary segments identified earlier in this step. All the large companies and small companies may also be car manufacturers, so this additional (SIC) information should be attached to their profiles. This will enable you to check later on in the process whether car manufacturers have, in fact, common needs, and whether the size of company is, in fact, irrelevant.

Before attaching additional demographic, geographic or psychographic information, you need to be able to answer 'Yes' to the following question.

Is this additional description applicable to all the buying units to be found in that particular preliminary segment?

You will also need to take into account your answer to the following question.

Can this description be found in any, though not necessarily all, of the buying units in any of the remaining preliminary segments?

If your answer to the second question is 'No', nothing further needs to be done. If, however, your answer is 'Yes', it is essential you attach this description to the appropriate buying units. An opportunity for doing this occurs in Chapter 5 (Step 4). Please, therefore, note this requirement on a separate piece of paper.

A useful structure for recording profiling information, both when adding further details to your preliminary segments and when listing the profiling information you may want to track throughout your project, is along the following lines:

Category: such as 'demographic', 'geographic' and so on.

Group: such as 'age', 'SIC', 'region', 'country' and so on.

Specification: such as 'under 18', 'services', 'Canada' and so on.

The 'specifications' form the profiling information used in the project.

A preliminary segment list with additional profiling information could therefore appear as in Table 3.3.

A worksheet for recording your preliminary segments, along with any additional profiling information applicable to them, appears in Table 3.4.

Table 3.3   Preliminary segments with additional profiling information

		Preliminary segments		
Additional profiling:		*A*	*B*	*C*
Category	*Group*	*Financial Officers*	*Administrators*	*Departmental Heads*
Demographic	Size of establishment	500+	100–500	Below 100
	Ownership	Private	Public	Public
Geographic	Area	Metropolitan	Urban	Rural

Note: The detailed descriptions, such as '500+', 'Public' and so on, are the profiling specifications.

Profiling: the practical dimension

The following lists of standard segmentation descriptions may be useful in completing the optional stage just outlined in this chapter. Putting together your own list is, however, essential, as being able to identify which customers are to be found in each of your concluding segments is critical to the success of the project. This is the most opportune stage at which to record the profiling information you may wish to use now and later on in the process, though it can, of course, be added to as the project progresses. A structure to follow when recording this information has already been suggested, namely category, group, specification. It is, of course, the profiling specifications you track throughout the project.

The descriptions you propose to record should focus on those you can use in your sales and marketing activity to identify customers. For example, although the size of garden may be appropriate in distinguishing between segments for garden equipment, unless there is a database somewhere which records this information for each address, it has no practical use for your sales and marketing activity. Certain postcodes may, however, correlate to particular garden sizes. Exploring the existence of such a relationship in any research you undertake would therefore prove useful. If a relationship between garden sizes and postcodes is then found to exist, the 'practicality' problem will have been overcome. Likewise, be careful about using psychographic profiles of customers as the method of distinguishing between segments, as this is often only suited to certain types of markets. Psychographic differences can be used in the creative execution of advertising and promotional campaigns in mass markets, thereby homing the offer into the target segment. Its use in other types of markets is not so easy.

Table 3.4 Worksheet – preliminary segments and additional profiling information

Junction segmenting: . . . .
Current view (or a new one) as to how the market segments at the selected junction:

Preliminary segment description	A	B	C	D	E

Note: Use a demographic, geographic or psychographic description (see text).

Additional profiling information applicable to the preliminary segment

Preliminary segment	A	B	C	D	E
Category – Group			*Profiling specifications*		
Demographic					
Geographic					
Psychographic					
Other					

Note: Within each category, structure the profiling information into a group, such as 'age', 'SIC', 'country' and so on, then write the applicable profiling specification under the preliminary segment. No more than eight preliminary segments are recommended.

Fortunately in many countries the range of profiling information with a practical application is growing, both for consumer and business-to-business markets. This is largely because companies are increasingly interested in the accurate targeting of their sales and marketing activity. As a result, many database companies have been spurred into developing ever-more sophisticated profiling packages. Occasionally, however, these sophisticated packages are seen as a method of *defining* segments. Segments, as already discussed, are defined by their particular needs, while profiling is the means by which you identify the membership of each segment.

MARKET RESEARCH NOTE	In any market research carried out as a requirement for segmentation, questions should be included which collect profiling information about each respondent. This will be used later in the segmentation process. Until you are at the stage where you know which characteristics can be used to distinguish between segments, the choice of profiling information you collect will have to be a matter of judgement.

Profiling data bank – a selection of standard approaches to profiling businesses

As suggested earlier in this chapter, a useful structure to follow when recording your lists of profiling information is as follows:

Category: such as 'demographic', 'geographic' and so on.

Group: such as 'age', 'SIC', 'region', 'country' and so on.

Specification: such as 'under 18', 'services', 'Canada' and so on.

A layout for accommodating this structure appears in Table 3.5.

Table 3.5   Recording information for your profiling data bank

Category	Group	Specification
Demographic	SIC	Manufacturing; Wholesale; Retail; Services; Government; Entertainment
	Company size	Up to 20 employees; 21–50; 51–200; Over 200
Geographic	Region	Scotland; Northern England; Midlands; Wales; Southern England; Northern Ireland
	Location	Rural; Urban; Metropolitan
Psychographic	Business stage	Start-up; Growing; Mature; Declining
	Style	Innovative; Conservative; Laggard

For profiling information which can be applied to individuals in a business, please refer to the profiling data bank for individuals.

Demographic characteristics

● Standard Industrial Classification (SIC)
The latest details are available from the appropriate statistical office. A summary appears below and a complete listing appears in Appendix II.

United Kingdom and Europe, 1992

Agriculture, Hunting and Forestry (01–02)
Agriculture, Horticulture and Hunting (01)
Forestry (02)

Fishing (05)
Fishing (05)

Mining and Quarrying (10–14)
Mining of coal and lignite; extraction of peat (10)
Extraction of oil, gas and incidental services (11)
Mining of uranium and thorium ores (12)
Mining of metal ores (13)
Other mining and quarrying (14)

Manufacturing (15–37)
Manufacturing of food products and beverages (15)
Manufacture of tobacco products (16)
Manufacture of textiles and textile products (17)
Manufacture of apparel and dyeing of fur (18)
Manufacture of leather and leather products (19)
Manufacture of wood and of wood products and cork (20)
Manufacture of pulp, paper and paper products (21)
Publishing, printing and reproduction (22)
Manufacture of coke, refined petroleum products and nuclear fuel (23)
Manufacture of chemicals and chemical products (24)
Manufacture of rubber and plastic products (25)
Manufacture of other non-metallic mineral products (26)
Manufacture of basic metals (27)
Manufacture of fabricated metal products, not machines (28)
Manufacture of machinery and equipment (29)
Manufacture of office machinery and computers (30)
Manufacture of electrical machinery (31)
Manufacture of radio, television and communications equipment (32)
Manufacture of medical, precision and optical instruments (33)
Manufacture of motor vehicles and trailers (34)

Manufacture of other transport equipment (35)
Manufacture of furniture and manufacturing not specified elsewhere (36)
Recycling (37)

Electricity, Gas and Water Supply (40–41)
Electricity, gas, steam and hot water supply (40)
Collection, purification and distribution of water (41)

Construction (45)
Construction (45)

Wholesale, Retail and Certain Repairs (50–52)
Sale, maintenance and repair of motor vehicles (50)
Wholesale trade except of motor vehicles (51)
Retail trade except of motor vehicles, and certain repairs (52)

Hotels and Restaurants (55)
Hotels and restaurants (55)

Transport, Storage and Communication (60–64)
Land transport and transport via pipelines (60)
Water transport (61)
Air transport (62)
Supporting and auxiliary transport activities (63)
Post and telecommunications (64)

Financial Intermediation (65–67)
Banking, leasing, credit and financial intermediation not specified elsewhere (65)
Insurance and pension funding, not compulsory social security (66)
Activities auxiliary to financial intermediation (67)

Real Estate, Renting and Other Business Activities (70–74)
Real estate activities (70)
Renting of machinery and equipment without operator (71)
Computer and related activities (72)
Research and development (73)
Other business activities (74)

Public Administration and Defence (75)
Public administration and defence (75)

Education (80)
Education including driving schools (80)

Health and Social Work (85)
Health and social work including veterinary activities (85)

Other Social and Personal Services (90–93)
Sewage and refuse disposal (90)
Activities of membership organisations (91)
Recreational, cultural and sporting activities (92)
Other service activities (93)

Private Households with Employees and Miscellaneous (95–96)
Private household with employees (95)
Residents property management (96)

Extra-territorial Organisations (99)
Extra-territorial organisations (99)

United States of America

Agriculture, Forestry and Fishing (01–02, 07–09)
Agricultural production – crops (01)
Agricultural production – livestock (02)
Agricultural services (07)
Forestry (08)
Fishing, hunting and trapping (09)

Mining and Construction (10–17)
Metal mining(10)
Anthracite mining (11)
Bituminous coal and lignite mining (12)
Oil and gas extraction (13)
Mining, quarrying non-metallic minerals, excluding fuels (14)
Building construction – general contractors (15)
Construction, excluding buildings, general contractors (16)
Construction – special trade contractors (17)

Manufacturing (20–39)
Food and kindred products (20)
Tobacco products (21)
Textile mill products (22)
Apparel and other finished fabric product manufacturers (23)
Timber and wood products, excluding furniture (24)
Furniture and fixtures (25)
Paper and allied products (26)
Printing, publishing and allied industries (27)
Chemical and allied products (28)
Petroleum refining and related industries (29)
Rubber and miscellaneous plastics products (30)
Leather and leather product manufacturers (31)
Stone, clay, glass and concrete products (32)
Primary metal industries (33)
Fabricated metal products, excluding machinery and transportation equipment (34)
Machinery manufacture, excluding electrical machinery (35)
Electrical, electronic machinery, equipment and supplies (36)
Transportation equipment manufacture (37)
Measuring, photographic, medical instruments, watches and clocks (38)
Miscellaneous manufacturing industries (39)

Transportation and Communications (40–49)
Railway transportation (40)
Local public transport and intercity buses (41)
Road freight transportation and warehousing (42)
Postal services (43)
Transportation by water (44)
Air transport (45)
Pipe lines, excluding natural gas (46)
Transportation services (47)
Communication (48)
Electric, gas and sanitary services (49)

Wholesale and Retail (50–59)
Wholesale trade – durable goods (50)
Wholesale trade – non-durable goods (51)
Building materials, garden supply, mobile home dealers (52)
General merchandise retailers (53)
Food retailers (54)
Motor vehicle dealers and petrol stations (55)
Clothing and accessory retailers (56)
Furniture, home furnishings and equipment retailers (57)
Eating and drinking places (58)
Miscellaneous retail trade (59)

Finance, Insurance and Real Estate (60–67)
Banking (60)
Credit agencies other than banks (61)
Security, commodity brokers, dealers, exchanges and allied services (62)
Insurance (63)
Insurance agents, brokers and service (64)
Real estate (65)
Combination of real estate, insurance, loans, law offices (66)
Holding and other investment offices (67)

Services (70, 72–73, 75–76, 78–79)
Hotels, guest houses camps and other lodgings (70)
Personal services (72)
Business services (73)
Automotive repair, services and garages (75)
Miscellaneous repair services (76)
Motion pictures (78)
Amusement and recreation services, excluding cinemas (79)

Services continued (80–84, 86, 88–89)
Health services (80)
Legal services (81)
Educational services (82)
Social services (83)

Museums, art galleries, botanical, and zoological gardens (84)
Membership organisations (86)
Private households (88)
Miscellaneous services (89)

Public administration (91–93, 95, 97, 99)
Executive, legislative, general government, excluding finance (91)
Justice, public order and safety (92)
Public finance, taxation and monetary policy (93)
Administration of environmental quality and housing programmes (95)
National security and international affairs (97)
Unclassified establishments (99)

- Size of company

Very small	Small	Small–Medium	Medium
Medium–Large	Large	Very Large	Very Large+

- Ownership

Private, public; quoted, private; independent, wholly owned, subsidiary

- Department/section

Manufacturing	Distribution	Customer Service
Sales	Marketing	Commercial
Financial	Bought Ledger	Sales Ledger
Personnel	Estates	Office Services
Planning	Contracts	Information Technology (IT)

Where appropriate, use more specific descriptions, such as specialist purchasing units, general purchasing units.

Geographic

- Postcode (the 124 postcode areas of Great Britain are listed in Appendix III)
- Metropolitan, urban, rural; city, town, village
- County
- Region: frequently defined in the UK by TV region (See below: Profiling data bank – a selection of standard approaches to profiling individuals)
- Country
- Economic/political union or association (for example, ASEAN)
- Continent

Psychographics

- Personality: stage in its business life cycle (start-up, growth, maturity, decline, turn-round); style/age of staff (formal, authoritarian, bureaucratic, disorganised, positive, indifferent, negative, cautious, conservative, old-fashioned, youthful); style of decision-making (centralised, decentralised, individual, committee).
- Attitude: risk takers or risk avoiders; innovative or cautious, and many of the adjectives used to describe different types of personality can also express a company's attitude towards your product line (as opposed to their distinctive personal character).
- Lifestyle: environmentally concerned; involved with the community; sponsor of sports/arts.

Profiling data bank – a selection of standard approaches to profiling individuals

A suggested structure for recording this information appears at the beginning of the business profiling section.

Demographic characteristics

- Age

| <3 | 3–5 | 6–11 | 12–19 |
| 20–34 | 35–49 | 50–64 | 65+ |

- Sex: male, female.
- Family life cycle: bachelor (young, single), split into dependants (living at home or full-time student) and those with their own household; newly married (no kids); full nest (graded according to the number and age of kids); single parent; empty nesters (children left home or a childless couple); elderly single.
- Family size

| 1–2 | 3–4 | 5+ |

- Type of residence: flat/house; terraced/semi-detached/detached; private/rented/council; number of rooms/bedrooms.
- Income (£k)

| <10 | 10–15 | 16–20 | 21–30 | 31–50 | >50 |

- Occupation: operative; craftsman, foreman; manager, official, proprietor; professional, technical; clerical, sales; farmer; retired; student; housewife; unemployed; white-collar (professional, managerial, supervisory, clerical); blue-collar (manual).
- Education (highest level): secondary, no qualifications; GCSE; graduate; postgraduate.
- Readership: newspapers, journals, magazines.
- Viewing and listening: news, drama, soaps, sports, current affairs, natural history.
- Leisure interests: football, rugby, cricket, squash, golf, gardening, theatre, cinema, classical music, opera.
- Religion: Christian; Jewish; Muslim; Buddhist; other.
- Ethnic origin: African; Asian; Caribbean; UK, Irish; other European.
- Nationality.
- Socio-economic (a guide on social grading appears in Appendix I). The following definitions are those agreed between Research Services Ltd, and National Readership Survey (NRS Ltd):

  A   Upper middle class (higher managerial, administrative, professional)
  B   Middle class (middle managerial, administrative, professional)
  C1 Lower middle class (supervisory, clerical, junior management, administrative, professional)
  C2 Skilled working class (skilled manual workers)
  D   Working class (semi and unskilled manual workers)
  E   Subsistence level (state pensioners, widows with no other earner, casual or lowest-grade workers)

- Multi-demographic: combining a selection of demographic criteria. For example, Research Services Ltd have combined each of four life cycle stages (dependent, pre-family, family and late) with the two occupation groupings of white-collar (A, B, C1) and blue-collar (C2, D, E) producing eight distinct profiles. They have then further split out 'family' and 'late' into 'better off' and 'worse off' producing a total of twelve distinct profiles in their 'Sagacity' model. The basic thesis of the model is that people have different aspirations and behaviour patterns as they go through their life cycle. Their definition of these life cycle stages is as follows:

  Dependent   Mainly under 24s, living at home or full-time student.
  Pre-family Under 35s, who have established their own household but have no children.
  Family   Housewives and heads of household, under 65, with one or more children in the household.

| *Late* | Includes all adults whose children have left home or who are over 35 and childless. |

Geographic

- Postcode (the 124 postcode areas of Great Britain are listed in Appendix III)
- Metropolitan, urban, rural; city, town, village
- Coastal, inland
- County
- Region (frequently defined in the UK by ITV regions – Carlton, Meridian, Central Independent, HTV Wales, HTV West, Westcountry, S4C, Anglia, Scottish Television, Grampian Television, Granada Television, Yorkshire, Tyne Tees, LWT, Border Television, Ulster Television, and Channel)
- Country
- Economic/political union or association (for example, NAFTA)
- Continent
- Population density
- Climate

Geodemographics

- A Classification of Residential Neighbourhoods (ACORN) produced by CACI Information Services Ltd is one of the longer established geodemographic classifications, updated in 1993 using the 1991 Census data. It classifies neighbourhoods according to a selection of factors such as home ownership, car ownership, health, employment, ethnicity, and lifestyle to produce a picture of consumer lifestyle. It consists of 54 types summarised into 17 basic groups which in turn are condensed into 6 broad categories. These six broad categories act as a simplified reference to the overall household classification structure. The categories are:

Category 'A' *'Thriving'*	Accounts for 19.8% of all households in the UK
Category 'B' *'Expanding'*	Accounts for 11.6%
Category 'C' *'Rising'*	7.5%

Category 'D'	24.1%
'Settling'	
Category 'E'	13.7%
'Aspiring'	
Category 'F'	22.8%
'Striving'	
(Unclassified	0.5%)

● PIN from Pinpoint, which combines geodemographics and financial data.

Other, more recent, classifications have been developed by some of the larger database companies which, as well as linking residential areas with selected demographics, also add psychographic factors (see 'Multi-dimensional' in the following section).

Psychographic characteristics

● Personality: compulsive, extrovert, gregarious, adventurous, formal, authoritarian, ambitious, enthusiastic, positive, indifferent, negative, hostile. Specific ones by sex have also been developed, such as Wells' eight male psychographic segments:

Quiet Family Man	Self-sufficient, shy, loner; lives for his family; practical shopper; low education, low income.
Traditionalist	Conventional, secure; has self-esteem; concerned for others; conservative shopper, likes well known brands and manufacturers; low education, low/middle income.
Discontented	Nearly everything (job, money, life) could be better; distrustful, socially aloof; price conscious; lowest educational and socio-economic group.
Ethical Highbrow	Content with life and work; sensitive to others; concerned, cultured, religious; social reformer; driven by quality; well educated, middle/upper socio-economic group.
Pleasure Oriented	Macho, self-centred; views himself as a leader; dislikes his work; impulsive buyer; low education and socio-economic group.
Achiever	Status conscious; seeks success (power, money and socially); adventurous in leisure time pursuits;

stylish (good food, music, clothes); discriminating buyer; good education, high socio-economic group.

He-Man   Action, excitement, drama; views himself as capable and dominant; well educated, middle socio-economic group.

Sophisticated   Attracted to intellectual and artistic achievements; broad interests; cosmopolitan, socially concerned; wants to be dominant and a leader; attracted to the unique and fashionable; best educated, higher socio-economic groups.

Source: W. D. Wells, *Lifestyle and Psychographics* (American Marketing Association, 1978).

- Attitude: degree of loyalty (none, total, moderate), risk takers or risk avoiders, likelihood of purchasing a new product (innovator, early adopter, early majority, late majority, laggard), and many of the adjectives used to describe different types of personality can also express an individual's attitude towards your product line (as opposed to their distinctive personal character). Some companies have also developed specific behavioural groups, such as 'Monitor' from Taylor Nelson Ltd which has seven social value groups, each with a distinct pattern of behaviour.
- Customer status: purchase stage (aware, interested, desirous, ready for sale), user classification (non-user, lapsed user, first time, potential).
- Lifestyle: consists of three main dimensions:

Activities   Work, hobbies, social events, vacation, entertainment, club membership, community, shopping, sports.

Interests   Family, home, job, community, recreation, fashion, food, media, achievements.

Opinions   Selves, social issues, politics, business, economics, education, products, future, culture.

In the UK, the three main providers of lifestyle data are NDL (National Demographics and Lifestyles), CMT (Computerised Marketing Technologies) and ICD (International Communications and Data). Each obtains its information from consumer questionnaires. NDL's 'question-naires' are product registration guarantee forms containing questions on household demographics, income and leisure interests, and distributed with durable goods such as electrical equipment. This has enabled NDL to collect over 10 million duplicated 'questionnaires' which can be matched up to census data in order to produce geographic profiles accurate for the census data.

- Multi-dimensional: combining psychographic profiles with selected demographic data and identifying geographic areas where the resulting segments are to be found. For example, CCN Marketing have developed 20 persona behavioural types using CMT's National Shoppers Survey database. These types range from so-called 'bon viveurs' to 'new teachers' and 'craftsmen and homemakers'. CCN's MOSAIC system now also extends into certain mainland European markets, classifying neighbourhoods into ten lifestyle types:

Elite Suburbs	Well-established suburban neighbourhoods in large and medium-sized cities, consisting of residential properties in large grounds. Wealthy but living in restrained luxury.
Average Areas	Average in age, income and family composition. Usually found in small market towns and local centres. Low poverty level.
Luxury Flats	Found in the centre of large conurbations, whose occupants set the country's fashion style and cultural agenda. Stylish accommodation for the political, artistic and media elite.
Low Income Inner City	Poor quality older housing, mixed with bars, cinemas, take-aways and football clubs, in the industrial and commercial inner city areas of large towns and cities.
High Rise Social Housing	Many social problems with a reliance on welfare caused by unemployment, divorce and illness.
Industrial Communities	Older terrace housing occupied by blue-collar workers in the traditional heavy industries.
Dynamic Families	Higher income families living in modern, privately-owned housing. Materialistic and up-to-date with the latest gadgets.
Lower Income Families	Living in both private and social housing in regional centres and average-sized towns. A good market for strongly branded packaged goods.
Rural/Agricultural Areas	Occupied by older, conservative, traditional people, not commuters, very dependent on agriculture, keen supporters of the independent retailer.

Vacation   Mix of tourists, second homers and the retired. Both
Retirement   seasonal and week day changes in population.

Process check

At the junction on the market map being segmented, a decision has been
made as to whether segmentation is to be focused on those who make decisions (have leverage) or whether it will look at all the customers at this junction. A decision has also been made as to whether the project is to test any
segmentation structures believed to exist at the junction. Finally, although
mostly used later in the process, lists have been drawn up of the profiling
data which it is believed may help distinguish between the customers found
in the concluding segments.

 Failure to record usable profiling information about the
customers found in your market will have serious implications
when attempting to target any offer put together for a specific
segment. Until you know which profiling characteristics can be
used to discriminate between segments, collect as much
pertinent profiling information as possible.

Case study and further examples

As already mentioned, a case study is used to illustrate each step in turn.
This case study is based on the case appearing in the last chapter of this
book but has been modified for reasons of commercial confidentiality and
to assist in demonstrating the process in practice. The company in the case
study is therefore referred to as 'Agrofertiliser Supplies'.

CASE 3.1   **Agrofertiliser Supplies**

Although not essential, it was considered to be helpful if the final users in
this segmentation project, the farmers, were identified at this early stage as
either 'arable' farmers, 'grassland' farmers (keeping dairy animals, beef
and/or sheep) or as farmers running a 'mixed' enterprise. This is illustrated
in Figure 3.3 which also presents the current status of the project.

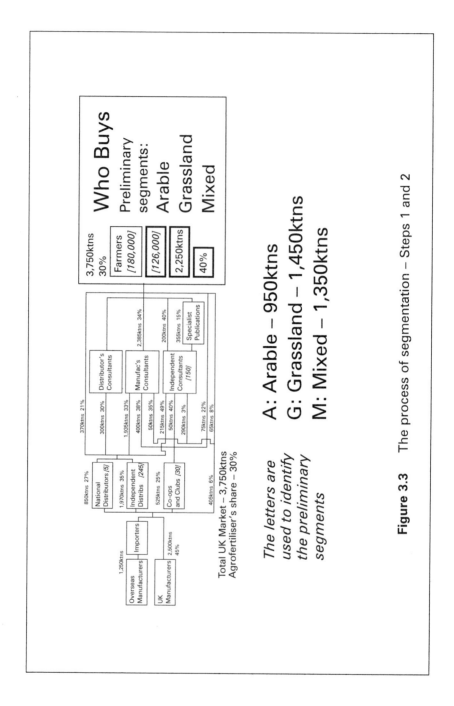

Figure 3.3 The process of segmentation – Steps 1 and 2

CASE 3.1   **Agrofertiliser Supplies (cont'd)**

It is worth noting that in classifying a farmer, for example, as an 'arable farmer', this did not always mean the farmer was exclusively growing arable crops. It also included farms which had, for example, grassland for beef cattle, but for whom that part of their overall business was less important than their arable crops. Conversely, some of the farmers classified as 'grassland' could also be growing some arable crops but, once again, their focus would be on the grassland part of their business.

Amongst a number of other profiling data tracked during the project, Agro-fertiliser Supplies was particularly interested to see if the concluding segments would be characterised by a farmer's formal level of agricultural training and/or size of farm. Interestingly, neither of these two characteristics could be used to distinguish between the segments.

A final decision concerned whether or not to include those farmers who relied on someone else along the market map to decide which product they should buy. As it quickly became apparent at a very early stage of the project that the company did not really understand the buying priorities of farmers, it was decided to include all farmers in the segmentation project.

Further examples

The range of possibilities, as would be expected, is quite large and depends a great deal on the company undertaking the segmentation project, as well as the market being segmented. In many mass markets looking for long-term relationships with customers, the life stage of the individual is of increasing interest as the basis for a market structure, while in business-to-business markets splits by business type (SIC) tend to be popular, as does the distinction between the private and public sector. More precise profiling of the individual decision-makers themselves within businesses is of increasing interest, particularly their profession and/or responsibilities. Whatever the choice for preliminary segments, it is important to remember that with this particular segmentation process it will not prejudice the outcome.

An interesting option for preliminary segments is to differentiate between customers according to the particular end use they have for the product or service, assuming this possibility exists within the confines of the market definition for the project. As a consideration within the segmentation-process, this is in fact looked at in more detail in the next chapter under the heading, 'End-use application'.

For those projects which have turned to market research in order to define their market(s), it has been possible to develop preliminary segments after listening carefully to the different buying preferences customers talked about during the discussion. The concluding customer types are then tracked throughout the remaining stages of the project.

4 *What, Where, When and How (Step 3)*

This chapter is Step 3 in the process of developing a segmentation structure for your market. It breaks down the current activity in the market into four categories: what is bought; where it is bought; when it is bought; and how it is bought.

In the example presented in Chapter 1 of a completed segmentation project for the users of toothpaste, the components of each purchase in terms of their features were identified for the concluding segments. For ease of reference this is repeated here in Table 4.1.

Table 4.1   Purchase components for segments in the market for toothpaste

		Segment name			
		Worrier	*Sociable*	*Sensory*	*Independent*
Who buys					
What is bought,	*Product examples*	Crest	McLeans UltraBrite	Colgate (stripe)	Own label
Where, When and How	*Product physics*	large canisters	large tubes	medium tubes	small tubes
	Outlet	supermarket	supermarket	supermarket	independent
	Purchase frequency	weekly	monthly	monthly	quarterly

Note: In this particular market, only what, where and when factors are actually listed. 'How' the product is bought is not a relevant factor.

Although this is the picture for a completed segmentation project, breaking down the market like this helps progress your segmentation project in two ways:

- it provides the framework for the most crucial stage in the market segmentation process, namely, identifying the range of benefits being sought by the market (described in detail in Chapter 6). Given that segments are based on groups of customers with similar requirements satisfied by a distinct marketing mix, this information is critical to the process;

● it enables you to build a model of your market based on all the different purchasing combinations that are known to take place within it, any of which could be reflecting a different customer requirement.

It is also useful at the end of a segmentation project to be able to review the actual purchasing practices of the customers found in each concluding segment.

As this step, therefore, provides the link with the needs-based buying requirements sought by the market (the benefits), it is essential that it is approached from the customer's perspective.

For some markets, the lists of different what, where, when and how factors can be quite extensive, so the chapter contains guidelines on how to restrict these lists without losing their contribution to the segmentation process. *It is, therefore, recommended that you read all of Step 3 before drawing up your list of the key features sought by your market.*

A summary of where this step lies within the segmentation process is presented in Figure 4.1.

Stage 1: Your market and how it operates

> **Step 1 – Market mapping**
> Structure and decision-makers

Stage 2: Customers and transactions

| **Step 2 – Who buys** | **Step 3 – What* is bought** |
| Customer profiling | Purchase options |

Figure 4.1   The process of segmentation – Step 3

Note: 'What*' is the abbreviation used to denote 'what, where, when and how'.

It is worth recalling at this stage that the process is presented primarily in a format designed to utilise information already held by or accessible to your company, and this is the approach we suggest you initially adopt. Information for this step potentially can be found in a number of areas and may require you to talk with a cross-section of representatives from the salesforce, customer services/enquiries and ordering, as well as from distribution. Revisiting appropriate past market surveys may also provide valuable input.

What is bought

Listing products and services

As a distinct activity for this step, list *all* relevant competitive products/ services purchased by customers in the defined market, whether or not you manufacture/supply all of them. Ensure you 'unbundle' all the components of a purchase so that you arrive at a comprehensive breakdown of 'what is bought'. Although this list will be reviewed later, an initial comprehensive list will ensure no important features are missed.

Avoid covering a number of different products/services with what is really a description of either the advantage or the benefit being provided. For example, 'next day delivery' is a description of what is obtained by buying first-class postage or certain types of courier service. The list should therefore contain 'first-class post' and 'next day courier service'. It may, however, assist you in drawing up the list of competitors' and your own products/services if they are categorised by the advantage or benefit being provided.

To assist in the distinction between a 'feature', 'advantage' and 'benefit' the following summary may help you:

- Feature: what it is, or is made from;
- Advantage: what it does;
- Benefit: what the customer gets that they explicitly need (or want).

A more detailed discussion of features, advantages and benefits occurs towards the end of Chapter 6.

The role of 'influencers', as defined in Step 1 (Chapter 2), along with technical advisers and consultants, should be included in the lists of 'what is bought' (as opposed to appearing in the list of 'who buys') when they are used by the junction being segmented (and are therefore located at junctions closer to your company on the market map). Influencers/advisers/consultants and so on should be separated out, where applicable, between those purposely brought into the buying process (independents), and those included in ('bundled' together with) the product package offered by the supplier (manufacturer), regardless of whether the buyer wants them or not.

Ensure the level of detail used to describe the products/services equates to the level of aggregation being looked at in the market map. A finely defined market would have the individual products listed, while a more generally defined market would have broader product/service groups listed, possibly using generic descriptions. For example, if looking at family cars, it is essential to list the different types and makes of car available. However, if looking at the passenger transport market between major cities, the types and makes of cars being used would be unnecessary as this level of detail adds nothing to understanding customer requirements and would, therefore, complicate the process unnecessarily (particularly in the next step). A list of alternative modes of transport would be more appropriate for this level of aggregation.

A useful structure for organising the information for this step is to consider 'what', 'where', 'when' and 'how' as four separate 'categories'. Within each of these categories it should then be possible to organise all the various specifications that are available into groups of alternatives. For example, within the 'what' category, 'colour' would be a feature group, while each of the colours available would be the alternative specifications in this group, in other words, the alternative features in that group. Information for this step would therefore be organised along the following lines:

Category: such as 'what', 'where' and so on.

Group: such as 'package type', 'colour', 'brand' and so on.

Specification: such as 'multi-pack', 'red', 'high tech' and so on.

An example of this structure appears in Table 4.2.

Table 4.2   Recording information on what, where, when and how

Category	Group	Specification
What	Speed	High; Medium; Low
	Loading	Top; Front
	Programme Standard	All three; Standard and high; Standard and low;
	Service	Under 4 hours; 4–8 hours; Next day; Within 2 days
Where	Retailer Catalogue	Superstore; Department store; Specialist shop;
	Buying club	Trade body; Affinity group; Local club
When	Frequency	Daily; Weekly; Monthly; Yearly
	Season	Spring; Summer; Winter; Autumn; All year
How	Credit	24 months; 12 months; 6 months; Not taken

This structure is the same as that suggested in the previous chapter for recording the profiling information.

It is important to be pragmatic when drawing up these lists. So, for example, if it is known that customers rely on what their supplier stocks, exclude those feature groups which customers are clearly indicating they have no interest in, such as manufacturer's brand. If, however, it is known that some customers do have an interest in a particular feature group but others are indifferent towards it, this can be captured by adding 'any (*feature group name*)' to the list of features specified in the group. For example, 'any brand', 'any size' or 'any colour', as appropriate.

These lists of features (for 'where', 'when' and 'how' it is bought as well as for 'what' is bought) can be drawn up for the market as a whole, or, if you prefer, for each of your preliminary segments in turn, assuming you elected to develop these in Step 2. Do whatever you feel most comfortable in doing.

The following are some of the feature groups to take into account when drawing up your list of what is bought, along with some possible features selected from a range of markets:

Type of product	Cleaners, galvanisers, installed, flat pack, ready made, on-call engineers, resident engineers, bundled with a service package and so on.
Specification	100% purity, 98% purity, tolerance levels, percentage failure rate and so on.
Colour	Red, white, blue, pastel, garish and so on.
Size of package	Single, multiple, family pack, 5 litre, 10 litre, 20 kgs, bulk and so on.
Space required	Small, medium, large, very large (or a more precise breakdown if appropriate).
Volume used	Small, medium, large, very large (or a more precise breakdown if appropriate).
Level/intensity of use	High, medium, low (or a more precise breakdown if appropriate).
Type of service	Testing service, design service, technical advice (which is sometimes, unintentionally, provided by the sales force), evaluation, analysis and so on.
Brand	Manufacturer's, own label, single brand only, any major brand, only local brands, high profile brand and so on.
Country of origin	UK, Germany, France, European Union (EU), Scandinavia, North America, Asia, Africa, Japan and so on.
Independent influencers	Advisers, consultants (complementing or competing with the technical/advisory services provided by the manufacturers/suppliers), specialist publications, consumer publications, accountants, financial advisers, financial consultants and so on, assuming they appear at junctions used by customers at the junction being segmented.

Type of delivery	Next day (or a listing of the competing products or services which provide this, for example, courier, first class), within four hours, collected, automatically triggered via links with the inventory control systems and so on.
Volume of purchase	Large, medium, small (or by a more precise breakdown if appropriate).
Value of purchase	High, medium, low (or by a more precise breakdown if appropriate).
Range bought	All, single, across the range, those at the top/middle/bottom and so on.

Although the features listed for a feature group would normally represent alternatives to each other, there may be occasions when combinations are possible. In these circumstances it is useful if each combination that is known to occur in the market is separated out and regarded as a distinct specification within the appropriate list of features. This will assist later stages in the process.

The following are extracts from the final, summary feature lists put together for three different markets:

Lawnmowers	Hover, cylinder, rotary, petrol driven, manual, electrically driven, 12 inch cut, 16 inch cut, any mower with a branded engine, extended warranty, with aftersales service and so on.
Paints	Emulsion, gloss, non-drip, one coat, 5 litre cans, 2 litre cans, environmentally friendly, bulk and so on.
Petrol stations	Self-service, forecourt service, with loyalty programme and so on.

Teasing out attributes

It is important when putting these lists together that essential details are not hidden behind some of the feature descriptions. For example, 'brand' and 'quality' are rather meaningless on their own and could be hiding a range of different specifications. Buying a 'good brand' for some customers could be associated with buying well-researched products while for others it could be associated with a company's technical support staff. It is important you list these more specific descriptions.

As a guideline, a description of a feature is meaningless if it does not describe what a company would need to do in order to offer it.

End-use application

Although not strictly a feature as such, it is opportune at this point in the process to extend the discussion on 'end-use application'. If it appears that in your market the competing products or services are used for different end uses, then it is highly likely that these different applications will have an important input into segmentation.

Whenever a single final user department or individual utilises any of the products or services available in the market for different end uses, these different applications should be listed here as if they were an extension to your feature list. For example, the office services department may require cleaning services, but the cleaning requirements of the public areas, general office areas and the manufacturing plant (particularly if the manufacturing process involves precision instruments) could all be different. Another example has been identified in the domestic paint market, where the selection process for paint differs according to the type of room it is being bought for (the buying criteria for gloss in the 'public rooms' being different from the buying criteria for gloss in the 'private rooms'). Hence, in this instance, end-use applications would include 'private room' decoration and 'public room' decoration. The buying of items for personal use or as a gift can also benefit from being listed separately.

As already mentioned in Chapter 3, some projects distinguish between preliminary segments by the different end-use applications a particular product and/or service is put to. In business-to-business markets different applications can often be associated with different industries or with different departments and, as a result, are captured in Step 2 of the process as different preliminary segments. Likewise, the different rooms in a house can be considered as being different 'departments' when the products or services bought for these rooms are being bought with a different 'application' in mind. If you are progressing a project for a market in which there are quite different applications but, as yet, have chosen not to run the project with a number of preliminary segments, it is recommended that you now regard these applications as distinct preliminary segments. The process you are following will, however, tease these differences out if pursued rigorously.

Where it is bought

As a further distinct activity for Step 3, and without attempting at this stage to link it with the previous section, list all the channels (if appropriate) where the listed range of products/services are bought. Please note that this only refers to the products/services supplied/manufactured by you and your competitors. It therefore excludes the sourcing details for independent influencers, advisers, consultants and so on. A suggested structure for recording the information for this category appeared in Table 4.2.

Depending on the detail contained in your market map in Step 1, you may be able to lift this information straight from the map.

Although the channels customers use to source the competing products or services are not necessarily 'manufactured' by you or your competitors, they are a component in the purchase as far as the customer is concerned. Being able to access the product through particular channels could be crucially important for some customers and may, therefore, be the key to distinguishing them from other customers in your concluding segments. The segmentation process must, therefore, take into account all the different channels used by customers at the junction being segmented.

The channels list could include:

> Direct telephone/mail order, distributor, department store, national chain, regional chain, local independent retailer, tied retailer, supermarket, wholesalers, shed, specialist supplier, street stall, through a buying group, through a buying club, door-to-door, local/high street/out-of-town shop and so on.

As with the list put together for what is bought, the channels list should be comprehensive and therefore include all the channels customers use to source their products regardless of whether they are included in your company's distribution strategy.

When it is bought

Now draw up a list which covers the different availability requirements that exist. This will be seen in the different frequencies of purchase experienced for your own and your competitors' products/services.

The purchase frequency list could include:

> Daily, weekly, monthly, seasonally, every two years, at 50 000 miles, occasionally, as needs, only in emergencies, degrees of urgency, infrequently, rarely, special events, only during sales, at the bottom of the market and so on.

Organising the features for this category into their appropriate groups, as suggested earlier, is a useful structure to follow (see Figure 4.2).

How it is bought

Finally, draw up a further separate list covering the different methods of purchase.

Examples which may help in drawing up your list include:

> Credit card, charge card, cash, direct debit, standing order, credit terms, direct transfer, outright purchase, lease-hire, lease-purchase, negotiated price, sealed bid and so on.

Although in most instances the full range of payment options is generally available, except for a few notable retailers in the UK who refuse to accept charge cards and credit cards other than their own, the ability (or otherwise) to include financing as part of the offer in some markets can win (or lose) a sale.

> In segmentation projects undertaken in some capital goods markets, the provision of financing packages has been a crucially important factor in deciding between alternative suppliers for the segments consisting of chief executive officers and/or chief financial officers. In such situations, having your own in-company financing facility or close liaison with a financing institution has been a critical factor for a successful bid.

Information for this category can be organised along the lines already discussed.

Reducing the complexity of the 'what', 'where', 'when' and 'how' lists

At this stage, *it is usually advisable to restrict the contents of each list to a more manageable number of variants*, as the list you will have generated by now may be quite detailed and extensive. The purpose of the next five sub-sections is to show you how to end up with a manageable number of 'whats*'.

 Suppliers know what they, and often what their competitors, offer in great detail. Customers in most markets, however, tend to look at the offer in much simpler terms. It is essential, therefore, that you ensure your feature lists reflect the views held by the market, otherwise you will unnecessarily complicate this and subsequent steps in the process.

Focusing your feature lists on to the discriminating items and ensuring the features are described in terms the customers would use can be achieved in a number of ways.

Removing basic entry requirements

In many markets there are certain features your product or service must have in order even to be considered by *any* customer. They are sometimes referred to as 'market qualifiers'. These features are those which the users expect to have as a matter of course, so much so that even if improvements are made to these features they are unlikely to generate any major gains in market share because they do not generate any major gains in customer satisfaction. However, once one company introduces improvements to these features, the entry level requirement moves up to this higher level. A good example can be found in the market for PCs where the constant improvement in processor speeds simply moves the market up a further notch in terms of the customer's standard level of expectation.

Over time, features that were once used by customers to decide between alternative suppliers become the norm and begin to be regarded as basic entry requirements. For example; radio and cassette players pre-installed in cars; advance programming for domestic video recorders (though it is predicted that it will take until 2015 before 80 per cent of domestic users will have worked out how to use this facility correctly!); built-in CD-ROM drives on desktop PCs; colour televisions (with digital televisions eventually becoming the norm); 'family size' packs and multi-packs of savoury snacks, confectionery items, cleaning products and so on; shrink-resistant clothes (apart from, so it still seems, certain brands of jeans); loyalty programmes with airlines and so on. It is important, therefore, that you periodically review your list of determining items, preferably through statistically sound research amongst customers.

This routine can be carried out for the market as a whole, but given the stage of the project you are now at, the distinction between basic entry requirements and determining features is best done for each of your preliminary segments, assuming you have developed these in Step 2.

Finally, a word of caution: if you are in a market in which customers can select from a range of features and, in effect, 'design' their own product, be cautious as to what you classify as 'basic entry items'. For example, in the car insurance market in the UK the basic product consists of 'third party' cover, a legal requirement. Every policy, therefore, provides third party cover, which would seem to qualify this feature as a basic entry requirement. For some customers, however, this feature is all they really buy, so it must therefore be left in the process. In the main, however, *features which are basic entry requirements can be omitted from your list*.

Focusing on the influential feature groups

It may be possible to narrow down the list of determining feature groups into those which have an important influence on the choice of product or service for *any* customer:

If there is data to hand, preferably based on market research conducted amongst a statistically sound representative sample of customers at the junction being looked at, which has identified the influential feature groups listed under 'what', 'where', 'when' and 'how' – in other words those which play an important part in the buying criteria (for example, packaging, size) and/or have a significant influence on the attitude of buyers (for example, brand, technical advisers) – all the other items in the various lists can be dropped.

To carry out this exercise, re-arrange the feature groups in descending order of importance. It may then be possible to decide a cut-off point that separates out those feature groups which play an influential part in the buying process from those which, to all intents and purposes, play only a secondary part.

If you have identified different applications in your feature lists, measuring the importance of the application against other feature groups is inappropriate. The applications should be carried forward to the next step, along with your final list of features, once they have been sized during the concluding part of this step.

To help decide the cut-off point, once you have re-arranged the purchase groups into a descending order of importance, allocate 100 points between them in a way which represents their relative importance to each other *from the market's perspective*. It is as if a value of £100 is placed on the feature groups as a whole and then this total sum is distributed between each of them to indicate their individual worth. An example appears in Table 4.3.

Table 4.3   Prioritising feature groups

Feature groups	Individual score	Cumulative score
'What' – colour	35	35
'What' – country of origin	25	60
'What' – product type	15	75
'Where' – retailer	10	85
'What' – brand	5	90
'What' – type of delivery	4	94
'How' – payment	3	97
'When' – frequency	3	100

Pinpoint accuracy in the distribution of the total sum between the feature groups is not essential. What is required is a clear distinction between those feature groups that really count in the decision and those which are less important.

As a general rule, it is quite in order to focus the segmentation project on to those feature groups which account for, say, 80 per cent of the decision. In the example appearing in Table 4.3, the cut-off point could therefore be after 'what – product type' or after 'where – retailer'.

As for the preceding section, this routine can be carried out for the market as a whole, but given the stage of the project you are now at, this prioritising of feature groups is best done for each of your preliminary segments, assuming, once again, you have developed these in Step 2.

If in carrying out this prioritising routine you do not believe all the individual customers in each preliminary segment would have the same feature groups below the cut-off point, split the preliminary segment up into the appropriate number of different groups. Produce a priority table for each of them and now regard them as distinct preliminary segments with their own identification prefix. This will also require you to re-allocate the volume/value figure attached to the original preliminary segment between the two (or more) resulting preliminary segments.

Narrowing down the range of features

Statistically sound research information could allow you to go even further in this review of your lists of 'what', 'where', 'when' and 'how'. You may have information to hand which enables you to restrict the list of features appearing in the feature groups. For example, one product could have eight different pack sizes and four different pack types. Research may show that only two are relevant in demonstrating differences between customers.

Once again, this routine is best carried out for each preliminary segment separately, if applicable.

Merging feature groups and features according to how customers categorise them and buy them

Further research data may be to hand which enables you to merge different features within any one feature group together. For example, you may have data which enables you to combine a number of similar products together because the specific product types have no relevance to market segmentation, as is suggested in the following example.

EXAMPLE 4.1

In the general drinks market, lemonade and orangeade could be grouped together as 'pop' because listed separately they indicate nothing more about possible segmentation splits. On the other hand, attitudes towards mixers, such as tonic water, are different from attitudes towards pop (as mixers are added to expensive spirits) and so would be listed under 'what' separately in a general drinks market.

This type of information can be established from listening to the way customers talk about the different features available. For example, rather than listing all the different 'bells and whistles' available with a particular product, customers who are interested in these features may simply refer to them as 'add-ons'. Capturing the applicable range of features this way in your feature list is therefore perfectly valid (even if the 'bells and whistles' were originally allocated to different feature groups). Likewise, the breakdown of retail outlets into specialist stores, department stores and so on may be irrelevant to the buying process when listed separately if 'local store' is the pertinent description.

Reducing the complexity of the feature lists this way is often possible in those markets where the options available are far too numerous for the customers to cope with. To 'put order into chaos', customers therefore simplify the options into more manageable sets.

It may also be possible to merge certain products or services into single feature specifications such as, 'full range' or 'premium services' for example, as long as these descriptions reflect buying patterns in the marketplace. Mergers of this sort may also be possible for your list of different purchasing organisations.

As for all the other routines in this section, restructuring your features should be looked at for each preliminary segment.

Merging correlated features

Finally, it may be the case that features in one group may be highly correlated with features in another group. For example, referring back to Table 4.2, one of the features listed under 'type of delivery' could be 'home delivery', and one of the features listed under 'where' could be 'direct mail'. Now it could well be that the only goods ever delivered to the home are those which are ordered by direct mail, therefore one or the other of these features could be removed. A similar combination could be carried out if, for example, it was only very rarely that any other outlet ('where') offered home delivery, as this would mean that for the overwhelming majority of customers 'direct mail' and 'home delivery' were highly correlated.

It is important to ensure that the correlation is a two-way exclusive correlation before removing one or the other feature. For example, even if it was the case that *all* goods ordered by direct mail had home delivery, if some department stores also openly offered a home delivery service, then the feature list would have to remain as it was.

Key discriminating features (KDFs)

The lists of features you now have are referred to in this book as the *Key Discriminating Features* (KDFs). The best method of arriving at these is by reference to statistically sound market research. It may also be possible to use your judgement to restrict the lists of features to a manageable number, but take great care to ensure the rationale behind any restriction is *market-based* and that features are not simply being removed because *you* would prefer them not to be there.

At this stage, do not attempt to list the real needs being met by the features. For example, some customers may be buying quality/reliability, which they obtain by buying well-known brands, or by buying goods produced in a particular country (for example, Japan): this will be covered in Step 5. Just list product types, channels used, purchase frequencies and buying methods *as you are making nothing more than comprehensive lists*.

For those projects which are excluding customers who do not have leverage at the junction being segmented, it is sometimes worth re-assessing this exclusion having gone through the lists of features. Non-leverage points should be included unless the reader is absolutely certain that it is pointless (in other words, there is nothing to learn about these customers and nothing will change their buying habits).

MARKET RESEARCH NOTE	In any research project commissioned to assist the segmentation process, an understanding of which features are the basic entry requirements, the importance of different features, the correlations that exist between features and how customers simplify complex offers are all important inputs to the process. In addition, it is important to collect the KDFs for each completed interview.

If you have identified different applications during this step and are recording them as 'features' (in other words, you have elected not to use them as preliminary segments), these should now be added to your list of KDFs and taken through the 'sizing' section of this step.

A worksheet for recording feature lists for each of your preliminary segments, which also caters for different applications, appears in Table 4.4. An example of this worksheet completed for a single preliminary segment appears in Table 4.8.

A brief comment about price

It is not appropriate at this stage in the process to include price in the list of 'what is bought', even though a number of customers in your market may simply buy the cheapest. Price is better covered in Step 5, 'why is it bought', when it can be allocated an importance rating, relative to the products/services being bought.

Sizing features

Now that you have arrived at the KDFs for your market, this is a useful point at which to size the various features found within each feature group. The detail you are putting together here can be used in a particular way during the next step of the process, depending on the particular approach you adopt for progressing through Step 4. You may, therefore, like to read the appropriate sections in the next chapter before spending too much time on it here, particularly if it appears as if it will be excessively time consuming. You may be able skip the detail here, though in doing so you will lose a method of checking some of the detail required in the next step. The appropriate sections to read are 'Building the customer base for your market (micro-segments)', in order to gain a quick understanding of what the next step is about, and 'Sizing micro-segments'.

Assuming you are going to size the various features within each feature group at this point, then, for each preliminary segment, allocate the volume or value you gave them in Step 2 between the features now appearing in each of their feature groups. *Therefore, if the total volume for a particular preliminary segment is 2 000, and you have listed three different features for 'what product' in this preliminary segment, you will need to split the 2 000 between these three features.* An example appears in Table 4.5 (it is based on Table 4.3).

In drawing up your table, you may need to take into account any particular relationships you know exist between various features. For example, if it was known that half the products in a pine colour (250) and all the products for painting/staining (550) came from the UK, then the UK accounts for 800 units.

If you have no information to assist you in how to split your volume/value figure between the features, either assume an even split and attach the

Table 4.4   Worksheet – end-use applications and KDFs by preliminary segment

Junction segmenting: ·
Key discriminating features in your selected market (overall or by preliminary segment)

Preliminary segment	A	B	C	D	E
Applications (*if appropriate*)					
Category – Group			KDFs		
What is bought					
Where					
When					
How					

Note: Within each of the feature categories, allocate the features into their respective feature groups as illustrated in Table 4.8. No more than eight preliminary segments are recommended.

appropriate figures or wait until you are attaching volumes or values to each micro-segment in the next chapter.

Table 4.5   Sizing features for a preliminary segment for which the total volume purchased is 2 000 units

Feature groups	Features		Volume
'What' – colour	Dark hardwood		750
	Light hardwood		200
	Pine		500
	For painting/staining		550
		Total	**2 000**
'What' – country of origin	Scandinavia/Germany		1 200
	UK		800
		Total	**2 000**
'What' – product type	DIY kits		500
	Made up		1 500
		Total	**2 000**
'Where' – retailer	Department stores		1 100
	Direct mail		200
	Sheds		700
		Total	**2 000**

Note: In some instances a feature group may be entirely optional, such as 'extended warranties', and contain features which some customers choose to have and others ignore. To accommodate this eventuality, add 'not purchased' to the list of features in the applicable group. This will ensure that the totals for each group are the same (being 2 000 in the above example).

It is appropriate to repeat here that if the features within a feature group are sometimes combined by customers, it is useful if each combination is listed as a distinct feature specification.

As a brief reminder, in those projects which have identified different end-use applications and are carrying these forward in their feature lists, these, too, should be allocated a volume or value figure, as appropriate.

Process check

Having mapped out the selected market and identified a particular junction to be segmented, profiling information which may help distinguish between the concluding segments at the end of the project has been recorded and a

decision made as to whether the project will test any segmentation structures already believed to exist there (preliminary segments).

Given that segmentation is about customers and their needs and that the
particular requirements customers are seeking to have satisfied are delivered
by the features of the product or service, the distribution channels, their
availability requirements and payment options, the project has drawn up a
list (or lists) of features customers use to discriminate between alternative
offers (KDFs). These KDFs can now be used to help identify the particular
benefits being sought by the market. They can also be used to build a model
of the market which represents the different customers found within it.

Although this step has drawn up the feature lists under the headings of
'what', 'where', 'when' and 'how', an alternative structure you may wish to
adopt for arriving at these lists is to look at the features under the headings
of 'core products/services', 'supporting services' and the 'intangibles', as
illustrated in Figure 4.2.

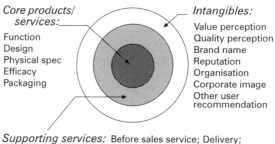

Figure 4.2   An alternative structure for arriving at the feature lists

Whichever approach you adopt for drawing up your feature lists, *it is essential they reflect the customer's point of view*.

Case study and further examples

CASE 4.1   **Agrofertiliser Supplies**

The potential list of features to be considered for Agrofertiliser Supplies
was quite large. The company itself had over 40 products on its list.
However, when these lists were looked at from the customer's point of

---

CASE 4.1   **Agrofertiliser Supplies (cont'd)**

view, they could be simplified quite substantially and with confidence. For example, although most bags of fertiliser contain three different fertiliser components which can be mixed (blended) in a wide variety of ratios, farmers tended to distinguish between the blends according to whether they were part of a range, therefore made up and bagged by the manufacturers (manufactured blends), or whether the farmer had specified the ratio they wanted and had the blend made up specifically for them (bespoke blends). It is rather like paint: paint can be bought in a particular colour and used as it is, or a customer can request a specific colour to be made up for them.

In addition to the blends, farmers also bought one of the fertiliser components (nitrogen) on its own, nitrogen being the nutrient in most demand by the crops. Nitrogen could be bought in one of two forms, ammonium nitrate (AN) or Urea.

Farmers were therefore seen to buy one of four product combinations:

(a) AN and manufactured blends
(b) AN and bespoke blends
(c) Urea and manufactured blends
(d) Urea and bespoke blends.

Thus a large range of product types could be captured quite simply.

Other feature lists were also looked at from the farmers' point of view and adjusted accordingly. For example, fertilisers could be purchased from three different types of distributor (national, independent or the co-operative), as well as from an importer or direct from the manufacturer. However, the three different types of distributor tended to be subsumed under the general description of 'local' distributor, regardless of ownership. The resulting feature list appears in Table 4.6.

Table 4.6   Feature list for the case study

Category	Group	Specification
What	Product	AN and manufactured blends; AN and bespoke blends; Urea and manufactured blends; Urea and bespoke blends
	Package	50 kgs; 500 kgs
	Brand	Well established; Any brand
	Quality*	High; Any quality
	Intensity	High nitrogen level; Low nitrogen level
	Consultant/ services	Manufacturer's; Distributor's; Independent; Not purchased**

CASE 4.1   **Agrofertiliser Supplies (cont'd)**

Category	Group	Specification
	Publication	Specialist technical; General
Where	Channel	Local distributor; Importer; Direct from the manufacturer
When	Frequency	As required; Bulk in advance
How	Payment method	Standard terms; Long-term finance from the manufacturer; Long-term finance from the bank

Notes: *Quality referred to the consistency of fertiliser granule size with no lumps or very fine particles.
**Consultancy, along with some agronomic services, was often available from the manufacturers and distributors at no charge. Even so, many farmers preferred to pay for independent advice while others chose not to use these facilities from any supplier: a situation captured by having a 'not purchased' option in the feature group.

As this list was still rather extensive, the next stage was to determine which feature groups contained the KDFs. This was done for each preliminary segment in turn. Table 4.7 shows the results for one of them, the grassland preliminary segment.

Table 4.7   Prioritising feature groups for a preliminary segment in the case study

Feature groups	Individual score	Cumulative score
'What' – product	20	20
'What' – brand	20	40
'What' – quality	15	55
'Where' – channel	15	70
'What' – intensity	10	80
'What' – consultant/services	8	88
'When' – frequency	5	93
'How' – payment	3	96
'What' – publication	2	98
'What' – package	2	100

Note: The dotted line indicates the suggested cut-off point. Given the closeness of the scores for 'intensity' and 'consultant' it would be perfectly in order to drop the cut-off point to 88 and continue the process with the inclusion of consultants in the KDFs.

CASE 4.1   **Agrofertiliser Supplies (cont'd)**

In arriving at this list, and those for the other preliminary segments, the segmentation team spoke to members of the salesforce and to a sufficient number of farmers to ensure they had discussed this topic with a representative sample from each preliminary segment.

After removing the particular features from each preliminary segment that weren't actually bought and after following some of the other routines discussed earlier in this chapter, the final lists of KDFs were drawn up, one for each preliminary segment. A completed list for one of the preliminary segments appears in Table 4.8. The worksheet appearing in Table 4.4 has been used as the format for this table.

Table 4.8   Completed KDF worksheet for a preliminary segment in the case study

Preliminary segment	M – Mixed farming enterprise
Applications *(if appropriate)*	*not appropriate*
Category – Group	*KDFs*
What is bought	
– Product	AN and manufactured blends; Urea and manufactured blends
– Brands	Well known; Any brand
– Quality	High; Any quality
– Intensity	Low nitrogen level
– Consultant/services	Manufacturers; Not purchased
Where	
– Channel	Local distributor
When	
– Purchase frequency	*not significant*
How	
– Payment method	*not significant*

To conclude this step for the case study, Figure 4.3 presents a summary of the project's status so far.

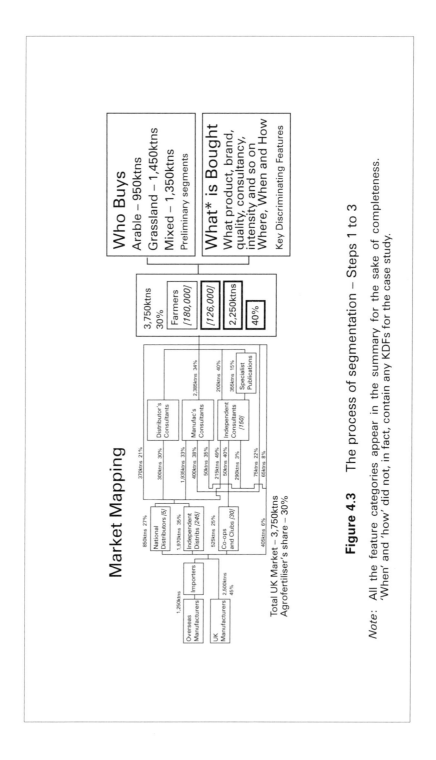

Figure 4.3 The process of segmentation – Steps 1 to 3

Note: All the feature categories appear in the summary for the sake of completeness. 'When' and 'how' did not, in fact, contain any KDFs for the case study.

Further examples

In general, it is by listening to customers, in addition to observing their buying practices, that companies arrive at the lists of key features for their market.

For one particular company, listening to their customers enabled them to simplify an extensive catalogue of components into those which were 'off-the-shelf' and those which were 'bespoke', further divided into those which were required to tolerate 'harsh' environments (varying temperatures and pressures, for example) and those which were required to function in 'benign' environments. In yet another market it quickly became apparent that the market split between those who sought the latest technology and highest specifications, those who concentrated on the productivity of the equipment (output), those who focused on the financing package, and those who simply relied on what was available through a particular distribution channel.

Some of the most extensive feature lists have been presented for markets served by companies in the financial services sector. However, by talking to representative samples of customers in these markets, all these lists have been reduced and simplified thus enabling their segmentation projects to progress by focusing on the *customer's* KDFs.

5 Who Buys What, Where, When and How (Step 4)

The main purposes of this chapter are:

- to provide guidance on how to construct a customer base for the market you are segmenting by using the information put together in Step 3;
- to link this customer base to the profiling information recorded in Step 2.

The relationship between this step and previous steps is illustrated in Figure 5.1.

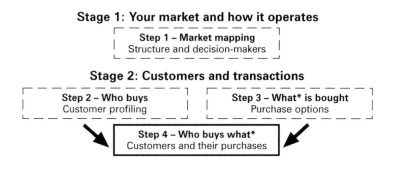

Stage 1: Your market and how it operates

> **Step 1 – Market mapping**
> Structure and decision-makers

Stage 2: Customers and transactions

> **Step 2 – Who buys**
> Customer profiling

> **Step 3 – What* is bought**
> Purchase options

> **Step 4 – Who buys what***
> Customers and their purchases

Figure 5.1   The process of segmentation – Step 4

For companies segmenting their market initially by using data available from within, or easily accessible by, their company, the most logical way of building a representative model of their market is to record the different ways in which customers are known to put together the features identified in Step 3 as the KDFs. Step 4 enables you to put together a comprehensive picture of the market as it is today by identifying for each preliminary segment listed in Step 2 all the unique KDF combinations known, or

118

believed, to occur. In this book we refer to each of these combinations as a *'micro-segment'*.

At the extreme, each of these combinations could be reflecting a different requirement and, therefore, a different segment. The reality is, however, that these different combinations tend to focus upon satisfying a smaller range of core requirements. It is just that different customers often satisfy these core requirements with different features. Therefore, in order to arrive at a segmentation structure for your market, *it is an important step in the process to list the different combinations known to occur in the market and then to understand them*.

In some instances, despite the procedures suggested in the previous step for determining the KDFs, the number of micro-segments can be of an order that makes it difficult to progress the project to the next step. Further routines are therefore included in Step 4 to scale the project back to a more manageable size. These include:

- checking that they depict real customers, or customers you have reasonable evidence to believe exist, as opposed to hypothetical customers;
- removing features found to occur across all the preliminary segments;
- removing micro-segments known to be unattractive to your company (segment attractiveness is looked at in Chapter 9); and by
- revisiting the routines suggested in the previous chapter.

While putting together micro-segments, profiling information is added to each of them: This is first approached by seeing if any specific features can be linked as a whole to any particular profiling characteristics; then followed by attaching to each micro-segment profiling characteristics known to be associated with them. This would be in addition to any profiling information 'inherited' by the micro-segment from its preliminary segment (Step 2).

Once your list of micro-segments is complete, a volume or value figure is attached to each of them.

For the segmentation projects which turn to market research in order to obtain a statistically sound sample of customers for their market, this process would regard each completed interview as a 'micro-segment'.

As a reminder, whenever you see 'what' followed by a star ('what*'), please assume that it also includes 'where', 'when' and 'how'.

It is strongly recommended that you carefully read the next two main sections before making a start on this crucial step in the segmentation process. You will almost certainly need to refer to them again once you get started.

Adding profiling information to the KDFs

Before building your micro-segments, this is a useful point at which to consider whether any KDFs can be associated with specific profiling characteristics. This can first be looked at across the market as a whole and then refined by looking at the KDFs for each preliminary segment. Micro-segments which then contain KDFs linked to a particular profile will therefore 'inherit' this profiling information. For example:

- it may be a known fact in your market that customers who buy the well-established brands, tend to be 'conservative' which, when translated into a marketing strategy, may mean they require the latest product developments to be proven before being targeted with these 'new' lines or enhancements;
- in a business-to-business market, customers who require very high levels of purity in the materials their components are made from or high levels of adherence to their technical specifications may be precision engineering companies;
- in a consumer market, customers who buy the retailers 'own branded' products may be associated with particular socio-economic groups.

Don't be concerned if you are linking a broad range of specific characteristics from one particular profiling group to a KDF by, for example, associating 'A', 'B', 'C1' and 'C2' from the socio-economic profiling group to, say, 'multi-packs'. An opportunity to refine the profiling is presented at the micro-segment level. In addition, don't be concerned if the same associations can be made in more than one preliminary segment. The process you are following is testing the validity of this preliminary structure and any duplication observed across the preliminary segments may be challenging this structure's validity. Finally, the associations you are highlighting need not be the case for 100 per cent of the purchases. What is being looked for at this stage are 'strong' associations, say, associations that are probably true for around 80 per cent of the time.

The profiling information added here is in addition to that already linked to the preliminary segments in Step 2.

At this stage, assuming it is your first segmentation project for the market in question, you are unlikely to know which characteristic(s) will come through as the discriminating identifiers between the concluding segments. This does not mean that linking features to particular profiling characteristics is an unnecessary activity. It is because of the importance of being able to associate particular customers to each of the concluding segments that, whenever an opportunity arises to link a particular stage of the project to customer profiling, it should be taken. Step 4 is the principal opportunity to make this link. (If this project is a review of a past, in-depth, segmentation project, you may already know which profiling characteristics to track.)

If different end-use applications have been brought through to this step alongside the KDFs, attach to each of them any associated profiling characteristics, just as may have been done for the KDFs.

A worksheet for associating specific profiling characteristics with the different end-use applications and the KDFs appears in Table 5.1.

Building the customer base for your market (micro-segments)

In most markets, the number of micro-segments you end up with in this step will almost certainly be too many in number to satisfy segmentation criteria. Step 6 in the process provides the mechanism for reducing the number of micro-segments, with Step 7 providing the test for satisfying segmentation criteria.

At the other extreme, and despite following the routines suggested in the previous step for determining the KDFs, you may find that the number of micro-segments being developed are of an order that makes it difficult to progress the project to the next step. Further routines are therefore included in this chapter to scale the project back to a more manageable size, in addition to suggesting a return to the routines appearing in Step 3.

If at any point during this section it looks as if you are developing an unmanageable number of micro-segments and need to scale back your project, refer to the later section in this chapter titled 'Managing micro-segments – keeping control'.

How to start

Micro-segments are developed for each preliminary segment in turn and a useful starting point is the KDF list put together in the previous chapter. A possible list may look like the one in Table 5.2. It is, in fact, based on Table 4.5 from the preceding chapter.

If you are dealing with different applications of the products or services in your market and captured these differences in your feature lists, it is recommended you start your KDF list with a feature group called 'applications' and list the different applications under the 'features' column.

Two observations made in the last chapter are worth reiterating at this point:

Table 5.1   Worksheet – adding profiling information to end-use applications and KDFs

Preliminary segment: . . . .

Profiling characteristics Category – group – specification	Applications (if appropriate)	KDFs* (What, Where, When, How)												
Demographic														
Geographic														
Psychographic														
Other														

Note: *It is useful to organise the KDFs by their respective feature groups and in their order of importance for the preliminary segment. Each profiling characteristic associated with a particular application/KDF is indicated by a ✔.

- If you know only some customers have an interest in a particular feature group, while others are indifferent towards it, you can capture this by adding 'any (*feature group name*)' to the list of features in the group. For example, 'any brand', 'any size' or 'any colour', as appropriate. This can still occur even though the feature groups have come through the screening procedures in Step 3.
- A further refinement you may need to consider is when some of the feature groups are entirely optional, such as, for example, pre-loaded software on a PC, extended warranties, loyalty points with petrol, groceries or air travel, and so on. To cover those purchase situations when the option is not taken, add 'not purchased' to the applicable feature list.

Table 5.2   A KDF list for a preliminary segment

Feature groups	Features
'What' – colour	Dark hardwood
	Light hardwood
	Pine
	For painting/staining
'What' – country of origin	Scandinavia/Germany
	UK
'What' – product type	DIY kits
	Made up
'Where' – retailer	Department stores
	Direct mail
	Sheds

Developing micro-segments in your market

The principle behind the structure of each micro-segment is the same; each contains a combination of features taken from the list of KDFs. However, the approach you take in how you arrive at your list of micro-segments may be different. This difference relates to the number of customers found at the junction being segmented:

(a) If you are segmenting a market in which there is a limited number of customers at the junction being segmented (and how you define 'limited' may depend on time and resources available to the project), you may wish to create a micro-segment for each individual customer and proceed through the next steps at this individual customer level.

(b) The next level would be to merge *known* customers together according to the similarities they demonstrate in the combinations of KDFs they put together, their use of the product and past buying history. (This is covered in more detail a little later in this section.)

(c) In many markets, when the company is segmenting their market initially by using data available from within, or easily accessible to the company, the customer base is built by recording the different combinations of features *known* to occur in the market, or which the company has reasonable evidence to believe occur in the market.

Whichever option you choose, it is important you record the particular KDFs associated with each micro-segment. This is used in later stages of the process.

Although mentioned earlier in this chapter, it is worth repeating here that in any research project commissioned to assist the segmentation process, each completed interview at the quantitative stage would be regarded as a micro-segment. Recording KDFs is still important when micro-segments are developed this way, a point briefly mentioned in the last chapter.

The simplest structure for recording the different feature combinations is as follows:

1. First ensure each preliminary segment has its appropriate list of KDFs (allocated to their respective feature groups).
2. Then progressively select one feature at a time from each feature group which, when put together, make up a particular purchase combination *known to occur in your market* or which you have reasonable evidence to believe occurs in your market.
3. Repeat the second part of the procedure for each customer or, if you are developing micro-segments following approach (c), until all the different purchase combinations *known* (or believed) to occur in your market have been recorded.

These combinations of features are now your micro-segments.

A simple example should serve to explain this procedure. Assume that for a particular preliminary segment in a market served by florists just two feature groups exist, 'colour scheme' and 'type of bouquet'. Within the colour scheme the KDFs are 'red-based', 'blue-based' and 'pastel-based', and the types of bouquet are either 'bespoke' or 'ready made'. One purchase combination that customers in this preliminary segment are known to put together is 'red-based, bespoke bouquets'. This particular combination of KDFs would therefore form one micro-segment. If, on the other hand, 'pastel, bespoke bouquets' were not put together by this particular preliminary segment, no micro-segment would be recorded for this customer group consisting of the 'pastel, bespoke bouquet' combination.

If you organised the feature groups in a descending order of priority in Step 3, it is useful if this hierarchy is copied for this procedure. This is in case you later need to rationalise the number of resulting micro-segments. One of the options is to remove the least important feature group(s), therefore removing any micro-segments which may only exist because of the alternatives this particular feature group introduced into the process. The suggested layout for developing micro-segments is illustrated in Table 5.3 which also shows a selection of micro-segments along with their particular combination of features.

Table 5.3   A selection of micro-segments recorded for preliminary segment 'A'

| | | Micro-segments | | | | |
Feature groups	Features	A1	A3	A9	A12	A18
'What' – colour	Dark hardwood	✔				
	Light hardwood		✔			
	Pine			✔	✔	
	For painting/staining					✔
'What' – country of origin	Scandinavia/Germany	✔	✔	✔		
	UK				✔	✔
'What' – product type	DIY kits				✔	✔
	Made up	✔	✔	✔		
'Where' – retailer	Department stores	✔	✔	✔		
	Direct mail				✔	
	Sheds					✔

Key: A1, A3, A9 and so on are the micro-segment labels, the prefix indicating the preliminary segment they originated from, the suffix the numeric identifier allocated to that micro-segment. The prefix on the label serves as a useful reference later on in the process because it identifies for each concluding segment the source of its micro-segments. Each feature associated with a particular micro-segment is indicated by a ✔.

The full list of micro-segments for this preliminary segment, being A1 through to A20, appears later in this chapter in Figure 5.2.

As a general rule, each micro-segment within a preliminary segment should have a unique combination of features. If, when recording known customers and their transactions, you find you are repeating micro-segments, question whether there really is a difference between these two customers in terms of the importance they attach to the different features, how they use the product/service (application) and their past buying history. If there is a difference, or you are unsure, list them as separate micro-segments for now. It may be necessary to revisit this later. If you decide to combine these micro-segments, note that for the consolidated micro-segment it covers two (or more) customers.

 For companies progressing their projects using information already available to them, ensure you only record micro-segments for purchase combinations which are *known* to occur in the market or which you have strong reasons to suspect occur in the market. This reality check is essential, otherwise you will unnecessarily complicate this and subsequent steps in the process.

A worksheet for drawing up micro-segments along the lines illustrated in Table 5.3 appears in Table 5.4.

Managing micro-segments – keeping control

Micro-segments are *not* created by generating every possible combination of features appearing under each preliminary segment. The principal controlling mechanism for companies segmenting their market by using data available from within, or easily accessible to the company, is to check that their micro-segments match with reality. An example can be taken from the market represented by Table 5.3.

EXAMPLE 5.1

It was suggested in the last chapter that it was known that when customers wanted to paint or stain an item themselves they always bought UK products. No micro-segment should therefore be listed which links the option of painting/staining with Scandinavia/Germany.

(Please note that in this particular example, the relationship between the two features is not an exclusive two-way correlation, see Chapter 4, 'Merging correlated features', as other coloured UK products can be bought, as is shown in Table 5.3.)

A reality check can have a significant impact.

Table 5.4 Worksheet – recording micro-segments

Preliminary segment: . . . .

Micro-segment		1	2	3	4	5	6	7	8	9	10
Application *(if appropriate)*											
Feature category – group	KDFs*										
What is bought											
Where											
When											
How											

Note: * It is useful to list the KDFs by their respective feature groups and in their order of importance for the preliminary segment in question, for example:

What – Size	Big			
	Small			
What – Colour	Dark			
	Light			

Note: Each application and KDF associated with a micro-segment is indicated by a ✔.

EXAMPLE 5.2

A recent segmentation project for a components manufacturer initially generated just under 150 micro-segments, but when challenged to match these micro-segments to transactions known to take place in their market, the number of micro-segments dropped to 49.

For some complex markets it may, however, be necessary to run the project with 150 to 180 micro-segments, but most markets can be adequately represented by substantially less than this.

Reducing the complexity of 'what*'

After completing your reality check, the first series of techniques to run through when looking to reduce the number of micro-segments are those appearing in Chapter 4 in the section, 'Reducing the complexity of the "what", "where", "when" and "how" lists'. The series of techniques covered were:

- Removing basic entry items; are there any others you could remove?
- Focusing on the influential feature groups; could you lower the cut-off point?
- Narrowing down the range of features; is any further focusing possible?
- Merging feature groups and features according to how customers categorise them and buy them; have you understated the rationalisation?
- Merging correlated features; are any further pairings (or more) possible?

If, after revisiting these techniques, you still find the number of micro-segments rather daunting, the following may finally bring them under control.

Consolidating micro-segments duplicated across the preliminary segments

As this particular section is concerned about micro-segments found in more than one preliminary segment it is only applicable if you are conducting the process with more than one preliminary segment.

At this stage of the process, you may be feeling confident that the preliminary segment structure arrived at in Step 2 is not really standing up to the scrutiny it has been receiving. This may well be the case if:

- the feature groups for two, or more, preliminary segments received similar scores when you were determining their relative importance to each other (Chapter 4 – 'Focusing on the influential feature groups'); and,
- similar micro-segments are being formed for these very same preliminary segments.

It may therefore be possible to remove one or other of the duplicated micro-segments.

Before arriving at any conclusions on this, it is essential that you are able to answer 'No' to *both* the following questions:

- Is the product/service applied in the same way?

  Although 'end-use application' was addressed earlier in the process, it is appropriate to revisit it here. An example given concerned the domestic paint market, where it has been determined that the selection process for paint differs according to the type of room it is being bought for – the buying criteria for gloss in the 'public' rooms, such as the lounge, being different from the buying criteria for gloss in the 'private' rooms, such as the family bedrooms.

- Is the product/service used to achieve the same end result in order to achieve the same benefit? (Although this second question was also addressed earlier in the process it, too, is appropriately revisited here, even though it is, in reality, a topic for the next chapter, 'Why it is Bought'. Do not, however, substitute at this stage any of the features by the benefit they deliver. This is better tackled in the next step, Step 5.)

EXAMPLE 5.3

Some people may buy first-class postage (the product feature) to secure next day delivery (the advantage) and therefore prompt receipt by the addressee (the benefit). Others may buy it for reasons of personal status or to imply importance (alternative benefits).

You may well find that you are able to answer 'No' to both questions and can therefore remove one or other of the duplicated micro-segments.

If you are reducing your micro-segments this way and still want to track your original structure, you could do this by either opening up another preliminary segment and transferring into it the 'surviving' duplicates or add to the profile of each survivor the preliminary segment identifier of their duplicate ('A' or 'B' or 'C' and so on, see Chapter 3). In addition, note at this stage for each 'survivor' any appropriate profiling information previously associated with its duplicate. The opportunity for adding profiling information to each micro-segment occurs later in this chapter.

Removing 'unattractive' micro-segments

If, despite the control routines, the number of micro-segments remaining is still too high, those which are known to be unattractive to your company may be removed from the detailed analysis which follows this step by combining them into one group. It is important that they are not removed from the process completely because to do so would distort the picture of the market being looked at.

Great care should be taken when removing micro-segments from the detailed analysis this way. *Micro-segments may be unattractive today, but could well be the attractive segments of tomorrow*, for example:

● some micro-segments may be currently unattractive because no supplier has put the right offer together to stimulate demand from this particular group and/or obtain the required margins from it;
● some micro-segments may be unattractive today because they only account for a small volume/value of business, but this may be because they are at an early stage of their development.

Individually, micro-segments may represent only a small volume/value, but their requirements may be the same as those of other micro-segments. Later stages of the process would see these micro-segments combined and, as a group, they may then represent a significant volume/value. To remove them from the detailed analysis appearing in later stages of this process would lead to this possibility being overlooked, especially as these 'similar' micro-segments would probably be combined in a group which also contained 'dissimilar' micro-segments.

Only combine micro-segments this way if you feel satisfied with the selection criteria you propose to use and/or you simply have to rationalise the number of micro-segments like this in order to progress with the next steps. The resulting group of micro-segments can always be revisited later, which is an option you may have to consider when looking for opportunities to achieve the company's revenue targets.

As you will need to attach a volume/value figure to this group, leave this method of reducing the number of micro-segments until after the next section. (Segment attractiveness criteria for your company is looked at in Chapter 9.)

Sizing micro-segments

It is important for later stages of the process to have a volume or value figure attached to each micro-segment, especially as this will be the only way in which you will be able to size each of the concluding segments. You may, however, already be in a position where you can attach a volume or value figure to each micro-segment. This will especially be the case if they represent known customers or they have been developed from individual respondents in a suitable market research exercise (which, in order to satisfy the requirements for segmentation, must include questions on the volumes or values bought). In such circumstances you can move straight to the next section. If this is not the case, the following procedure may assist you.

The starting point for sizing micro-segments is, of course, the volume or value figure you gave each of the preliminary segments in Step 2. This figure would then have been used in Step 3 if you opted at that stage of the process to size the final list of features appearing in each of their feature groups. The table used to illustrate this point is repeated here as Table 5.5 for ease of reference.

Table 5.5   Sizing features for a preliminary segment for which the total volume purchased is 2 000 units

Feature groups	Features		Volume
'What' – colour	Dark hardwood		750
	Light hardwood		200
	Pine		500
	For painting/staining		550
		Total	**2 000**
'What' – country of origin	Scandinavia/Germany		1 200
	UK		800
		Total	**2 000**
'What' – product type	DIY kits		500
	Made up		1 500
		Total	**2 000**
'Where' – retailer	Department stores		1 100
	Direct mail		200
	Sheds		700
		Total	**2 000**

Note: In the last chapter it was suggested that if you had no information to assist you in how to split your volume/value figure between the features, you could either assume an even split and attach the appropriate figures or wait until you are attaching volumes or values to each micro-segment in this chapter. The figures being brought forward into this step may not, therefore, be as complete as they are in the above table.

Table 5.5 can now be used to construct a best guess size for each micro-segment by transferring it into a simple cascade which mirrors the way in which the micro-segments were constructed for their respective preliminary segment, as in Table 5.3. Any particular relationships known to exist between various features, in addition to those now covered by the micro-segments, need to be taken account of when drawing up this cascade. For example, in Step 3 when sizing the features now repeated in Table 5.5, it was suggested that half the products in a pine colour (250) and all the products for painting/staining (550) came from the UK.

If you have no information to assist you in how to split your volume/value figure between the features appearing in the next level of the cascade, either assume a ratio based on that appearing in the feature list as a whole for the appropriate preliminary segment, or assume an even split if you were unable to size features in the previous chapter. For example, the ratio between department stores, direct mail and sheds based on the percentage they each account for is 55:10:35.

The suggested approach for sizing micro-segments is illustrated in Figure 5.2. A worksheet for recording the size of each micro-segment appears in Table 5.6. This table is also used for recording the profile of each micro-segment – see next section.

Sizing your micro-segments this way may raise questions about the validity of some of them. If any cannot stand up to scrutiny, remove them from the process. Revisions to the sizing of features may also come out of this procedure.

Completing the profile for each micro-segment

As it is essential that you are able to identify the customers found in each of the concluding market segments, it is important to review and, where possible, enhance the profiling information associated with each micro-segment.

By default, each micro-segment has already 'inherited' the profiling information associated with its originating preliminary segment (Step 2) and has picked up additional characteristics from the features it buys (and application, if appropriate), assuming you made any such links earlier in this chapter. This is the ideal opportunity to review these profiles and remove any characteristic not appropriate to specific micro-segments. In addition, having arrived at these micro-segments by relating them to known activity in your market, adding further profiling information should follow easily. For example, it may be the case that, in preliminary segment 'A', customers who buy 'dark hardwood' are to be found in households where the children have now left home, therefore all the micro-segments generated from this combination should have this additional profiling information attached to them.

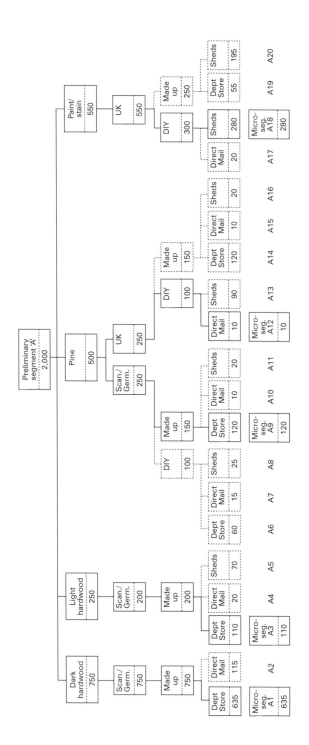

Figure 5.2 Sizing micro-segments

Note: The highlighted micro-segments are those appearing in Table 5.3. The 'route' followed to size each of them is also highlighted. In arriving at these figures for the micro-segments, overall ratios for Preliminary Segment 'A' in Table 5.5 were used to split the 'dark hardwood' and 'light hardwood' between the different outlets: 'dark hardwood' was split 85:15 between department stores and direct mail (based on 1 100:200); 'light hardwood' was split 55:10:35 between all three outlets (based on 1 100:200:700).

If this additional information is taken from a profiling category not yet used in the project, as could be the case with the family life cycle, it is also helpful if the other micro-segments have their profiles enhanced by attaching to them their applicable characteristic from this same category. Using the example given in the previous paragraph, this would mean attaching to the other micro-segments their applicable stage in the family life cycle (see Chapter 3). This particular piece of information may be useful in identifying the concluding segments for marketing purposes.

A worksheet for associating specific profiling characteristics with each micro-segment appears in Table 5.6. In compiling the profile of each micro-segment, first highlight the characteristics associated with its preliminary segment (Chapter 3) and then highlight any additional characteristics associated with its KDFs (and application, if appropriate) – see earlier in this chapter. Finally, review and enhance the profiling information associated with each micro-segment as befits the customer(s) it represents.

This is an important part of the segmentation process.

| **MARKET RESEARCH NOTE** | If interviews are used to arrive at the micro-segments, or just to verify them, ensure profiling information is captured about each respondent. Until you know which profiling characteristics discriminate between your segments, the profiling information collected at these interviews should be as extensive as possible. |

Process check

For the junction being segmented, a model of the market has been developed that represents the different customers found there. Each of these different customers, or micro-segments as they are called in this process, is associated with a particular combination of KDFs and, if appropriate, has been separately developed for each preliminary segment identified in Step 2. Such a comprehensive model of the market is essential if the intention is to arrive at a sound segmentation conclusion which can be used to develop your marketing objectives and strategies. In addition to recording the KDFs, each micro-segment has been associated with profiling information that can be used to identify who they are in the market. This is crucial to understanding which customers should be targeted with each of the resulting segment-specific offers.

We can now look at developing a framework which can be used to compare each of the micro-segments with one another. Given that segmentation is about customers and their specific needs, this framework should be based on a detailed understanding of why customers buy the particular features they regard as important.

Table 5.6   Worksheet – adding the size and profiling information to micro-segments

Preliminary segment: . . . .

Profiling characteristics		Micro-segments									
Category – group	– specification	1	2	3	4	5	6	7	8	9	10
		vol/val	vol/val	vol/val	vol/val	vol/val	vol/val	vol/val	vol/val	vol/val	vol/val
Demographic											
Geographic											
Psychographic											
Other											

Note: Each profiling characteristic associated with a particular micro-segment is indicated by a ✔.

<table>
<tr><td>

MARKET RESEARCH NOTE

</td><td>

In arriving at sampling quotas for the quantitative stage of any research project commissioned to assist the segmentation process, account should be taken of appropriate quantified information put together so far in the project, assuming it has a reasonable degree of confidence around it. This could be based on profiling or features. Basing quotas on micro-segments is unlikely to be cost effective – the number of micro-segments and the sample size required to verify each one resulting in an uneconomic number of total interviews. A statistically sound sample size should pick up the range of purchase combinations found in the market being researched.

</td></tr>
</table>

Case study and further examples

CASE 5.1   Agrofertiliser Supplies

Following on from the KDFs identified in Table 4.7, Table 5.7 shows a small selection of the micro-segments developed from these KDFs, all of which were based on known transactions in the market for the grassland preliminary segment. For the sake of completeness, Table 5.7 shows the complete list of KDFs for this preliminary segment, even though some of them appear to be redundant. All the KDFs listed in Table 5.7 were applicable to at least one grassland micro-segment.

A total of 13 micro-segments were identified for the grassland preliminary segment, a further 17 identified for the arable preliminary segment and a final 4 for the mixed preliminary segment. All 34 micro-segments represented purchase combinations observed in the market.

It is worth noting that if preliminary segments had not been introduced into the case study in Step 2, the different farming practices they cover most probably would have been picked up as different applications in Step 3. With the segmentation process suggesting that each KDF list should be headed by the different applications known to exist in the market, the Agrofertiliser project would have ended up with exactly the same micro-segments.

Sizing for the five micro-segments in Table 5.7 appears in Figure 5.3.

Although some guesswork inevitably went into arriving at the size of each micro-segment, the availability of sales figures from the industry trade body and estimated usage levels from government statistics proved to be of great help. Many markets, however, are not so fortunate, but it is important to all segmentation projects that at least some reasonable approximations are arrived at as this information becomes essential when assessing the commercial viability of each concluding segment.

The status of the case study as it now stands is summarised in Figure 5.4.

CASE 5.1   **Agrofertiliser Supplies (cont'd)**

Table 5.7   **A selection of micro-segments for a preliminary segment in the case study**

Feature groups	Features	Micro-segments				
		G1	G2	G3	G4	G5
'What' – product	AN & manuf. blends AN & bespoke blends Urea & bespoke blends	✔	✔	✔	✔	✔
'What' – brand	Well established Any brand	✔	✔	✔	✔	✔
'What' – quality	High Any quality	✔	✔	✔	✔	✔
'Where' – channel	Local distributor Importer	✔	✔	✔	✔	✔
'What' – intensity	High nitrogen level Low nitrogen level	✔	✔	✔	✔	✔
'What' – consultant	Manufacturer's Distributor's Independent Not purchased	✔	✔	✔	✔	✔

Key: 'G1', 'G2' and so on are the individual identifiers for the micro-segments, the 'G' indicating that they come from the grassland preliminary segment. Each feature associated with a particular micro-segment is indicated by a ✔.

Note: Due to the closeness of the scores for 'intensity' and 'consultant' when the feature groups for this preliminary segment were prioritised in Step 4 (see Table 4.7) it was decided to continue the process with the inclusion of consultants, even though they fell below the suggested cut-off point.

Further examples

For many companies this step is progressed by working in close liaison with the salesforce along with other customer contact staff, each micro-segment being based on known customers and prospects. For other companies this step is progressed by referring to customer databases when they are fortunate enough to have records of the different features selected by various customers. However, an often incorrectly held belief is that one company's

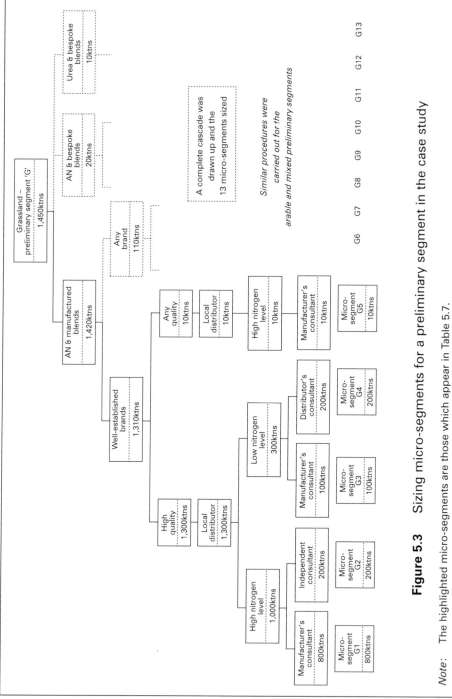

Figure 5.3   Sizing micro-segments for a preliminary segment in the case study

Note: The highlighted micro-segments are those which appear in Table 5.7.

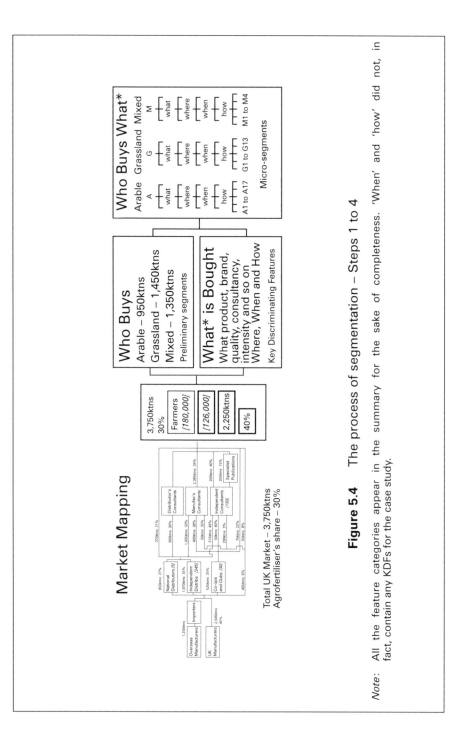

Market Mapping

Who Buys
Arable – 950ktns
Grassland – 1,450ktns
Mixed – 1,350ktns
Preliminary segments

What* is Bought
What product, brand,
quality, consultancy,
intensity and so on
Where, When and How

Key Discriminating Features

3,750ktns
30%

Farmers
[180,000]

[126,000]

2,250ktns

40%

Who Buys What*

Arable	Grassland	Mixed
A	G	M
what	what	what
where	where	where
when	when	when
how	how	how
A1 to A17	G1 to G13	M1 to M4

Micro-segments

Overseas Manufacturers 1,250ktns
Importers
UK Manufacturers 2,500ktns 45%

National Distributors [5] 850ktns 27%
Independent Distribs [245] 1,970ktns 36%
Co-ops and Clubs [36] 525ktns 25%

370ktns 21%
300ktns 30%
1,005ktns 33%
400ktns 38%
50ktns 26%
215ktns 40%
50ktns 40%
200ktns 3%

Distributor's Consultants
Manufac's Consultants
Independent Consultants [750]
Specialist Publications

2,385ktns 34%
200ktns 40%
355ktns 15%

75ktns 22%
60ktns 8%
400ktns 6%

Total UK Market – 3,750ktns
Agrofertiliser's share – 30%

Figure 5.4   The process of segmentation – Steps 1 to 4

Note: All the feature categories appear in the summary for the sake of completeness. 'When' and 'how' did not, in fact, contain any KDFs for the case study.

customers form a microcosm of the market as a whole and can therefore be regarded as forming a representative sample of the complete market. Slipping into this belief without some independent validation could well result in the company failing to identify new opportunities in their market.

However, even if you know that the micro-segments you have put together are not truly representative of the market as a whole, and given the stage that the project is now at, it is still worth progressing the project through the remaining three steps. This will enable you to gain an appreciation of what is involved in the segmentation process as a whole, and to compare the results of this first pass with those from the more statistically sound study which should, of course, follow.

When drawing up micro-segments initially by using data available from within, or easily accessible to, the company, there has been a tendency in a number of projects to generate micro-segments which don't really exist. Challenging each micro-segment in turn and insisting it must relate to a known customer transaction has seen micro-segments reduced by well over 50 per cent for some projects. In one extreme case, this reality check reduced the number of micro-segments to less than 20 per cent of the original total! Instead of matching micro-segments to *known* transactions in the market, this company had been looking at all the possible combinations of KDFs that *could* exist in the market.

An inevitable question at this stage of a project concerns the number of micro-segments a market *should* have. There is, unfortunately, no simple answer. In theory, if the number of concluding segments for a market usually total between 5 and 8, then, for any market understood in depth, the number of micro-segments generated should not be too far off this number! In many projects the number of micro-segments required to represent a market have been well under 100, though some companies have found it necessary to consider higher numbers of micro-segments. If your project is exceeding 150 micro-segments it is worth reconsidering the number of features you are using for this step. It could also be worth reviewing your market definition as it may, in fact, be too broad. Both of these checks have re-injected sanity into more than one project.

If, despite what has been said so far, your project is still considering a large number of micro-segments, it may help in progressing the project if, when entering the final stage of the next step (scoring the needs-based buying requirements for each micro-segment), you initially take only around 50 to 80 of them through this particular sequence and then through Step 6. Once this initial batch has been through Step 6, repeat this sequence for the remaining micro-segments, not forgetting to consider each new batch taken into Step 6 alongside the results already established in that step.

For those projects reverting to market research in order to generate micro-segments it is important you first progress through the final steps of this process before writing the final research brief. This will ensure the researchers have a comprehensive brief and that their research programme will provide the information required for successful segmentation.

Careful and thoughtful consideration of the segmentation steps presented so far, assisted by a healthy dose of realism, will ensure your company is ready to take its project into the next step.

6 *Why it is Bought (Step 5)*

Step 5 puts together the framework that will be used to compare each of the micro-segments with one another. This framework consists of the needs-based buying requirements of the market, identified by referring to the KDFs listed in Step 3 (Chapter 4).

The first part of Step 5 is designed to ensure the real needs in your market are fully understood and, in doing so, seek to uncover any unmet needs. The second part then identifies the key needs across all the preliminary segments in order to arrive at an overall list for the market being segmented. Once this list is finalised, 'price' is introduced into the process in order to complete the picture.

Part 3 of this step then requires relative values to be attached to the key needs-based buying requirements of the market, along with price, for each of the micro-segments developed in the previous chapter.

The relationship between this step and previous steps is illustrated in Figure 6.1.

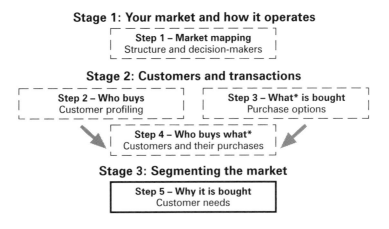

Stage 1: Your market and how it operates

Step 1 – Market mapping
Structure and decision-makers

Stage 2: Customers and transactions

Step 2 – Who buys
Customer profiling

Step 3 – What* is bought
Purchase options

Step 4 – Who buys what*
Customers and their purchases

Stage 3: Segmenting the market

Step 5 – Why it is bought
Customer needs

Figure 6.1   The process of segmentation – Step 5

This chapter also contains a detailed look at features, advantages and benefits in order to highlight the difference between them. In addition, there is a section which looks at some of the techniques which can be used to uncover the possibility of unmet needs existing in your market.

Identifying the real needs-based buying requirements, the real benefits

The primary purpose of this first part is to develop the benefits list required later in this step and to highlight the possibility that there may be unmet needs in your market. This will help in correctly capturing the importance of 'price' in the buying process.

 The importance of looking at the needs-based buying requirements of your market (the benefits) should not be underestimated. Additionally, the difficulty of ensuring you are identifying the real benefits should not be underestimated. This difficulty should not, however, provide a reason for excluding benefits from the process.

First, draw up, separately, a complete 'benefits' list which covers all the reasons the market has given for buying, including the reasons given by those who depend on another junction in the market map to select the products they eventually purchase. This benefits list should cover both tangible and intangible benefits.

To ensure the distinction between 'feature', 'advantage' and 'benefit' is clear, a section on features, advantages and benefits is included towards the end of this chapter. The sequence suggested in this section for moving from a feature to a benefit will ensure that the benefits you list are deliverable by the features.

This first look at benefits could be taken from past research and by talking with representatives of your customer contact staff. If your company also follows the practice of putting together lost sales reports, a review of these could also prove to be a useful source of information.

In order to ensure this list is both thorough and comprehensive it is useful if you directly relate this list of benefits to the KDFs identified in Step 3 and used to build your micro-segments in the last chapter. This is best achieved by listing the feature groups, along with their features, and then attaching to each group the benefits delivered by their respective features. A suggested structure for recording this information appears in Table 6.1.

In arriving at your list of benefits it is important to note that a single feature can deliver different benefits to different customers and more than one benefit to the same customer. For example, canned dog food provides easy storage (no special storage conditions) and reduces the frequency of shopping trips (long shelf life). Different features can also deliver the same benefits, for example, dried dog food also reduces the frequency of shopping trips.

Table 6.1   Recording benefits

Feature groups	Features	Advantages	Benefits
'What' – colour	Dark hardwood Light hardwood Pine For painting/ staining		
'What' – country of origin	Scandinavia/ Germany UK		
'What' – product type	DIY kits Made up		
'Where' – retailer	Department stores Direct mail Sheds		

Note: An example of a completed 'benefit analysis sheet' appears in Table 6.4.

Although 'attributes' were looked at in Step 3 (Chapter 4) it is worth revisiting this topic again here to ensure that none of the feature descriptions are 'hiding' more specific features. For example, 'quality' could mean scratch proof and/or stain proof, 'brand' could mean service and/or reliability, and so on. As highlighted in Chapter 4, a description of a feature is meaningless if it does not describe what your company would need to do in order to offer it.

If on running through your feature lists you come across a description which is covering more than one attribute you may need to accommodate this variation by splitting the applicable micro-segments and re-specifying the features they look for. The volume/value will also need to be redistributed between them and their profiling information reviewed and amended if necessary.

If your segmentation project has introduced preliminary segments into the process, separate benefit lists should be drawn up for each preliminary segment in turn. Although this approach will undoubtedly lead to the duplication of some benefits, it is better to be thorough than to miss out a benefit that could be an important differentiator between concluding segments. A worksheet which can be used for this stage of the project appears in Table 6.2. It is based on the completed benefit analysis sheet which appears in Table 6.4.

Table 6.2   Worksheet – recording benefits

Customer appeal	Feature	Advantage	Benefit
What issues are of particular concern for the customer? For example, availability, safety, reliability, simplicity, leading edge, fashionable and so on.	What features of the product/service best illustrate these issues? What are they? How do they work? (As in your list of KDFs.)	What advantages do these features provide? In other words, what do they do for the customer?	How can tangible benefits be expressed to give maximum customer appeal? In other words, what does the customer get that they explicitly need?

Preliminary segment: . . . .

		which means that:	which means that:
		which means that:	which means that:
		which means that:	which means that:
		which means that:	which means that:
		which means that:	which means that:
		which means that:	which means that:

In addition to looking at each feature in turn, also look at the various feature combinations appearing in the micro-segments. It is sometimes particular combinations of features that deliver the benefits customers are looking for. Add to the list any new benefit this reveals by attaching it to one of the appropriate features.

Further, if different end-use applications are being considered in your project alongside the KDFs (as opposed to the different applications being used as preliminary segments) it is important to consider whether different benefits are being delivered by the various KDFs when they are applied to a different end use. It is, however, unusual to be able to identify specific benefits for the different applications as they tend to be an overall statement of purpose for the purchase.

It is important you spend as much time as necessary in compiling these benefit lists as they will be used to determine the segmentation structure of your market.

If you created preliminary segments for lapsed buyers and/or prospects in Chapter 3, an understanding of their unmet needs should be developed in this step using the procedures suggested.

Looking at 'Why it is bought' really only provides answers to the status quo. To help uncover the real needs, we must be able to answer the question, 'What are they trying to achieve?' For example, in the agricultural market covered by the case study, the focus of some farmers was to buy products which produced lush, green grass for their livestock to graze on. For another group of farmers, their concern was how well their livestock looked (the appearance of the grass being a minor concern). In the arable sector, one group of farmers concentrated solely on producing crops which met the needs of the market they were selling into, again regardless of how the crop looked whilst in the field. This particular group also demonstrated another important point when looking at the reasons 'why' particular products are bought.

This point concerns the 'market orientated' arable farmers, who bought a great deal of this product in its constituent parts, rather than already mixed (which was how the majority of it was sold in various standard combinations), and they always looked for the cheapest buys. The initial conclusion was that this group bought on price, a conclusion which, it was later discovered, combined them with another group of farmers who *were* driven by price. However, on probing what they were really trying to achieve, it became apparent that they were combining the constituent parts in a variety of ways to make up a number of different mixes. This was being done because the standard, off-the-shelf combinations produced by the manufacturers were not sophisticated enough for the needs of this particular group of farmers. These bespoke combinations improved their farm's output and had nothing to do with price. In addition, a further driving force for this group of farmers was innovation, and their own bespoke mixing operation was also seen to be innovative.

In yet another market, one segment was found to consist of unenthusiastic buyers who stated they were not really interested in the product class and only made purchases in this product class for the functional needs it satisfied. For example, they bought cars simply to travel between 'A' and 'B'. However, a research project discovered that this segment did have aspirations, in addition to the functional requirements, which could be met by the product if only it was designed and specifically targeted at this distinct group (which, usefully, had a distinct demographic profile). An example of this would be a car specifically designed to meet the requirements of business-women and specifically positioned to appeal to this segment. A motor manufacturer who has pursued a strategy similar to this is Jaguar (Ford), who in the USA positioned the XJS model as one targeted at (wealthy) women.

Thus, it is crucial at this stage to be alert to any possible unsatisfied needs manifesting themselves in the guise of something else, rather than accepting the status quo. For example, 'price' may be given as the sole or major criterion for choice, but it *could* be hiding the fact that customers/consumers are currently dissatisfied with the present alternative offers available, as their real needs are not being met. What they are currently having to buy in order to meet a functional need is, therefore, second rate, for which they certainly would not pay a premium. For example, there is a functional need of (most) garden owners to mow the grass. To meet this need, there used to be only cylinder mowers available. Despite a close cut, a collecting box and roller providing an attractive finish, the cylinder mower was regarded as cumbersome by some gardeners and, because of this, they would buy cheap versions. Then came the hover mower, which was light and quick, thus enabling a substantial amount of the time previously allocated to a chore to be better spent. This group, therefore, has a need for a fast method of keeping their grass in check. In contrast, the group choosing to use a cylinder mower, has a need, in many instances, to present the lawn as a 'show piece'.

To assist in identifying whether there are any unsatisfied needs in a market, two techniques are available, 'needs gap analysis' and 'perceptual mapping'. The former looks at what is available today in terms of features, while the latter looks at what is available today in terms of views or attitudes. In doing so, these techniques highlight where there are unfilled *potential* opportunities. They may be unfilled, of course, because there is no demand. Details of these two techniques appear later in this chapter.

If, at this stage, you now consider your company's understanding of its market is inadequate, there is clearly a need to fill the information gaps by commissioning some independent market research from an agency skilled in carrying out and interpreting in-depth qualitative discussions. It is, however, recommended that you finish reading through Step 5 before finalising your research brief, as there may well be other areas you would want to include in the brief.

To cover the existence of unmet needs, such as those uncovered by market research – which, in turn, could include those of lapsed buyers and prospects (potential buyers who appear to be suited to the products/services available in the market but who aren't buying anything yet) – further micro-segments should be opened up to account for these potential new marketing opportunities. Each should have a unique alphanumeric label attached to it (with the letter selected from either the appropriate preliminary segment, or from a newly introduced preliminary segment).

It is now essential to enhance the information as best you can for each new micro-segment with the following actions:

(a) attach any specific profiling information you can associate with them;
(b) list the features they require, which, in some instances, may not yet be available, but could certainly be made available;
(c) as best as possible attach volumes or values to each, made up, if appropriate, of volumes/values from other micro-segments, or preliminary segments, along with any potential extra volume/value which could be generated by meeting these currently untapped needs.

Your list of benefits should now be complete.

Identifying the critical purchase influences (CPIs) for the market

Although your benefit list has been developed by reference to the KDFs, it may be known that some of these benefits are relatively unimportant in the decision-making process across the market. To continue the segmentation process with these particular benefits will therefore add very little to the final conclusion. Part 2 of this step therefore provides the opportunity to focus the final stage of your project on to the key benefits, in other words, those that are critical in influencing the purchase decisions in the market. In this segmentation process we refer to such benefits as CPIs.

This second part also brings 'price' into the process and introduces an optional refinement of allocating the final list of purchase requirements into either 'buying criteria' or 'attitude' groups.

If you do not need to reconsider your benefit list(s) you can move straight to the next section, 'Creating market CPIs'.

Ranking the benefit list(s)

For each preliminary segment, if appropriate, including any new ones created earlier in this step, re-arrange their benefits into a descending order of importance. Use statistically sound market research data or reasoned judgement to do this, ensuring your judgement is *market based* and that benefits are not simply dropped to the bottom of the list because *you* would prefer them to be unimportant.

It may now be possible to decide a cut-off point which separates out those benefits that play a decisive part in the buying process (the CPIs) from those that, to all intents and purposes, play only a secondary part.

Although the procedure used to determine the CPIs is the same as that used to determine the KDFs, here is a quick refresher: once you have re-arranged the items into a descending order of importance, allocate 100 points between them in a way which represents their relative importance to each other *from the market's perspective*, as illustrated in Table 6.3. Draw the cut-off point at, say, where the score comes to 80.

Table 6.3   Prioritising benefits

Benefits	Individual score	Cumulative score
Maintains 'pioneering' status	35	35
Enables precision work	25	60
Reduces labour requirement	15	75
Occupies little floor space	10	85
Easy to move	7	92
Payments match usage level	5	97
Available for local viewing	3	100

In this particular example, the cut-off point could be after 'reduces labour requirement' or after 'occupies little floor space'. All the items up to the cut-off point would now be regarded as CPIs.

It is important to note that if, when carrying out this prioritising routine you do not believe that all the micro-segments within a particular preliminary segment would have the same benefits falling below the cut-off point, only those benefits known to fall below the cut-off point across all these micro-segments should be excluded from the CPI list. If necessary, note the different orders that occur in separate tables, attach to them their relative values and determine the cut-off point for each table.

You now have a series of CPI lists, one (or more) for each preliminary segment.

Creating market CPIs

Now compile one CPI list for the whole market by bringing together the separate preliminary segment lists. Duplicates should be omitted so that each benefit in the list is unique. *These are now your market CPIs.*

If you only had one list, this now becomes your list of market CPIs.

Price

Clearly, 'price' has an important part to play in the buying activity of segments and is obviously a component of 'buying criteria'. Everything has its price!

However, 'price', as a distinct topic, has been deliberately kept out of the process up until now because it can too easily be used as a 'catch all' or 'get out' in answer to some of the more difficult questions posed by this segmentation process. All too often, 'price' is given as the reason for particular buying activity. Not everyone buys the cheapest, and for those that do, it could be because there is nothing available in the market that really meets their requirements, as was pointed out earlier in this chapter. Produce the product/service they are looking for, and price becomes less of an issue.

'Price' is simply a measure of value placed by the buyer on both the tangible and intangible components of a purchase. A simple example should suffice to illustrate this point.

EXAMPLE 6.1   Price as a measure of value

A company launched a new pure juice product on the market after tests had indicated an overwhelming acceptance by the target group. When sales fell far short of expectations, research indicated that the target group simply did not believe that the claims on the can about the product could be true at such a low price. So the company doubled the price and relaunched it, and the product was a resounding success.

For the purposes of segmentation, we are concerned with the relative importance of price to the other components of the purchase: in other words, to what extent will the purchaser let their requirements be bought out by lower prices? Alternatively, when will they start trading in their requirements in order to keep the price at an acceptable level? The ability of one supplier to supply the market at lower prices than everyone else is not the issue we are addressing here, or need to address, when segmenting markets and the failure to recognise this often leads to the wrong conclusions. For example, in a market characterised by buyers phoning round for the cheapest price, such as in the car insurance market, it would be wrong to instantly conclude that this market was dominated by price chasers. Many will be phoning round a selected list of alternative suppliers, having rejected other possible suppliers, therefore indicating they attribute some value to particular brands. Many will also be phoning round their group of suppliers with a particular list of requirements they regard as being important. In this market, therefore, segmentation would need to focus on the lists of alternative suppliers and the lists of requirements, the phoning round basically indicating that they regard their list of suppliers as all being very similar to each other. They are, therefore, comparing one with another in order to obtain the best value. Inevitably, of course, some of those phoning round will be looking for the cheapest, willing to take a policy out with any supplier and ready to sacrifice any of their requirements in order to get a lower price (assuming they have any requirements other than the basic legal minimum).

MARKET RESEARCH NOTE	It is extremely important that in any research project commissioned to assist this step of the process, the questionnaire and/or interviewer makes it very clear to the respondent what is meant by 'price' and how it is therefore to be related to the other benefits (market CPIs) in the list.

To conclude these comments on price, it is worth noting that, in some instances, the role played by price can be distorted (as in the case, for example, of company car purchases by individuals). This will certainly be true when none of the options available are really what the employee wants, yet they 'have' to spend their allowance! Hopefully, however, this will have been picked up earlier in this chapter.

Allocating the market CPIs into 'buying criteria' or 'attitudinal' lists (optional)

This optional part of the process allows you to test segmentation results obtainable from the data by separately grouping your micro-segments by buying criteria and by attitude.

Re-arrange your market CPIs into two groups. The first group, 'buying criteria', should be made up of the physical components of the purchase such as size, packaging, channel and so on. The second group, 'attitudinal', should be made up of the intangible components of the purchase, such as brand.

Attaching the CPIs and their values to the micro-segments

This is achieved by apportioning a total score of 100 between *all* the market CPIs for every micro-segment, thus giving a relative value relationship to the CPIs. Wherever a particular market CPI is irrelevant, attach a zero score. *Do not forget to include a relative score for price.* The total is allocated between all the market CPIs, along with price, for every micro-segment in order to ensure that each micro-segment can be directly compared with all the other micro-segments. This comparison routine occurs in Step 6.

 At this point, you may have identified another area of weakness in the data currently available in your company. It is now timely to complete your research brief and commission some independent market research. Information gaps identified earlier in the process should also be included in this research project. In addition, and assuming it has not been already identified as an information gap in the process so far, it will help Step 7 if the research gathers demographic, geographic and psychographic profile data from the companies/individuals interviewed.

As the market research project progresses, the implications of any new findings should be incorporated into the segmentation steps taken so far and the necessary amendments made. The 'buying criteria' and 'attitudinal' data can then be fed directly into the process so that the clustering routine detailed in Step 6 can take place. Alternatively, it may be possible to include this clustering procedure in the specification for the research project, with the resulting segments tested against the checklist appearing in Step 7.

This stage may be helped by identifying for each micro-segment the top three to five market CPIs – in other words, the three to five most important – and list them in rank order, along with price, with the most important first. (Three to five is a guideline figure. It could be more, or it could be less: what you are focusing on at this stage are the CPIs which account for around 80 per cent of the micro-segment's decision. Only on very rare occasions is the number likely to be above this.) Then apportion a total of 100 between the appropriate CPIs and price for each micro-segment in turn in order to remove the linear relationship implied by the rank order (which is unlikely to be the case), ensuring that the distribution of the 100 points indicates the relative value relationship *from the micro-segment's perspective*.

For example, the three most important CPIs for one micro-segment could be:

1. Brand – leading R&D.
2. Built-in carrying mechanism.
3. Environmentally friendly packaging.

The relative values of these three CPIs to each other, along with price, may have been found to be:

1. Brand – leading R&D:	40
2. Environmentally friendly packaging:	35
3. Built-in carrying mechanism:	15
4. Price:	10
Total 100	

All the other market CPIs that may have been listed for this market would then be given a zero value for this particular micro-segment.

It is crucially important to ensure that the relative importance score attributed to 'price' reflects the micro-segment's willingness to sacrifice their other requirements in order to get a lower price. If this is not made clear at the outset the segmentation findings will be misleading. This, in turn, will result in marketing objectives and strategies failing to deliver the best financial returns available to the company.

The role of price was discussed earlier in this chapter.

MARKET RESEARCH NOTE

At the interview stage it can become rather tedious for the respondent if they are requested to 'tidy up' their scores because they don't exactly add up to 100. Once the respondent has begun to distribute their 100 points, ensure they concentrate on indicating the relative importance to them of the market CPIs rather than become distracted by also having to consider their running total. The scores can be recalculated back to 100 after the interview has been completed.

When conducting this part of the research it can assist the respondent if they are asked to first select their most important requirement from the list of market CPIs, and then requested to give this particular CPI a score out of 100 to indicate its importance to them. The respondent is then asked to allocate scores to the remaining CPIs using the first score as a reference point. A variation on this approach is to suggest the respondent gives their most important requirement a score of 100, and then score the remaining CPIs in relation to this. In either case, the scores can be recalculated back to 100 after the interview has been completed.

For some respondents, coping with 100 points can be rather daunting and they would prefer to consider the distribution of a lower total. Clearly the preference of the respondent should be adopted as it is important they feel comfortable with what they are being asked to manage. This flexibility is also more likely to produce a more accurate reflection of the respondent's buying priorities and, therefore, a more accurate segmentation result.

If market research data is available, particularly if it has used the technique of requesting respondents to allocate between their buying criteria a pre-specified sum, such as 100, attach the values obtained through this work to the CPIs. If such research is not available and you wish to continue the process for the sake of completeness and experience while the research is being conducted, the following exercise could be adopted.

Let each member of the segmentation team (assisted, whenever possible, by other members of staff with direct contact with the market) adopt the stand-point of each of the micro-segments in turn and guesstimate the relative values the micro-segment would give to the CPIs. This would enable you to progress the process through the final two steps.

Be careful not to let this hypothetical exercise be misinterpreted and adopted as fact!

While scoring the CPIs you may discover that the CPIs and their values for the different products are almost identical. If this is the case, segmentation by product bought is irrelevant and you should reduce the number of product types at this micro-level.

MARKET RESEARCH NOTE Depending on how accurate the micro-segments are in representing the market, it is possible to use them in the design of the sampling frame for the research. However, it could well be that in doing this the total number of interviews required to provide a representative sample of each micro-segment would be far too large in terms of cost and/or in terms of the sample size required to accurately represent the market as a whole. If this is the case, revert to interviewing a statistically valid sample size and assume this will 'capture' all the significant features and purchase combinations found in the market. If, however, there are certain features and/or micro-segments you particularly want to understand (for whatever reason), supplement the general sampling frame with quotas which ensure your research will include them.

A key question to re-address at this point is: are you absolutely sure that the reasons listed are not hiding any underlying needs which are not being met? If your answer is 'No', it is recommended that you, or a professional market research interviewer, conduct face-to-face interviews with a small sample (five or six) of those customers you are still unsure about. This should be sufficient to indicate whether or not there are any unmet needs yet to be discovered. If necessary, this check should then move on to a larger-scale project in order to quantify the extent and value of these unmet needs.

An alternative method of scoring can be to rate each CPI (or the top three to five, if appropriate) on a scale of 0 to 10 where '0' means the CPI is of no relevance at all, '1' means it is considered but is of very little importance and '10' means it is extremely important. The same scaling can be applied to price. This approach to scoring is often suggested as the preferred approach at the research stage because it is simpler to administer, particularly if telephone interviews are being conducted. Although this approach does not prevent the data from being taken through the next step of the process, its simplicity has a downside.

Assume there is a micro-segment that is not very price sensitive and values five CPIs, one of which is very dominant. The highest score that can be given to the dominant CPI is 10. As this micro-segment values four more CPIs, the inclination will be to give each of them a reasonable score in order to indicate their individual importance to the micro-segment. If we assume the scores for these four CPIs range from, say, 6 down to 4, averaging out at a score of 5, the total for these four CPIs comes to 20. Add a score for price of, say, 2 and the total for these less dominant criteria comes to 22. Although the dominance of one CPI when compared with everything else still remains, its true relative importance to the micro-segment is highly likely to be masked. A very dominant CPI could well account for 50 per cent or more of a decision. This could have crucial implications for the marketing strategy put together for a particular segment. Table 6.4 summarises the example presented in this paragraph and illustrates how the 'rating' approach to scoring can hide the true relative importance of CPIs. The benefits listed as the CPIs are those which appeared in Table 6.3.

Table 6.4   The 'rating' approach to scoring a micro-segment's CPIs

CPIs and price	Individual rating: 0 to 10	Rescored to total 100*
Maintains 'pioneering' status	10	31
Enables precision work	6	19
Reduces labour requirement	5	16
Occupies little floor space	5	16
Easy to move	4	12
Price	2	6
Total	**32**	**100**

* Calculated by expressing each individual rating as a percentage of the total for the ratings column (being 32 in this example).

Note: Although the dominance of 'maintains pioneering status' survives, its true relative importance, which in the example given could mean it accounted for over 50 per cent of the decision, is masked.

It should be re-emphasised that this alternative approach to scoring does not prevent the segmentation project from progressing through the next steps of the process. Segmentation, as pointed out earlier in this book, is not an end in itself. It is only by developing and implementing strategies targeted at your chosen segments that the real benefits of segmentation can be realised. The total sum preference approach to scoring CPIs and price is better able to identify where the priorities for your marketing strategies should lie.

Testing the validity of current SBU structures

If you are in a business with a number of SBUs, and have, so far, been looking at only one of them, though the intention is to take all the SBUs through the process, this point can be a useful stage in the process to take stock and tackle the remaining SBUs, bringing them through Steps 1 to 5. This is because Step 6 is where the process seeks to group common micro-segments. If all your SBUs are, therefore, included in Step 6, it will enable you to see whether your current SBU structure is the most appropriate for the market, or whether a re-organisation of your business is required. You may, of course, prefer to take the first SBU through the whole process in order to become familiar with it, after which, the remaining SBUs are taken through Steps 1 to 5, with the first SBU taken through Step 6 again, once the remaining SBUs are ready.

Features, advantages and benefits

Customers buy products and services because they seek to acquire a range of benefits that go with them. For example, the motivation behind employing a surveyor when contemplating moving into a new house is not to preserve the sub-species *Homo sapiens 'surveyorcus'*; analgesics are not bought to keep the pharmaceutical manufacturers in business; and the do-it-yourselfers do not buy drill bits out of an interest in preserving the precision engineering industry of the Lower Don Valley! Purchasers are rarely motivated in the first instance by the technical features or attributes of a service or product, but rather by the benefits those features or attributes bring with them. Therefore, the surveyor is employed because the buyer wants to be assured the proposed new property is structurally sound; analgesics are bought to relieve pain; and, as a drill manufacturer is quoted as saying, 'Last year we sold one million quarter-inch drills, not because people wanted quarter-inch drills, but because they wanted quarter-inch holes' (although this could be seen as a blinkered understanding of the need, which is usually to attach two items together and could therefore be achieved by using an appropriate glue!) Understanding benefits is therefore as important as knowing about the products or services themselves. It is equally important to realise that different customers may attach different values to these benefits.

Standard benefits

These are the basic benefits that arise from the features of the product, but are not in any way unique to any particular manufacturer/supplier: for example, 'the aerosol propellant is one that does not damage the ozone layer'. Even if all aerosols contained such propellants, it is still worth noting as it could be an important consideration in the purchasing decision for your market. Its importance may also differ between segments.

Company benefits

Whenever a purchase is made, the transaction links the customer to the company supplying the item. Links will be forged between the two at many levels. For example, in business-to-business transactions their accounts departments will be in contact to deal with payment or financial matters; people on installation work or aftersales servicing will interact with the personnel at the buyer's company; delivery men with storekeepers; designers with technicians, and so on. When a buyer selects one of a number of competing suppliers, there ought to be some benefits to that buyer for making that choice.

Customers will prefer to deal with companies that, for example, provide better customer service, inspire confidence, have a reputation for fair trading policies, are known to be flexible, or even have a particular image associated with them. Company benefits are a means of differentiating your products/services from competing ones if, to all intents and purposes, they are similar. Take UK banks, for example: some are trying to establish specific identities for the benefits they supply. Hence there is the 'action bank', the 'listening bank', a bank which follows certain ethical policies when determining who they will do business with, and there once was a bank with a strapline that described them as the bank that liked to say 'yes'. There are now even banks which are 'open when their customers want them to be'!

Differential benefits

In a competitive marketplace, most suppliers vying for the available customers will not be able to claim that their standard, or company, benefits are, in truth, regarded as being a great deal different from those of the competition. The benefits that only your products or services provide, which are also benefits in the eye of the customer, give your company its competitive advantage and are known as 'differential benefits'. To understand your market dynamics fully, however, particularly in the context of developing a segmentation structure for it, you not only need to be able to list your own company's differential benefits, you also need to list those differential benefits of your competitors which attract some of the market to them, as opposed to you. Differential benefits could include, for example:

- the only breakdown service genuinely open 24 hours a day and therefore available at any time to get the customer back on the move;
- the only product with self-cleaning heads, so once installed there are no maintenance worries.

It is important to note, however, that a particular feature may have more than one benefit, and the most appropriate benefit(s) to highlight could well differ by segment. For example, an airline's non-stop service between two cities could mean:

- a better use of time because less of it is spent at 35 000 feet;
- less opportunity to go missing at transit airports and get left behind (an important concern for expatriates sending their children back home for a school term);
- a better chance of arriving on time (a transit stop is an opportunity for delaying incidents to occur).

Distinguishing between features, advantages and benefits

To get from a feature to an advantage, and then to a benefit, the phrase 'which means that' can be helpful. For example, 'This product is coated in new formula paint (*feature*) which means that the colour will never fade (*advantage*)'. If you *know* this is what the customer *needs*, then you have also arrived at a *benefit*.

Sometimes the expression 'which means that' can sound rather clumsy. When this happens, an alternative linking word is 'because': for example, 'You can be sure of personal attention from us because we are a small family business'.

To check if you have arrived at a benefit and not just an advantage, apply the 'so what?' test. Ask this question after the benefit. If the 'so what?' prompts you to go further, it is likely you have not yet reached the real benefit: for example, 'The products are hand made (*feature*), which means they are better quality than machine-made ones (*benefit?*)' – 'so what?' – which means they last longer (*the real benefit*).

Developing the benefits list for your market

In arriving at the pertinent list of benefits for the whole market you will initially need to concern yourself with 'customer appeal'. The first step in arriving at the final benefits list is, therefore, to determine what issues are of particular concern to the customer. This can then be developed into a list of the feature(s) that enable the product/service to appeal to the customer, then the advantage(s) they provide and, finally, the benefits. Table 6.5 contains a structure for a benefits analysis sheet which will assist this process, and three examples.

Table 6.5   Benefit analysis sheet

Customer appeal	Features	Advantages	Benefits
What issues are of concern for this customer? For example, reliability, availability, safety, simplicity, fashionable, leading edge and so on.	What features of the product/ service best illustrate these issues? What are they? How do they work?	What advantages do these features provide? In other words, what do they do for the customer?	How can tangible benefits be expressed to give maximum customer appeal? In other words, what does the customer get that he/she *needs*?
Credit cards			
Ease of use. Safer than carrying money. Less bulky than cash or cheque book. Speedy transaction. Provide credit. International.	MasterCard credit card.	Enables purchases to be made world wide.	Eliminates the need to carry large amounts of cash. Eases cash problems and so on.
Saucepans			
Ease of use. Ease of washing up. Attractive end product.	Teflon coated.	Non-stick.	Trouble-free cooking. Quicker washing up. Better presentation of food and so on.
Office Service Bureaux			
Accuracy. Speedy turnaround of work.	Latest software. Very skilled staff.	Extremely versatile.	Minimum of errors. Always meet deadlines.

Summary

- Feature: what it is, or is made from;
- Advantage: what it does;
- Benefit: what the customer gets that they explicitly need (or want).

Techniques for uncovering unsatisfied needs

Two techniques are looked at here, 'needs gap analysis' and 'perceptual mapping'.

Needs gap analysis

This concept is best described using examples.

EXAMPLE 6.2   Needs gap analysis in motor car manufacturing

A simple example of needs gap analysis occurred in the 1960s when Bayerische Motoren Werke, a motor company struggling to survive, desperately set out to uncover whether there were any unmet market opportunities in an already seemingly saturated market.

After undertaking extensive market research to uncover both the needs of car buyers and how well the models available at that time met these needs, it became apparent that buyers of motor cars in the 1960s made their choice of model based mainly on two criteria, speed and price. The company then sat down and plotted out on a simple, two-dimensional, matrix a 'picture' of the total car market as it was then, as shown in Figure 6.2.

The resulting picture revealed that there was a gap in the market, a gap with sufficient sales potential to justify the required capital investment, so the company set about building cars for it.

Today this motor company has only a small share of the total motor car market, but has a large share of the particular segment its namesake brand has become associated with. Only once has the brand stepped outside its specialist segment, but it quickly withdrew the specific model in question. Today, the major car manufacturers have fluctuating financial results, but BMW, as it is better known, continues to be a profitable, niche car brand.

EXAMPLE 6.2   (cont'd)

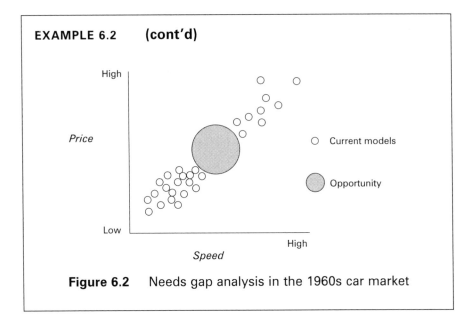

Figure 6.2   Needs gap analysis in the 1960s car market

EXAMPLE 6.3   **Needs gap analysis in the market for photocopiers**

Another example of needs gap analysis can be seen in Figure 6.3.

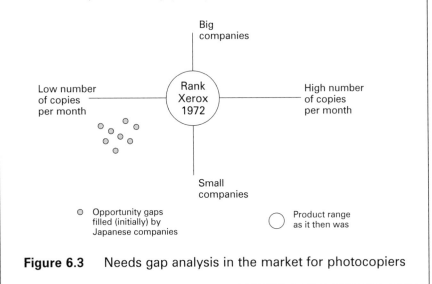

Figure 6.3   Needs gap analysis in the market for photocopiers

---

EXAMPLE 6.3   **(cont'd)**

In 1972, Rank Xerox (as it was then called) had an 80 per cent market share and a margin of 40 per cent. In 1977, it had a 10 per cent market share and a 10 per cent margin. With the lapse of Xerox's technology patent in 1972, Japanese companies were able to enter the market and satisfy unmet needs.

Since then, Xerox has recovered and formed separate divisions satisfying different market segments.

The axes could easily have been adapted for the BMW example with Price: High and low; Speed: High and low.

A further technique which can be used to identify where there are needs not being fulfilled is to construct what could be termed a 'needs cascade'. This is simply a build up of needs based on an analysis of functional requirements: in other words, requirements that do not take into account the less tangible aspects of buying such as attitudes and perceptions. In the pharmaceuticals market, for example, a needs cascade for the 'relief of pain and inflammation' could be constructed as illustrated in Figure 6.4.

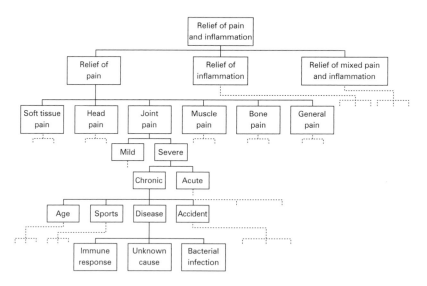

Figure 6.4   Extracts of a 'needs cascade' for the 'relief of pain and inflammation'

Source: J. Lidstone, 'Market Segmentation for Pharmaceuticals', *Long Range Planning*, **22**(2) 1989, 54–62 (Oxford: Pergamon Press).

The precise structure of this cascade may differ, of course, by sex, and further differ by age. Separate cascades would therefore need to be constructed for each of these different user groups, who could well have entered the segmentation process earlier as preliminary segments.

As with all routines that list possible permutations, the resulting number of distinct needs (segments) could very well be too many in number to satisfy segmentation criteria. However, for well-defined, and quantifiable, functional needs, as in the example above, some of these needs could be combined with others simply because, on their own, they are not large enough to justify a distinct marketing strategy. This particularly applies to the development of specific products/services, when the investment demanded to achieve this level of requirement could not be justified by the anticipated return. The first stage in this type of screening process is to look at the total market size for this particular functional need (that is, across all the preliminary segments). If that still does not justify product development costs, then these tightly defined needs should be merged into the next logical group in the cascade (often the next level up). If it does justify the cost, leave the segments as they are.

The second stage in this screening process is, in many respects, similar to the routine in Chapter 5 when the option of removing unattractive micro-segments was discussed. This second stage of screening, if necessary, requires you to determine whether any parts of the cascade are, in truth, going into areas which have no interest to your company at all (for whatever reason). In such circumstances, merge the different needs together to the point of aggregation where your lack of interest starts. Do not, however remove them from the market. They should continue through the process to ensure you have a full picture of the market being looked at. You may want to reconsider your company's policies towards the market at a later stage! Many computer manufacturers who ignored PCs have learnt this lesson the hard way.

Perceptual mapping

Perceptual maps have the additional advantage of being able to illustrate the changes which can occur in a market's view of what a particular product line can represent. The only difference is that they represent views, or attitudes, rather than functions, as in the previous examples. By plotting the position of currently available products on this map, opportunity gaps can be seen for positioning new products in the market, or even repositioning current brands.

Examples are used once again to illustrate this concept.

EXAMPLE 6.4 **A perceptual map of the soap market**

The example in Figure 6.5 looks at the soap market in terms of soap being positioned between feminine brands and family brands, and between soaps with medical benefits and those with cosmetic benefits. Clearly, other dimensions are possible.

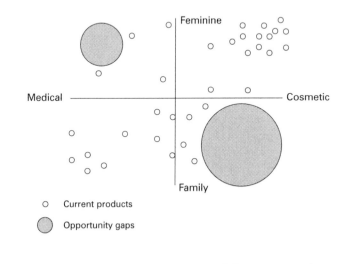

Figure 6.5 A perceptual map of the soap market

There appear to be two areas of opportunity in the soap market as represented above. These new opportunities clearly would have to be evaluated before resources were committed to developing and launching suitable products (in case they were actually representing areas where little or no demand existed). It is interesting to note that in the male toiletries market, there is an increasing flow of new products positioned as having a cosmetic value. There has clearly been a major shift in this market which has opened up the 'cosmetic' area of the male's perceptual map.

EXAMPLE 6.5   Tabloid newspapers in the UK as a perceptual map

The dimensions used for the map in Table 6.6 show the extremes of 'up market' and 'down market' (which can, in some cases, be associated with socio-economic group) and 'serious' or 'entertaining', the latter often being associated with 'exclusive' reports highlighting the activities of individuals which the individuals concerned would often prefer not to have highlighted!

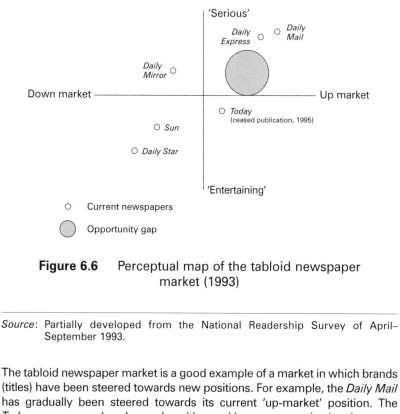

Figure 6.6   Perceptual map of the tabloid newspaper market (1993)

Source: Partially developed from the National Readership Survey of April–September 1993.

The tabloid newspaper market is a good example of a market in which brands (titles) have been steered towards new positions. For example, the *Daily Mail* has gradually been steered towards its current 'up-market' position. The *Today* newspaper also changed position and became more 'serious', a move which possibly contributed to its demise. It is important, however, that we don't confuse deliberate repositioning with drifting. The danger of drifting is that it can often take a product into the weak, middle ground.

Process check

The KDFs identified in Step 3 have been used in this step to identify the needs-based buying requirements of the market (market CPIs) at the junction being segmented. To ensure there is a comprehensive and thorough list of CPIs, KDFs have been looked at in isolation, in combination and by each preliminary segment. This step has also seen 'price' finally introduced into the process.

The market CPIs provide a framework that can be used to compare the micro-segments with one another, but before this can be done, the relative importance of each market CPI and price has to be recorded for each individual micro-segment. This is achieved by allocating a total of 100 points between the market CPIs and price, either directly or through a procedure that will allow this allocation to be calculated.

The project is now ready to uncover the segments that exist in the market being segmented, segmentation being a process which splits customers (or potential customers) in a market into different groups, called segments, within which customers have the same or similar *requirements* which can be satisfied by a distinct marketing mix.

Case study and further examples

CASE 6.1	**Agrofertiliser Supplies**

In order to identify the needs-based buying requirements of their market and understand what the farmers were really trying to achieve, the segmentation team in Agrofertiliser Supplies had to resort to market research. This was done through an independent research company skilled in this particular aspect of market research.

A selection of features and their associated benefits appear in Table 6.6.

Table 6.6   A selection of benefits for a preliminary segment in the case study

Feature groups	Features	Benefits
'What' – product	AN & manuf. blends	Proven/traditional (re-assurance) Healthy looking crop

CASE 6.1	**Agrofertiliser Supplies (cont'd)**	
Feature groups	*Features*	*Benefits*
	AN & bespoke blends	Innovative/new Sophisticated
	Urea & bespoke blends	Innovative/new Sophisticated
'What' – intensity	High nitrogen level	Maximum growth and output
'What' – brand	Well established	Proven/traditional (re-assurance) Service (qualified help) Also linked to high quality
	Any brand	No direct benefit as such, more related to not needing the above and, therefore, not needing to pay for it (price)
'What' – quality	High quality	Healthy looking crop Easy to handle
	Any quality	As for 'any brand'

Note: This particular preliminary segment only applied high nitrogen levels, hence why there is no mention of low nitrogen levels in 'What – intensity'.

As can be seen in Table 6.6, features can deliver more than one benefit, and the same benefit can be delivered by more than one feature.

Once the benefit lists had been drawn up for each of the preliminary segments, consideration was given to prioritising each list and then merging the more important benefits from each of these lists in order to produce the market CPIs. However, it was apparent that this exercise would not, in fact, remove a single benefit from the process as each benefit would find itself positioned above the 80 per cent cut-off point for one or more of the preliminary segments. All the benefits would therefore be carried through to the consolidated list. In addition, the overall total of different market benefits from across the preliminary segments came to what was considered to be a manageable number. Reducing the list was therefore unnecessary. This resulted in nine market CPIs, along with price, proceeding to the next stage.

A selection of micro-segments and their scores for the final list of CPIs and price appears in Table 6.7. They are the same micro-segments that appeared in Table 5.7.

| CASE 6.1 | **Agrofertiliser Supplies (cont'd)** |

Table 6.7 **Benefit scores for a selection of micro-segments in the case study**

Market CPIs	Micro-segments				
	G1	G2	G3	G4	G5
Innovative/new	9	11	–	–	20
Proven/traditional (re-assurance)	5	4	21	20	–
Healthy looking crop (includes grass)	27	24	–	–	–
Healthy looking animal stock	–	–	26	25	–
Sophisticated	–	–	–	–	5
Maximum crop growth and output	18	22	–	–	10
Easy to handle (quality)	16	15	9	8	–
Service (qualified help from manuf.)	11	9	–	–	–
Distributor – convenient local supply	11	8	39	42	–
Price	3	7	5	5	65
Total	**100**	**100**	**100**	**100**	**100**

Key: 'G1', 'G2' and so on are the individual identifiers for the micro-segments, the 'G' indicating that they come from the Grassland preliminary segment.

Note: Although the recommended approach is to limit scoring to the top five CPIs for each micro-segment, this particular project, when it was conducted, allowed the total to be distributed among all of them. Analysis conducted later demonstrated that if each micro-segment had been asked to focus on their five most important CPIs, and price, the conclusions would not have changed.

In the first instance, scoring for the micro-segments was conducted by the segmentation team in association with the salesforce. Once the potential implications of the results were realised, the initial conclusions were tested by commissioning a detailed market research project. The results from this illustrated that while the team had miscalculated in some areas, their overall conclusions were not too short of reality. The research project, however, provided not just accuracy, but also the robustness the team would need when presenting the results and the strategic messages it carried.

The status of the case study at the end of Step 5 is summarised in Figure 6.7.

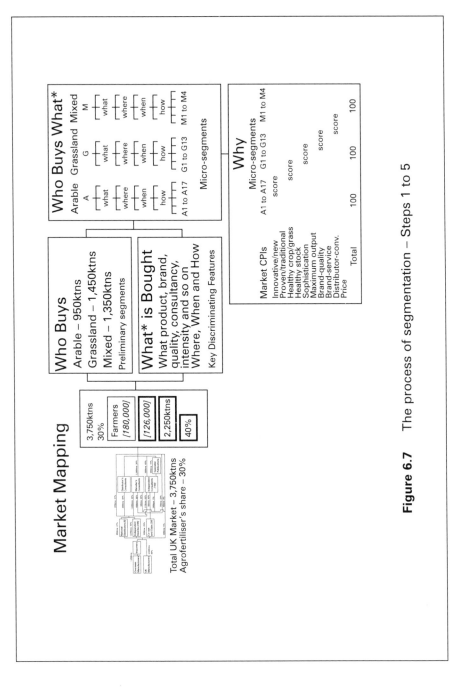

Figure 6.7 The process of segmentation – Steps 1 to 5

Further examples

Success in identifying the real benefits being sought by different groups of customers (segments) in a market can lead to remarkable increases in market share when the right offer is put in place. The following extract from an article which appeared in the mid-1980s illustrates the point. Here we see one overseas tour operator has correctly identified a growing preference in the UK market for self-catering holidays while some of its competitors have not caught on so quickly. In fact, one of the competing tour operators makes an overall assumption that the holidaymakers buying this type of holiday have traded down and bought on price. This fails to acknowledge that there could well be other benefits associated with self-catering holidays which are more important to these holidaymakers than price, such as the freedom to eat *what* they want, at a place *where* they want and at a time *when* they want.

> Shrewd anticipation of holiday trends has paid off for Intasun by nearly doubling its share of the Greek market.
>
> By buying heavily into the Greek self-catering sector for 1985 the leading operator has captured a 17 per cent stake compared to the nine points held last year.
>
> According to the latest figures produced by the British Market Research Bureau this means it is breathing down the necks of flagging front runner Thomson Holidays which has plunged from 28 points to 19.
>
> Horizon's share has fallen five points to 11, while Olympic Holidays has dropped two points to four.
>
> Apart from Intasun, the other star performers are Sunmed – whose share has doubled to ten points – and Grecian which is up to 11 from eight.
>
> Commenting on overall trade, the managing director of Olympic Holidays said that holidaymakers had traded down and bought on price.
>
> 'Specialists at the bottom of the market such as Grecian and Sunmed and Intasun have done well, while those offering more expensive hotel holidays are down on last year.'
>
> 'But only 35 per cent of the Greek market is self-catering, and Sunmed is probably around 70 per cent sold out, so the hotel holidays will have to start filling soon.'

The managing director of Olympic Holidays warned that if the British did not fill up the beds in Greece, then hoteliers would start to look for clients from other European countries.

Source: Travel Trade Gazette, UK.

The understanding of customer needs and the provision of holidays to match them has moved on a great deal since this article appeared.

7 Forming Segments (Step 6)

This step discusses the procedure required for building the micro-segments back up into market segments. A summary of where this step lies in relation to the process as detailed so far appears in Figure 7.1.

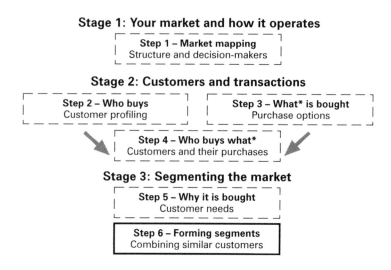

Figure 7.1 The process of segmentation – Step 6

With a manageable number of micro-segments it is possible to carry this out manually. Details of a manual procedure are discussed in this chapter. However, in most instances the assistance of a suitable computer-based support package is required. A PC-based support package for this already exists. It is called *Market Segment Master*, the registered trade mark for this process, and it allows you to build up the information required for segmentation step by step, exactly as described in this book. In addition, this package will accommodate responses from completed interviews, utilising the appropriate information categories.* We should stress, however, that progressing your segmentation project does not depend on the use of a PC-based support package. It is possible to carry out this key step manually.

Please note that when we refer to 'segments' in the text we are referring to 'market segments'.

Size and number of market segments

Before proceeding to combine similar micro-segments, two important questions should be considered.

● What is the economical value or volume of sales, or the economical minimum number of customers, needed for each segment?

Ensure whatever 'measurement' you use corresponds to that used so far in the process, particularly when sizing the micro-segments.

You should at this point, however, be alert to micro-segments which presently only have a small volume/value, but which are seen as offering growth potential for the future and therefore are of great strategic importance. It is an option at this stage to 'protect' these micro-segments from being overlooked by attaching to them a projected volume/value figure to reflect their potential. Note the alphanumeric reference of all the micro-segments that have their size increased this way. This enhancement could be particularly important for those micro-segments you may have developed for customers whose needs are not currently being met in the market. Similarly, you can adjust the size of those micro-segments which are known to be in decline to reflect their projected volume/value. Also note the alphanumeric reference of these micro-segments. If you choose not to make these adjustments at this stage you can, of course, bring these considerations into the process when reviewing the concluding segments.

The future size of segments is a topic covered in Chapter 9.

● What is the manageable number of segments the business can handle?

Although most markets tend to form into between five and eight segments, it is still worth reflecting on what number of different marketing strategies (segment-specific offers) your company could realistically handle. Whatever the number you arrive at, increase it by, say, one-third. If this number is close to the resulting number of micro-segments,

---

*   Contact Professor Malcolm McDonald or Ian Dunbar (details on page xvii) for further information.

you will have arrived at an ideal conclusion. This is simply because it is unlikely you will be able to operate in all the resulting segments success-fully and will need to select the most promising segments for your business. Chapters 9 and 10 contain routines which enable you to select the most appropriate segments.

It is important to stress here that we are *not* implying you should force a preferred conclusion on to the market. If the concluding number of segments falls outside your preferred range, it is worth recording this result and then rerunning the consolidation routine until the number of segments falls within your range. Both results can then be separately taken through Step 7.

For most companies, the most difficult of these two questions concerns the number of segments they will be able to support with different marketing strategies.

Building micro-segments into market segments (clustering)

The micro-segments should now be subject to the first clustering routine (the mechanics of a clustering routine are discussed later in this chapter).

Routine 1   This routine brings micro-segments together into distinct groups (segments) based on the similarity of their scores for the market CPIs. In addition, this 'best fit' routine consoli-dates for each segment the profiling information attached to the micro-segments it contains. You will have to do this manually if you do not have the PC-based support package.

Although we refer to the 'similarity' between micro-segments, what is actually calculated for this routine (and those that follow) is the 'difference' between micro-segments. To be more accurate, therefore, each segment should be described as consisting of micro-segments which have an acceptable level of difference between them. Calculating 'differences' is covered later in this chapter.

Depending on how satisfied you are with the degree of 'fit' obtained in this first clustering routine, you may wish to explore alternative clustering routines to see whether or not this 'fit' can be improved upon. Up to three further clustering routines can be available if you followed the process in its entirety (only one if you did not opt to divide the CPIs between 'buying criteria' and 'attitude'). The three clustering routines are as shown below.

Routine 2   A selective CPI clustering routine which follows the principles of the first routine except that you select which particular market CPIs to include, and even whether to include price. This may be a useful routine if the score for one, or more, of the clustering criteria is/are similar across the micro-segments. It can also be useful if one, or more, of the benefits is, in fact, becoming an expected part of the offer and less of a differentiator. Seeing what would happen when this CPI becomes a market 'qualifier' (and therefore removed from the segmentation equation) can provide you with an interesting future vision of the market – a vision which could provide you with a valuable strategic advantage. A profiling report should also accompany the output of this routine.

Routine 3   As for the first routine except that the micro-segments are clustered using only the market CPIs identified as being the buying criteria. A profiling report should also accompany the output of this routine.

Routine 4   As for the first routine except that the micro-segments are clustered using only the market CPIs identified as being the attitudinal criteria. A profiling report should, once again, accompany the output of this routine.

A final routine which is sometimes interesting to look at concentrates on the profiling information of each micro-segment.

Routine 5   This routine brings micro-segments together into distinct groups (segments) based on the similarity of their profiling information. In addition, the similarity (or otherwise) of the scores for the market CPIs and price are shown for each of the concluding 'segments'.

If segments are, however, about groups of customers with the same or similar requirements, the value of this fifth routine is often limited to simply satisfying curiosity. However, if your company is currently following a segmentation structure built around customer profiles, such as industry types, and this approach to segmentation has identified that this is not in fact the case, being able to produce the results based on a current view held by the business can help the segmentation team persuade the company to change.

Two options can be looked at when running these clustering routines with the aid of a computer:

- Option 'A': taking the clustering routine through its various stages, step by step. This is the only routine available if you are carrying out this routine manually.
- Option 'B': leaving a PC-based clustering routine to proceed straight to a pre-specified level of 'difference' before reviewing the results and deciding whether to:

    (a) evaluate these segments using the checklist in Step 7; or
    (b) rerun the clustering routine to a higher level of difference (often because the number of segments after the clustering run was too high *and* the level of difference was too strict); or
    (c) rerun the clustering routine to a lower level of difference (often because the number of segments after the clustering run was too low *and* the level of difference was too generous).

Progressively building your market segments (Option 'A')

The clustering routine you wish to follow can be built progressively using this option.

The example which follows relates to Routine 1 and suggests one approach which could be adopted for manual clustering. You may, however, prefer to adopt a slightly different approach, but one which follows the same principle of gradually merging the micro-segments together. Results for the other routines would be built in a similar way.

Given the degree of work which has undoubtedly gone into your segmentation project so far, the procedure you adopt for this step needs to be rigorous and capable of standing up to scrutiny. With this in mind, one of the most useful mathematical procedures for comparing micro-segments is detailed first of all as this will ensure you arrive at a sound conclusion. This procedure does, however, involve a large number of mathematical calculations so your willingness to follow it as a manual routine will very much depend on:

(a) the number of micro-segments you are having to consider;
(b) the number of market CPIs you have; *and*
(c) the amount of time you can spare!

As a first step, cluster together all the micro-segments that have the same scores for all the CPIs and price. No mathematics are required here, other than determining the total size of the cluster, as there is no difference between the micro-segments. Give each of the resulting clusters a label, such as CL1, CL2 and so on, and note which micro-segments it contains.

An example is used to demonstrate the next steps.

Table 7.1 contains a sample of five micro-segments taken from a particular market, along with their scores for the CPIs in this market. However, to help in the explanation of this procedure, only price, and three other market CPIs are used.

Table 7.1   Micro-segment details for a clustering routine

Market CPIs		Micros-segments and their CPI scores				
		A1	A2	A3	A4	A5
	Value	£30k	£20k	£20k	£20k	£30k
Local availability		40	50	45	30	30
Biodegradable pack		30	25	30	20	15
Well-known brand		20	20	15	40	45
Price		10	5	10	10	10
Total		**100**	**100**	**100**	**100**	**100**

The difference between each of these micro-segments needs to be calculated. The method of doing this is illustrated in Table 7.2, using micro-segments A1 and A2 from Table 7.1 as the example.

Table 7.2   Calculating the difference between micro-segments

Market CPIs	Micros and CPI scores		Absolute difference between scores	Difference squared	Square root of total difference
	A1	A2	(A1–A2)		$\sqrt{}$
Local availability	40	50	10	100	–
Biodegradable pack	30	25	5	25	–
Well-known brand	20	20	0	0	–
Price	10	5	5	25	–
Total	**100**	**100**	**–**	**150**	**12.2**

Note: This particular routine is known as 'squared Euclidian distances'.

The difference between A1 and A2 following the method appearing in Table 7.2 is, therefore, '12.2'.

This is then repeated for A1 and A3, then A1 and A4, followed by A1 and A5, then for A2 and A3, A2 and A4 and so on until all the micro-segments have been compared with each other (a total of 100 calculations in this example). A worksheet for following this method appears in Table 7.3.

Table 7.3   Worksheet for calculating the difference scores between micro-segments/clusters

Market CPIs	Micros/ Clusters and CPI scores (a) (b)	Absolute difference between scores (a) – (b)	Difference squared	Square root of total difference √
				–
				–
				–
				–
				–
				–
				–
				–
Total	100 100	–		

The results of all the difference calculations required for the micro-segments appearing in Table 7.1 are summarised in Table 7.4. For ease of reference, Table 7.4 is presented along the same lines as a distance chart in an atlas.

Table 7.4   Difference scores for the micro-segments

		Micro-segments				
		A1	A2	A3	A4	A5
	A1	0	12.2	7.1	24.5	30.8
	A2		0	10.0	29.2	33.9
Micro-segments	A3			0	30.8	36.7
	A4				0	7.1
	A5					0

The closest matching micro-segments in the example are A1 and A3, with a difference calculated at 7.1, along with A4 and A5, which also have a difference calculated at 7.1. There is much less similarity, however, between either A1 or A3 and A4 or A5 (the difference scores ranging from 24.5 for A1 versus A4, to 36.7 for A3 versus A5).

The first cluster is formed by combining the micro-segments with the least difference between them. In the example, two sets of micro-segments have the lowest scores, meaning two sets of micro-segments can be combined on this first run. Therefore, assuming a difference of 7.1 is acceptable, A1 and A3 can be combined, which will now be referred to as 'cluster 1' (CL1), and A4 and A5 can be combined, which will now be referred to as 'cluster 2' (CL2). The issue of 'acceptability' is discussed after Table 7.5.

For the procedure to progress, a single set of CPI scores needs to be calculated for each new cluster. The simplest method of doing this is to calculate the weighted average scores of the CPIs, with the 'weighting' based on the size of each constituent micro-segment. For example, in CL1 micro-segment A1 accounts for £30 000 and micro-segment A3 for £20 000, therefore the CPI scores in A1 have a weighting of $1^{1}/_{2}$ times the CPI scores in A3 (£30k/£20k = 1.5). Alternatively, the weighting attributed to each micro-segment can be expressed as a percentage of the total size of the new cluster. Using percentages, the CPI scores in A1 have a weighting of 60 per cent (£30k/£50k = 60 per cent), leaving A3 accounting for 40 per cent. Calculating CPI scores for a new cluster using percentages is illustrated in Table 7.5.

A worksheet for calculating weighted average CPI scores using percentages appears in Table 7.6.

Table 7.5 Calculating weighted average CPI scores for a cluster

Market CPIs	Micro-segment/ cluster A1 weight – 60%			Micro-segment/ cluster A3 weight – 40%			New cluster (CLI) size: £50 000 100%
	CPI score (a)	Volume/ value £30 000 weight (b)	CPI score x weight a x b (c)	CPI score (d)	Volume/ value £20 000 weight (e)	CPI score x weight d x e (f)	CPI score c + f
Local availability	40	60%	24	45	40%	18	42
Biodegradable pack	30	60%	18	30	40%	12	30
Well-known brand	20	60%	12	15	40%	6	18
Price	10	60%	6	10	40%	4	10
Total	100	–	60	100	–	40	100

Table 7.6   Worksheet for calculating weighted average CPI scores for a cluster

	Micro-segment/ cluster	Volume/ value	CPI score x weight	Micro-segment/ cluster	Volume/ value	CPI score x weight	New cluster (CL)
		weight – %			*weight –* %		*size:*
							100%
Market CPIs	CPI score (a)	weight (b)	a x b (c)	CPI score (d)	weight (e)	d x e (f)	CPI score c + f
Total	100	–	100	100	–		100

The updated status for the market as originally illustrated in Table 7.1 appears in Table 7.7.

Table 7.7   Clustering update

Market CPIs		Clusters, micro-segments and weighted average market CPI scores		
		CL1 (A1 and A3)	A2	CL2 (A4 and A5)
	Value	£50 000	£20 000	£50 000
Local availability		42	50	30
Biodegradable pack		30	25	17
Well-known brand		18	20	43
Price		10	5	10
Total		**100**	**100**	**100**

Note: There are more rigorous routines which do not calculate the weighted average scores for clusters but retain the highest and lowest scores that exist for each CPI from the micro-segments in the cluster. When calculating differences, these routines work out the *maximum* difference for each CPI. This means that when comparing a CPI for two clusters, the difference score is determined by the greatest difference that exists between the highest or lowest scores in one cluster and the highest and lowest scores in the second cluster. If, therefore, we were to compare CL1 with CL2 using this approach, the difference between them on 'well-known brand' would be 45 minus 15 (the A5 score less the A3 score).

This is an opportune point at which to briefly cover the issue of 'acceptable differences'. The most useful method of assessing 'acceptability' is your own judgement. The main consideration for this judgement concerns the effect the combination would have on the marketing strategy you would put together to win their business. If, by combining two micro-segments/clusters, the resulting scores for the market CPIs would have little impact on the type of offer best suited to one or the other as they currently stand, then the level of difference between them is acceptable. If, on the other hand, the combination would weaken a good offer you could put together for one or both of them separately, the level of difference is *usually* not acceptable. The exception would be if one of the micro-segments/clusters was only quite small while the other was quite large, as the smaller of the two would not justify a distinct offer for itself anyway. Finally, if you are only addressing this problem at the last stages of clustering and simply trying to sweep up some currently 'homeless' micro-segments/clusters, too small to form their own segments, note which cluster they would join, add their volume/value figure to that cluster, but don't change the cluster's current market CPI scores. The overriding rule is, however, if in doubt, don't combine them, as you can always revisit this decision later.

For analysis purposes in Step 7 of the segmentation process, profiling information would need to be listed for each cluster. In addition, alongside each individual profiling item there would need to be a figure indicating its importance within the cluster. Therefore, if we knew that both A1 and A3 were in the age range of 18 to 25, the value of this particular profiling data for CL1 would be £50k. However, if A1 was female and A3 was male, the value of females in the cluster would be £30k, and the value of males would be £20k.

A further refinement, and one which is particularly useful at the strategy stage, is to keep track of the KDFs by cluster, with the importance of each KDF within the cluster indicated by its value or volume figure, as appropriate. Clearly, however, when progressing this step manually, this is a refinement you can come back to later.

Ideally, the calculations illustrated in Table 7.2 should be repeated, in the first instance, across all the micro-segments in a project before any clustering takes place, and this is the approach adopted by the PC package. A shortcut for those approaching this manually is detailed shortly.

Once this first run has been completed, the new clusters are then required to have their difference scores calculated against all the remaining micro-segments and against all the other clusters, after which the clustering sequence detailed above is repeated once again. This should continue until:

- the size of each remaining cluster and micro-segment is equal to or greater than the economical minimum value/volume decided upon at the beginning of this step; or
- the number of clusters and micro-segments remaining is in line with the preferred number of concluding segments decided upon at the beginning of this step; or
- the level of difference you are now having to consider before bringing further clusters or segments together is at such a level it appears you are having to combine dissimilar groups.

To make this routine more manageable when conducted manually, it can speed up the process if the micro-segments are arranged initially so that all of those with the same top-scoring CPI are arranged in groups. Each group can then be visually scanned to see where the most obvious best fits occur. Where there are very clear similarities between two or more micro-segments the calculation of difference between them can be skipped, with just their new, overall market CPI scores and total size for the cluster being calculated.

Likewise, calculating the difference scores between micro-segments which are clearly dissimilar can be skipped. The difference calculations can then be limited to:

- confirming similarities between micro-segments/clusters, or otherwise, when it is visually unclear; and
- determining where a particular micro-segment/cluster should move to next when there is more than one contender and it is visually unclear where the best fit occurs.

At some stage you may need to calculate differences between all the remaining clusters and micro-segments but, by following the routine detailed here, the number of occasions on which you will have to do this will be limited. The project should continue along this path until a conclusion is reached.

After each completed cluster run it is useful to briefly record the project's status in case you need to refer back to it later. It is particularly useful to have a record of the size of each cluster as it grows, as well as the micro-segments and, as will eventually happen, the clusters it contains. Number each run in sequence and record it on a separate sheet. A suggested worksheet for recording the results of a cluster run appears in Table 7.8.

If mathematics is really not your forte but you still want to approach this manually, a less demanding, but less rigorous, suggestion for clustering is to follow the manual procedure just outlined, but when debating what to do with a particular micro-segment or cluster, expand the value attributed to each market CPI score by one point either side, thus changing each of them into a range. A score of '15' would therefore become '14–16'. This should be done for all the micro-segments or clusters you are unsure about. See if this brings any of them closer and resolves the uncertainty. This review can then be progressed by simply expanding the range now attached to each market CPI by a further point either side, and so on. Whenever a cluster is generated following this procedure (including clusters generated without having to turn their market CPI scores into ranges), note for each cluster the full range of scores attributable to each market CPI. You can then use these ranges to visually assess the levels of similarity.

As stated earlier, this iterative process should continue until you have reached a conclusion.

If, at any stage during your clustering routine:

(a) a cluster is developed that matches or exceeds the sizing specification determined at the start of this step *and*
(b) by further including this cluster in the process you will have to weaken what is currently a clear focus around one, or more, market CPIs in this cluster,

Table 7.8   Worksheet – clustering record

Cluster run no:					
Cluster generated CL . . .		Cluster generated CL . . .		Cluster generated CL . . .	
Micro-segments/clusters contained in each new cluster, and size					
Micro/CL	*Size*	*Micro/CL*	*Size*	*Micro/CL*	*Size*
Total		**Total**		**Total**	
Profiling summary					
Profile	*Size*	*Profile*	*Size*	*Profile*	*Size*
Total		**Total**		**Total**	
KDF summary					
KDF	*Size*	*KDF*	*Size*	*KDF*	*Size*
Total		**Total**		**Total**	

put this particular cluster to one side and exclude it from consideration in further cluster runs. However, for thoroughness, review its position with reference to the changes generated by each cluster run to reconfirm, or otherwise, its independence.

Process check

The micro-segments which represented your market have been built back up into potential segments based on the similarities between them on their market CPI scores. The resulting clusters can each be reviewed in terms of:

(a) the average score for each market CPI they contain, based on the scores given to these market CPIs by the micro-segments in this cluster;
(b) the volume/value they represent, based on the individual volumes/values associated with each of its constituent micro-segments;
(c) the overall profile of the customers found within the cluster, based on the profiling information associated with each micro-segment it now contains;
(d) the volume/value which can be attributed to each profiling description in the cluster, based on the individual volumes/values associated with each of its constituent micro-segments and their individual profiles; and
(e) the KDFs and their individual volumes/values in the cluster, based on the KDF information associated with each micro-segment (though it is possible to defer putting this detail together until looking at marketing strategies).

The end of this first phase of the segmentation process, developing segments, is in sight!

Case study and further examples

CASE 7.1   Agrofertiliser Supplies

The segmentation team at Agrofertiliser Supplies reverted to using the support of technology for this step of the process. With the first run of the clustering process alone requiring a possible total of 12 870 calculations, this was understandable.

Manual clustering would, however, have been possible for part of this step, as is clear from Table 7.9, which is a repeat of Table 6.7 in the last chapter.

Without resorting to mathematics, G1 and G2 can be combined as a cluster, as can G3 and G4. The reality, however, is that it is not always as obvious or as simple as it appears in the above table. Only a small selection of micro-segments are listed in the above table, whereas in practice, all the micro-segments would need to be analysed at the same time. In addition, the example has deliberately brought two pairs of similar micro-segments together for illustrative purposes, whereas in practice, if you were conducting this routine manually, the grouping would not be done for you. Finally, in practice, the micro-segment CPI scores are not always so nicely matched, or as clearly different, as they appear for the five micro-segments in Table 7.9!

CASE 7.1	Agrofertiliser Supplies (cont'd)

Table 7.9   Benefit scores for a selection of micro-segments in the case study

Market CPIs	Micro-segments				
	G1	G2	G3	G4	G5
Innovative/new	9	11	–	–	20
Proven/traditional (re-assurance)	5	4	21	20	–
Healthy looking crop (includes grass)	27	24	–	–	–
Healthy looking animal stock	–	–	26	25	–
Sophisticated	–	–	–	–	5
Maximum crop growth and output	18	22	–	–	10
Easy to handle (quality)	16	15	9	8	–
Service (qualified help from manuf.)	11	9	–	–	–
Distributor – convenient local supply	11	8	39	42	–
Price	3	7	5	5	65
Total	**100**	**100**	**100**	**100**	**100**

Key: 'G1', 'G2' and so on are the individual identifiers for the micro-segments, the 'G' indicating that they come from the grassland preliminary segment.

For the 34 micro-segments generated in the case study, Figure 7.2 illustrates where they started from (in terms of preliminary segments) and how they ended up.

As can be seen from the final clusters, the preliminary segment structure, which basically distinguished between the final users according to their different application for the product, was a good starting point. Most of the final clusters are based on important differences that existed between the members of a preliminary segment. Only one of the final clusters, Segment 7, covers more than one preliminary segment, a cluster which, interestingly, is the segment that is very price sensitive – a purchase priority that will often bring together members from different preliminary segments. The final segments and their market CPI scores appear in Table 7.10.

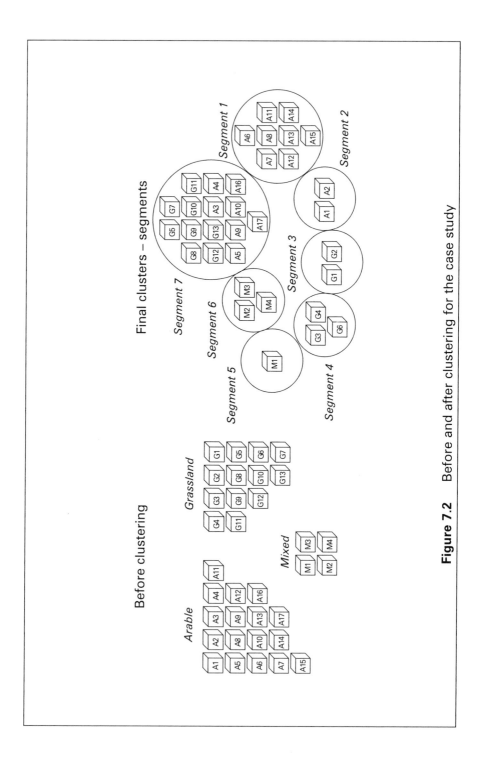

Figure 7.2 Before and after clustering for the case study

CASE 7.1   **Agrofertiliser Supplies (cont'd)**

Table 7.10   **The concluding segments and their market CPI scores for the case study**

| | Segments and their market CPI scores | | | | | | |
Market CPIs	S1	S2	S3	S4	S5	S6	S7
Innovative/new	40	5	10	–	–	–	20
Proven/traditional	–	20	5	20	35	30	–
Healthy crop/grass	–	5	25	–	5	–	–
Healthy stock	–	–	–	25	5	–	–
Sophistication	15	–	–	–	–	–	5
Maximum output	30	–	20	–	–	–	10
Brand – easy handling	–	20	15	10	25	–	–
Brand – service	–	25	10	–	15	5	–
Distributor – convenience	–	15	10	40	10	20	–
Price	15	10	5	5	5	45	65
Total	**100**	**100**	**100**	**100**	**100**	**100**	**100**

Key: 'S' = segment.

A diagrammatic presentation of the results in Table 7.10 appears in Figure 7.3.

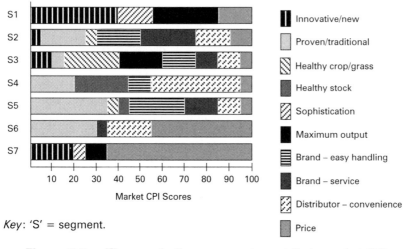

Key: 'S' = segment.

Figure 7.3   The concluding segments and their market CPI scores for the case study in diagrammatic form

Note: Output from *Market Segment Master* PC support package, modified for monochrome printing.

CASE 7.1   Agrofertiliser Supplies (cont'd)

As you will have noticed, one of the segments consisted of only one micro-segment (Segment 5). It may well be a segment in terms of the different requirements it is looking for, but is it a big enough segment to warrant its own marketing strategy? With respect to the volume of product bought by each of the concluding segments, Figure 7.4 summarises this as a pie chart.

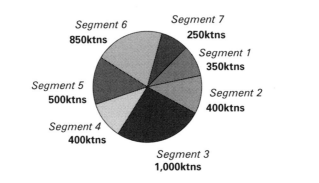

Figure 7.4   The volume attributed to each segment for the case study

Note: Output from *Market Segment Master* PC support package, modified for monochrome printing.

Segment 5, although only consisting of a single micro-segment, is, in fact, one of the larger segments.

Before declaring segments, however, one final step remains before the concluding clusters can be regarded as legitimate segments. Figure 7.5 (overleaf) presents a summary of the project's status so far. This figure also shows the formal titles given to each of the segments by Agrofertiliser Supplies. Each title represents the best overall description for their particular segment. A more detailed insight into these segments appears in the last chapter of this book, specifically Table 13.1.

Further examples

Not all projects cluster as cleanly as seen in the Agrofertiliser Supplies case study. The three most often mentioned concerns with the results at this stage are as follows:

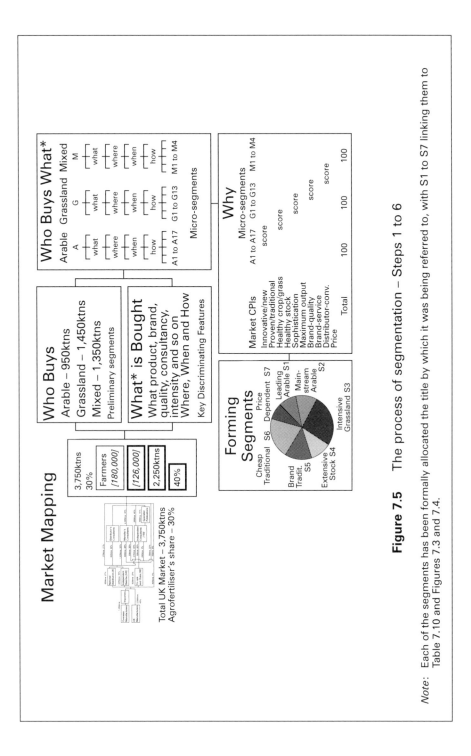

Figure 7.5 The process of segmentation – Steps 1 to 6

Note: Each of the segments has been formally allocated the title by which it was being referred to, with S1 to S7 linking them to Table 7.10 and Figures 7.3 and 7.4.

- a number of micro-segments do not appear to have a natural fit with any cluster;
- the resulting clusters are fewer in number than expected or, a small number of the concluding clusters account for a high proportion of the market;
- the best result in terms of producing clusters with very clear market CPI preferences between them produces too many clusters, but taking the clustering routine further will blur the distinctiveness.

Each project clearly has to be looked at individually, but the following may help you through these issues if you are having to address any of them.

'Homeless' micro-segments

First check the size of these micro-segments, as a single micro-segment could be large enough to form a segment in its own right, as was illustrated in the case study. If this isn't the case for any of them, consider the potential future size of these micro-segments (a point discussed earlier in this chapter). If this would qualify any of them as a segment in the future, take advantage of that possibility *now*.

For any which are of a reasonable size, but not large enough to qualify as a segment, and don't currently appear to demonstrate any future growth, revisiting them at a later stage is an option you could consider for any follow-up work.

If you are still left with a number of 'homeless' micro-segments, add up the total volume/value they account for and if this total is, say, less than ten per cent of the market, then you can usually put them to one side without having to face any major repercussions in the market. No specific marketing strategies will be targeted at them, unless there is a niche operator in the market for whom they represent a worthwhile marketing opportunity.

As a final resort, it often helps if you, or your research agency, talk with a representative sample of these micro-segments to ensure you have a full understanding of their buying requirements. They are, after all, active in the market today and it is unlikely any supplier is putting together a bespoke offer for them (and thus qualifying them as a segment/segments). On the other hand, they may represent a group, or groups, in the market whose needs are not being satisfied by any supplier and who are currently having to compromise on what they buy. Build this understanding into the segmentation process and they may well form into a new cluster.

This same approach would be applicable if your project was ending up with homeless, small, clusters.

Too few clusters

This usually means that only two or three market CPIs have attracted high scores from the micro-segments and/or a large number of micro-segments seem to want a portion of everything.

In these cases it can often mean that the prominent market CPIs require further investigation in the market in order to establish if, at the qualitative research phase, the real requirements were teased out. For example, if one of the prominent CPIs was, say, 'large, reputable company', it would be useful to establish a clearer understanding of what exactly was meant by this. At the time of the qualitative work for the project, assuming you required such research, the CPIs arrived at may have appeared to be adequate. You could not have known at that stage its true level of 'popularity'. This doesn't, however, prevent the segments you have arrived at from being taken through to the next step and into the second phase of the process. What can be usefully done in the meantime is to revisit this CPI with customers represented by the micro-segments giving this CPI a high rating. You can check with these customers whether or not there are some more specific requirements being delivered by this CPI which, if introduced into the segmentation project, would lead to a more focused result.

A 'large *reputable* company' could mean to some customers that the companies they associate with this description deliver a 'conservative' line of products or services. To others it could represent companies that are innovative, while to a further group of customers it could mean 'strong ethical business policies', and so on.

A useful clue as to whether you may have overlooked more exacting requirements could be in the KDF information attached to the micro-segments. If this CPI covers a range of different features, such as different brands, these different features may be delivering different benefits. A wrong assumption may have been made earlier on in the project.

Too many clusters

The first check would be on the size of each cluster to see if any could qualify as a segment (including future growth, if appropriate). If a large number of them qualify by size in their own right, you may have to accept that your market divides into more than the average number of segments. If, however, you are having to consider more than, say, ten clusters, all of which qualify as a segment by their size, as well as by having distinctive requirements, the first question would concern the market definition; is the market definition too broad?

Too many clusters may also be generated when the CPIs are not really reflecting the real needs-based buying requirements of the market.

Finally, if only some of the clusters qualify as segments in terms of size, check the other clusters to see if any of them are, in fact, growing into the market segments of tomorrow. For the clusters which are tomorrow's new segments, these should progress to the next step in their own right. For the remaining clusters which, we can now assume, are quite small, refer back to the earlier section which looked at 'homeless micro-segments' (the second and subsequent paragraphs).

Conclusion

As will be clear, each particular project needs to be looked at in turn as the range of possibilities could go beyond those summarised above. Those discussed in this section tend to be the most frequently observed.

It is worth emphasising, however, that *most* markets tend to split into between five and eight segments.

8 *Segment Checklist (Step 7)*

To conclude this phase of the segmentation process, the final clusters in Step 6 are individually checked against size, differentiation, reachability and company compatibility. If they pass this 'reality check', they can then proceed into the second phase of the segmentation process.

The complete list of steps for developing segments appears in Figure 8.1.

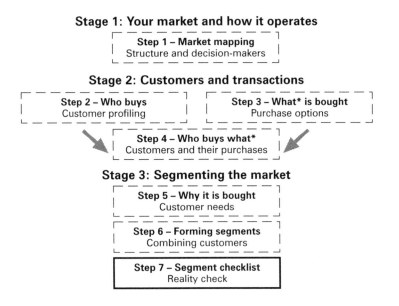

Stage 1: Your market and how it operates

Step 1 – Market mapping
Structure and decision-makers

Stage 2: Customers and transactions

Step 2 – Who buys
Customer profiling

Step 3 – What* is bought
Purchase options

Step 4 – Who buys what*
Customers and their purchases

Stage 3: Segmenting the market

Step 5 – Why it is bought
Customer needs

Step 6 – Forming segments
Combining customers

Step 7 – Segment checklist
Reality check

Figure 8.1 The process of segmentation – Step 7

Segment checklist

For the concluding clusters/segments in Step 6, apply the checklist as follows:

Volume/Value	The 'size' test for each segment should already have been cleared in Step 6. Segments have to be measurable.
Differentiated	Is the offer required by each segment sufficiently different from that required by the other segments? This is where the marketing strategies appropriate for one segment are checked to ensure they are distinguishable from the marketing strategies developed for the other segments.
Reachable	This is where the different marketing strategies are checked to ensure that they can be directed towards their applicable segments. Each segment must therefore have a distinctive profile, for example:

- distinct television viewing, radio listening, newspaper or magazine reading profiles, and/or
- distinct characteristics which can classify them by who or what they are, such as socio-economic group, type of company, and/or
- distinct characteristics which can classify them by a geographic area, such as postcodes, and/or
- distinct characteristics which can classify them by their purchasing preferences, such as purchasing patterns, distribution channels, distinct benefits looked for, distinct response to prices.

This is discussed in more detail after the final item on the checklist.

Compatibility	This is where you rigorously check your own company's ability to focus on the new segments by structuring itself around them organisationally, culturally, in its management information systems and in its decision-making processes. Such changes may not be possible immediately, therefore the organisation's ability to evolve to the required structure should be tested.

Before answering the checklist questions appearing towards the end of this section, a final revisit to the issue of profiling and reachability would be useful.

Profiling as an issue in segmentation has been covered throughout the process and numerous opportunities have been presented to increase the amount of profiling information carried through to this particular step. In some markets, of course, it is possible to distinguish between segments in your marketing strategy by their differences in distribution requirements, by differences in how you can communicate the offer to them, or even by price bands. If it is therefore not clear whether your segments meet the requirement of reachability, first check that you have explored all the possible distribution and communication alternatives available. Once this is complete, it may be necessary to review the profiles of each micro-segment appearing in the final clusters. You then need to use your judgement to decide whether the cluster is reachable.

When reviewing the profiling information you have put together, it is important to remember that it is not necessary to have the identical profile for *all* the customers in a segment, as we are just looking for one distinctive, but usable, characteristic, or one particular distinctive set of 'conditional', but usable, characteristics, such as 'telecommunications companies *and* privately owned'. It is also not necessary for *all* the customers in a segment to have this single, or conditional, set of distinctive characteristic(s), as long as the majority have. Table 8.1 provides an example.

Table 8.1   Segment age profiles in a market

	Segment 1 (2 200 units)			Segment 2 (3 050 units)		
Micro-segments	Vol/val by age: Age ranges			Micro-segments	Vol/val by age: Age ranges	
	31–40	41–50			31–40	41–50
A2	150			A1	250	
A3		1 250		A4	350	
B2	300			A5	200	
B3		500		B1		250
				C1	2 000	
Total	**450**	**1 750**			**2 800**	**250**
	0.5%	**79.5%**			**91.8%**	**8.2%**

From the above table you could now state that, 'Segment 1 was predominantly in the age group 41–50', and that 'Segment 2 was predominantly in the age group 31–40'. These distinctions could therefore be used to reach one or the other segment. If, however, the concluding segments had a less focused age structure, you would then conclude that 'age' was not a profiling discriminator between segments in the market being looked at and an alternative would have to be found. This alternative may, of course, be a 'conditional' set of profiling characteristics which could include age (see Example 8.1).

EXAMPLE 8.1

Let us assume that for the market represented by Table 8.1 you were *not* satisfied with the result when using age profiles as a means of distinguishing between segments. If it was known that in this market all of the micro-segments from preliminary segment 'B' did not own a car, namely 'B2' and 'B3' in Segment 1, along with 'B1' in Segment 2, then a more targeted description of customers found in Segment 1 would be, '41–50 year olds *and* 31–40 year olds *with no car*', which would give you a 93.2 per cent hit rate. This would, of course, have no effect on the hit rate for Segment 2, though it already stands at a very acceptable 91.8 per cent.

Before rejecting any cluster that is not sufficiently homogeneous in terms of its profiling, ensure that there are not some different descriptions that you have overlooked that would enable it to be reached cost effectively by your marketing effort, such as:

- demographic characteristics;
- geographic characteristics;
- psychographic characteristics.

The lists appearing in the segmentation summaries in Chapter 3 (Step 2), supplemented by the Appendices could be of use here.

To help you through this checklist, the following procedure may be of use. For *every* segment generated, carry out the following (of the five questions, questions 2, 4 and 6 are the most important; it is therefore *essential* they each can be answered by a 'Yes'):

1. Can this segment be sized by a set of measurable parameters? (For example, volume, value, number of customers.)   Yes ☐   No ☐

2. Has the segment achieved sufficient size to make it worth being considered a significant business opportunity? (This should have been covered in Step 6, which will also have ensured you have not excluded those segments with strategic potential, either because of unmet needs, or because they are at an early stage of their growth curve.)   Yes ☐   No ☐

3. Can this segment be served by a common sales and distribution channel? Please note that if there is any reason why you do not want a 'No' answer to reject this segment (for example, customers with similar requirements may use different distribution channels), mark the answer 'Yes'. Yes ☐ No ☐

4. Can you identify and reach customers in this segment by means of a distinctive and cost effective communications strategy (for example, promotion, selling, direct marketing, advertising)? Yes ☐ No ☐

5. Can this segment be clearly identified by a set of common characteristics and can you describe it? Yes ☐ No ☐

6. Can your company adopt a structure and information system which will enable you to serve this segment effectively? Yes ☐ No ☐

Process check

Developing the segments for the market in which your business operates is now complete. You can now move on to Chapters 9 and 10 which enable you to prioritise and select the segments in which your business should focus its resources.

Case study and further examples

CASE 8.1   **Agrofertiliser Supplies**

When assessing each of the seven segments against the four criteria on the checklist, it was clear that two of the criteria could be met without any further consideration. All the segments were large enough to justify a distinct marketing strategy, and they all were quite different from each other in terms of what they required. The difficulty, at least initially, appeared to be with the profiling characteristics of the final users in each segment, and with the company's ability to adopt this new segmented approach in its activities.

| CASE 8.1 | Agrofertiliser Supplies (cont'd) |

Although some profiling criteria were tracked throughout the Agrofertiliser Supplies project, the two of most interest being farm size and formal educational attainment in agriculture, none came through as being really distinctive identifiers for the different segments. The reality was that the segmentation team had not given profiling sufficient thought and attention. Fortunately, however, most of the segments by their very nature narrowed down the possible range of farms that would be found within them. This shortfall, therefore, was easily surmountable for Agrofertiliser Supplies.

At a later date, once the findings and implications with respect to a new marketing strategy had been presented, the segmentation team (working alongside the salesforce and assisted by a simple series of questions about the farm and the farmer's buying practices) began to allocate farmers to segments, concentrating first on the customers of Agrofertiliser Supplies.

Agrofertiliser Supplies was quite fortunate, as this opportunity does not exist in all markets.

The only item now remaining on the checklist was company compatibility.

Although presenting different offers in the market was not new to the company (after all it already had two brands), rigorously following this approach for a larger number of segments looked too difficult, particularly as the company had, in fact, largely dismissed its two brand strategy on the grounds of its ability to deliver any commercial advantage, and its belief that the farmers could see through it anyway. The reality here, however, was that the *company* didn't like running with a two brand strategy. Research for Agrofertilser Supplies' segmentation project found that farmers clearly differentiated between the two brands, seeing them targeted at different requirements. To convince the company of this fact, tapes made during some of the group discussions were played at a sales and marketing conference, attended by senior executives from across the company. They 'heard', but it was still going to prove difficult.

The next difficulty originated from the product-focused structure of the company. What was being called for now was a segment-focused structure at the 'front end', in other words, at the customer-facing end of the business. Critically, the 'power' of the product managers looked to be under threat. Segment managers would begin to control the external marketing activity of the business and start specifying the product requirements, with the product managers focusing on the crucial link that is required between marketing and production. This was *not* acceptable! Not immediately, anyway.

CASE 8.1   **Agrofertiliser Supplies (cont'd)**

The majority of staff in Agrofertiliser Supplies, however, signed up to the conclusions enthusiastically. This included staff in one of the most critical links with the marketplace, the salesforce.

In a matter of only a few months, after a very successful test of the conclusions in the marketplace with a new product targeted at one of the segments, the company took its leap of faith.

The *market* had won!

Case study conclusion

As was mentioned in Chapter 2 when first introducing the case study, although Agrofertilser Supplies is based on the company featured in the last chapter of this book, certain facts have been modified for reasons of commercial confidentiality and to assist in demonstrating the process in practice. This has enabled us to bring into this case study observations made in the many other segmentation projects with which we have been involved.

The status of the project for Agrofertiliser Supplies at the end of this first phase of the segmentation process is summarised in Figure 8.2.

Although the segmentation team took this project through the steps featured in Chapters 9 and 10 before putting together their marketing objectives and strategies, we shall have to leave Agrofertiliser Supplies at this point. However, the output from these next steps, a segment portfolio, can be found towards the end of Chapter 10 in Figure 10.5, as well as in the last chapter of this book (Figure 13.3).

For a more detailed insight into Agrofertiliser Supplies as it really was, please refer to the last chapter.

Further examples

Identifying which customers are to be found in the concluding segments, along with the ability, or even willingness, of companies to structure themselves around segments, are the two most frequent problems companies have with the checklist.

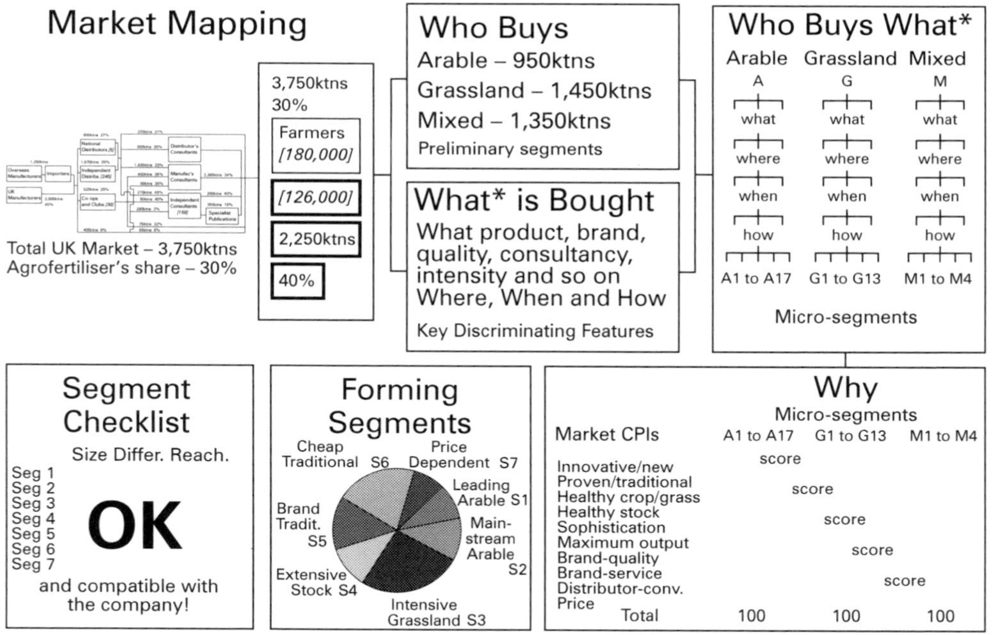

Figure 8.2 The process of segmentation – Steps 1 to 7

Although in one recent case in the distribution sector the company carrying out the project completely overlooked the need to collect profiling information, in most instances where profiling is a problem it is because the information collected wasn't extensive enough. This is because it is difficult at the outset of a project to know what profiling information will enable you to distinguish between segments. The only solution when the project has reached this far in the process is to go back and investigate further.

It may, however, be the case that a segment does consist of all types of customers, from all walks in life. Thus far, this has only been encountered once.

EXAMPLE 8.2

Some years ago an airline wished to investigate whether a 'segment' existed which consisted of customers with a fear of flying. It was considered at the time that an improved offer could be put together to better meet their requirements! A research project was commissioned and reported back. There was certainly a group of customers who did have a fear of flying. The difficulty was, however, that they did not fly in any particular class, did not watch any particular programmes or read any particular papers, they did not come from any particular socio-economic group, were not of any particular age group, neither were they from any particular part of the country, and so on. They were to be found everywhere and could not therefore qualify as a market segment.

The research project did, however, establish what their real needs-based buying requirements were. Unfortunately, only Scotty on the Starship Enterprise had the technology!

For a more down-to-earth project, Table 8.2 presents a summary of demographic profiles for the concluding segments in a study of the USA's historical romance novel market.

With respect to the difficulty companies may have in focusing on to the concluding segments, the most productive approach is to anticipate this problem at the very beginning of the project and start pre-empting it at an early stage. It is often by involving a wider audience in the project, through actively seeking their contribution and sharing with them the project's progress from the earliest stages, that difficulties associated with the 'mindset' of the business have a more than equal chance of being overcome. This should be one of the key responsibilities of the segmentation team, who should be kept regularly informed of progress by the core group conducting the detailed work (see Chapter 1).

Table 8.2 **Segment demographics of the historical romance novel market (USA)**

	Segment 1 (Movers and shakers)	Segment 2 (Isolated readers)	Segment 3 (Young swingers)	Segment 4 (Laggards)
Age	Average age: 31–40	Average age: 41–50	Average age: 30 and under	Average age: over 50 years
Children	One or no children	At least one child	Most have no children	Most have grown children
Education	High school education	High school education	One-third have college degree	Least education
Employment and income	Most employed; family income of $20 000	Half are employed; family income of $20 000	Most employed; income less than $20 000	More unemployed; lowest income

Source: S. P. Schnaars and L. G. Schiffman, 'An application of segmentation design based on a hybrid of canonical correlation and simple cross tabulation', *Journal of the Academy of Marketing Science*, **12**, Autumn 1984).

With an enthusiastic following across the business, and no big surprises, even structural changes that may be required can be moved from the 'can't be done' box into the 'leave it with me' category.

9 Segment Attractiveness (Steps 8–11)

Now the segments in your market have been defined, it is essential that you determine how attractive each segment is to your company. This, along with an analysis of your competitiveness in each segment (Chapter 10), will help you decide how best to distribute your financial and managerial resources between them.

The position of this stage in the segmentation process is illustrated in Figure 9.1.

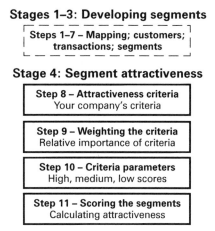

Stages 1–3: Developing segments

Steps 1–7 – Mapping; customers; transactions; segments

Stage 4: Segment attractiveness

Step 8 – Attractiveness criteria
Your company's criteria

Step 9 – Weighting the criteria
Relative importance of criteria

Step 10 – Criteria parameters
High, medium, low scores

Step 11 – Scoring the segments
Calculating attractiveness

Figure 9.1 The process of segmentation – Steps 8–11

In this chapter, we start by suggesting some attractiveness factors you may wish to consider and then move on to attach weightings to your selected factors in order to gauge their relative importance to each other. 'High', 'medium' and 'low' parameters are then defined for each attractiveness factor, with each segment finally scored against the selected factors. The chapter starts, however, with a summary of portfolio analysis, followed by a brief discussion about the planning period over which you should be assessing the segments.

Portfolio analysis

Portfolio analysis, for the purposes of this book, is simply a means of assessing a number of different segments, first of all according to the potential of each in terms of achieving an organisation's objectives, and second according to the organisation's ability to take advantage of the identified opportunities.

The idea of a portfolio is for a company to meet its objectives by balancing sales growth, cash flow and risk. As individual segments grow or shrink, then the overall nature of the company's portfolio will change. It is, therefore, essential that the whole portfolio is reviewed regularly and that an active policy towards the move into new segments and the exiting of old segments is pursued.

Widely referred to as the *Directional Policy Matrix* (DPM), portfolio analysis offers a detailed framework which can be used to classify possible competitive environments and their strategy requirements. It uses several indicators to measure the dimensions of 'segment attractiveness' on the one hand, and 'company competitiveness' on the other. These indicators can be altered by management to suit the operating conditions of particular markets.

The purpose of the matrix is to diagnose an organisation's strategy options in relation to the two composite dimensions outlined above.

However, before describing in detail how to use the DPM, it is worth considering its antecedents.

Portfolio analysis initially came out of the work of the Boston Consulting Group, began in the 1960s, and it has had a profound effect on the way management think about their market and their activity within it.

There are basically two parts to the thinking behind the work of the Boston Consulting Group. One is concerned with *market share* and the other with *market growth*, which we would translate into *segment share* and *segment growth*. These are brought together into a single matrix (the Boston matrix), which has important implications for the firm, especially in respect of *cash flow*. Cash is a key determinant of a company's ability to develop its segment portfolio.

The Boston matrix can be used to classify a firm's position in each segment found in the market according to their cash usage and their cash generation along the two dimensions described above, namely relative segment share and rate of segment growth. This is summarised in Figure 9.2.

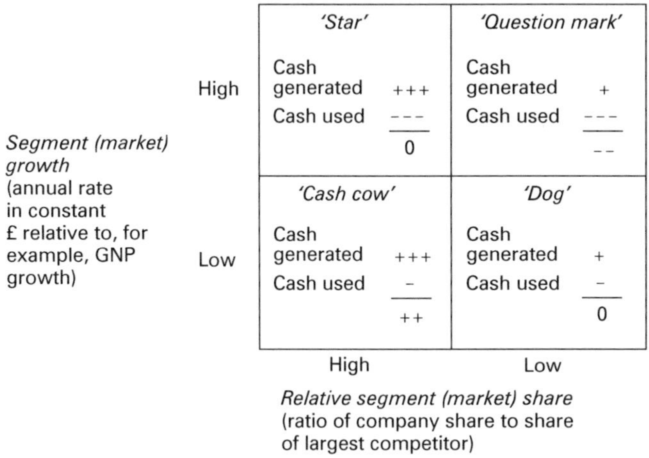

		'Star'		'Question mark'	
	High	Cash generated	+++	Cash generated	+
		Cash used	– – –	Cash used	– – –
Segment (market) growth (annual rate in constant £ relative to, for example, GNP growth)			0		– –
		'Cash cow'		'Dog'	
	Low	Cash generated	+++	Cash generated	+
		Cash used	–	Cash used	–
			++		0
		High		Low	

Relative segment (market) share
(ratio of company share to share
of largest competitor)

Figure 9.2   The Boston matrix

The somewhat picturesque labels attached to each of the four categories give some indication of the prospects for the *company* in each quadrant. Thus, the 'question mark' is a segment in which the company has not yet achieved a dominant position and, therefore, a high cash flow, or perhaps it once had such a position but has slipped back. It will be a high user of cash because it is a growth segment. This is also sometimes referred to as a 'wildcat'.

The 'star' is probably a newish segment in which the company has achieved a high share and which is probably more or less self-financing in cash terms.

The 'cash cows' are leaders in segments where there is little additional growth, but a lot of stability. These are excellent generators of cash and tend to use little because of the state of the segment.

'Dogs' often have little future and can be a cash drain on the company. They are probably segments the company should exit, although it is often very difficult to leave 'old friends'.

The art of managing segments as a portfolio now becomes a lot clearer. What we should be seeking to do is to use the surplus cash generated by the 'cash cows' to invest in our 'stars' and to invest in a selected number of 'question marks'.

The approach of the Boston Consulting Group is, however, fairly criticised because of its dependence on two single factors: relative segment share and segment growth. To overcome this difficulty, and to provide a more flexible approach, General Electric (GE) and McKinsey jointly developed a multi-factor approach using the same fundamental ideas as the Boston Consulting Group.

The GE/McKinsey approach uses *industry attractiveness* and *business strengths* as the two main axes, and builds up these dimensions from a number of variables. When applying this to segments, the first (vertical) axis is relabelled *segment attractiveness*. We have also relabelled the horizontal axis, *company competitiveness*. Using these variables, and some scheme for weighting them according to their importance, segments are classified into one of nine cells in a 3 × 3 matrix. Thus, the same purpose is served as in the Boston matrix (namely, comparing investment opportunities among segments) but with the difference that multiple criteria are used. These criteria vary according to circumstances, but generally include some, or all, of those shown in Figure 9.3.

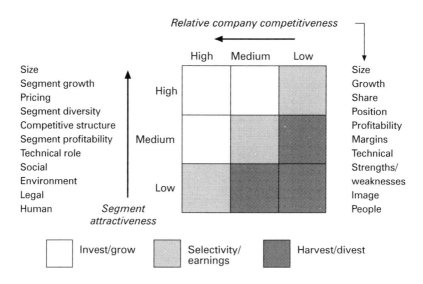

Figure 9.3   The nine-box portfolio matrix

It is not necessary, however, to use a nine-box matrix, and many managers prefer to use a four-box matrix similar to the Boston box, while using the GE/McKinsey definitions for the axes. This is the preferred methodology of the authors as it seems to be more easily understood by, and useful to, practising managers.

The four-box matrix is shown in Figure 9.4. Here, the circles represent sales into a segment, with each circle being proportional to that segment's contribution to turnover. The position of each segment on the matrix is determined by its attractiveness and the company's competitive position within it.

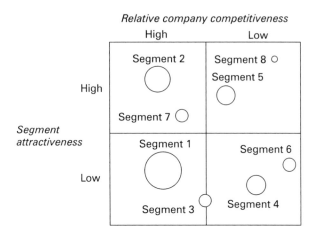

Figure 9.4   The four-box matrix

The difference in this case is that, rather than using only two variables, the criteria which are used for each axis are totally relevant and specific to each company using the matrix. It shows:

- segments categorised on a scale of attractiveness to the company;
- the company's relative strengths in each of these segments;
- the relative importance of each segment to the company.

An example of an actual segment portfolio directional policy matrix is presented in Figure 9.5. The procedures contained in this chapter and Chapter 10 will equip you to produce your own directional policy matrix.

Portfolio analysis is discussed in more detail in Chapter 5 of *Marketing Plans – How to Prepare Them: How to Use Them*, Malcolm McDonald, (4th edn) Oxford, Heinemann, 1998.

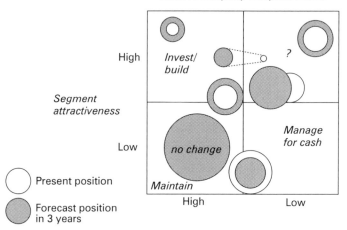

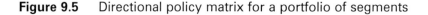

Figure 9.5   Directional policy matrix for a portfolio of segments

Time horizon

Prior to commencing the analysis of segment attractiveness, it is important to define the time period being scored. Three years is recommended. A segment that is attractive today will not automatically be equally attractive in the future. A particular change that can occur is the size of segments. Some segments could have shrunk in size by the end of the time period, while others, including any anticipated new segments, could have increased in size, and therefore increased their attractiveness. It is essential that you have up-to-date forecasts available to help determine both the size of the segments by the end of the time period and the size of your presence within them, which will help you in the next chapter. To this end, you will require sales forecasts for the current products/services, and for any new products/services your current policies plan to introduce during the time period.

Although it is perfectly acceptable to determine how attractive each segment will be at the *end* of the planning period only, it is quite useful to assess attractiveness at two points in time; today (Year 0) and in Year 3. This gives the resulting portfolio matrix a visual indication of each segment's dynamics. The directional policy matrix presented in Figure 9.5 has segment attractiveness calculated only for the final year. In such circumstances, segments can only move horizontally – that is, along the same level of attractiveness – with their direction of movement determined by your own company's activity within them (and therefore your company's changing relative business strength within each segment).

This chapter covers both options and therefore looks at determining segment attractiveness for today (Year 0), and for the end of the planning period, which we will assume to be Year 3.

Segmentation team

To ensure that the appropriateness of the selected attractiveness criteria is high and that the scoring is realistic, it is recommended that the same cross-functional team suggested for the segmentation process should continue with this part of the segmentation work. This mix will continue to encourage the challenging of traditional views during their discussions. There will also be the continuing need for a core group of two to three individuals to carry out the detailed work, the core group reporting back to the full team for consultation, comment and guidance, just as they did during the development of segments itself.

Circumstances may also be such that the continuing presence of an outsider to act as a facilitator for the process and to continue offering an objective and alternative viewpoint to the discussion could still be warranted.

Definition

Segment attractiveness in Year 3 is a measure of the potential of a segment to yield growth in sales and profits during the next three years (that is $t0$ to $t+3$, where t represents time), with Year 0 representing the current attractiveness of a segment based on the past three years (that is $t-3$ to $t0$). It is important to stress that this should be an *objective* assessment of segment attractiveness using data *external* to the organisation. The criteria themselves will, of course, be determined by the organisation carrying out the exercise and will be relevant to the objectives the organisation is trying to achieve, but the criteria should be *independent* of the organisation's position in its segments.

Put another way, imagine you have a measuring instrument, something like a thermometer, which measures not temperature but segment attractiveness. The higher the reading, the more attractive the segment. The instrument is shown in Figure 9.6. Estimate the position on the scale *each* of your segments would record (should such an instrument exist) and make a note of it.

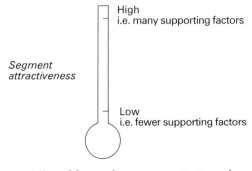

Figure 9.6   Measuring segment attractiveness

Segment attractiveness factors (Step 8)

Here, you should list the factors you wish to consider in comparing the attractiveness of your segments. This will be a combination of a number of factors, though they can usually be summarised under three headings.

Growth rate   Average annual forecast growth rate of revenue in that segment (percentage growth of 1998 over 1997, plus percentage growth of 1999 over 1998, *plus* percentage growth of 2000 over 1999, with the total divided by three: in other words, the number of years being looked at). If preferred, compound average growth rate could be used. Clearly, in determining segment growth rates, you will need to take into account the supportiveness (or otherwise) of the overall business environment.

Accessible   An attractive segment is not only large, it also has to be
segment size   accessed. One way of calculating this is to estimate the total revenue of the segment during the selected time span, less revenue impossible to access, *regardless of investment made*. Alternatively, total segment size can be used, which is the most frequent method, as it does not involve any managerial judgement to be made that could distort the true picture. This latter method is the method advised here.

Profit   This is much more difficult to deal with and will vary consid-
potential   erably, according to segment. For example, Porter's Five Forces model could be used to estimate the profit potential of a segment, as illustrated in the example appearing in Table 9.1. The factors for this table are taken from *Competitive Advantage – Creating and Sustaining Superior Performance*,

M. E. Porter, New York, The Free Press, 1985. The table itself, however, and the methodology shown, were devised by the authors.

Table 9.1   Porter's Five Forces model

Profit potential sub-factors	Segment rating 10=Low 0=High	Sub-factor weightings (Total–100)	Weighted factor scores (rating × weight)
1. Intensity of competition		50	
2. Threat of substitutes		5	
3. Threat of new entrants		5	
4. Power of suppliers		10	
5. Power of customers		30	
		Profit potential factor score	

Alternatively, a combination of these and segment specific factors could be used. In the case of the pharmaceutical market, for example, the sub-factors could be those appearing in Table 9.2.

These are clearly a proxy for profit potential. Each is weighted according to its importance. The weights add up to 100 in order to give a *profit potential factor score*, as in the Porter's Five Forces example (Table 9.1).

Table 9.2   Profit potential sub-factors in the pharmaceutical market

Sub-factors	High Med. × Weight Low	Weighted sub-factor score
Unmet medical needs (efficacy)	30	
Unmet medical needs (safety)	25	
Unmet medical needs (convenience)	15	
Price potential	10	
Competitive intensity	10	
Cost of segment entry	10	
	Profit potential factor score	

Naturally, growth, size and profit will not encapsulate the requirements of all organisations. For example, in the case of an orchestra, artistic satisfaction may be an important consideration. In another case, social considerations could be important. In yet another, cyclicality may be crucial.

It is possible, then, to add another heading, such as 'risk' or 'other' to the three headings listed earlier.

A generalised list of possible attractiveness factors is shown below. It is advisable to use no more than an overall total of five or six factors between your selected headings, otherwise the exercise becomes too complex and loses its focus.

Market factors
Size (money, units or both)
Growth rate per year
Sensitivity to price, service features and external factors
Cyclicality
Seasonality
Bargaining power of upstream suppliers
Bargaining power of downstream suppliers

Competition
Types of competitors
Degree of concentration
Changes in type and mix
Entries and exits
Changes in share
Substitution by new technology
Degrees and types of integration

Financial and economic factors
Contribution margins
Leveraging factors, such as economies of scale and experience
Barriers to entry or exit (financial and non-financial)
Capacity utilisation

Technological factors
Maturity and volatility
Complexity
Differentiation
Patents and copyrights
Manufacturing process technology required

Socio-political factors
Social attitudes and trends
Laws and government agency regulations
Influence with pressure groups and government representatives
Human factors, such as unionisation and community acceptance

Source: Malcolm McDonald, *Marketing Plans – How to Prepare Them: How to Use Them,* (4th edn) Oxford, Heinemann, 1998.

A worksheet for use with this step, as well as for Steps 9 to 11, appears in Table 9.3.

Table 9.3   Worksheet – segment attractiveness

Segment 1:	Description	Segment 2:	Description	Segment 3:	Description	Segment 4:	Description
Segment 5:		Segment 6:		Segment 7:		Segment 8:	

Segment Attractive-ness Factors	Weight	Parameters			Segment 1		Segment 2		Segment 3		Segment 4		Segment 5		Segment 6		Segment 7		Segment 8	
		High 10–7	Med 6–4	Low 3–0	Score	Total	Score	Total	Score	Total	Score	Total	Score	Total	Score	Total	Score	Total	Score	Total
Total	100				Total		Total		Total		Total		Total		Total		Total		Total	

Weighting the factors (Step 9)

For each of the factors for segment attractiveness, weight their relative importance to each other according to your own particular requirements by distributing 100 points between them.

Given that the overall aim of a company is usually represented in a profit figure, and that profit is a function of:

Segment Volume × Margin × Growth

it would be reasonable to expect a weighting against each of the attractiveness factor headings listed earlier in this chapter to be along the lines shown below:

Growth Rate	40
Accessible Segment Size	20
Profit Potential	40

Total 100%

An even higher weighting for growth could be understandable in some circumstances (in which case, the corresponding weightings for the others should be reduced). These factors could then be combined with market specific factors, resulting in a table along the lines shown in Table 9.4.

Table 9.4   Weighting segment attractiveness factors

Market: ABC	
Segment Attractiveness Factors	*Weight (%)*
1. Volume growth potential	25
2. Profit potential	25
3. Potential segment size (vol/val)	15
4. Vulnerability	15
5. Competitive intensity	10
6. Cyclicality	10
Total	**100%**

It is important to note that the segment attractiveness factors and their weightings for the market being evaluated cannot change whilst constructing the DPM. Once agreed, under no circumstances should they be changed, otherwise the attractiveness of your segments is not being evaluated against common criteria and the matrix will become meaningless.

Defining the parameters for each attractiveness factor (Step 10)

You now need to determine high, medium and low parameters for each of the factors selected, where very high scores 10 and very low scores zero. An example is given in Table 9.5.

Table 9.5   Weighting segment attractiveness factors

	Market: ABC		
Segment Attractiveness Factors	Parameters		
	High (10–7)	Medium (6–4)	Low (3–0)
Growth	GNP* + 5%	GNP	GNP – 5%
Profitability	> 15%	10–15%	< 10%
Size	< £5m	£1m–£5m	< £1m
Vulnerability	Low	Medium	High
Competitiveness	Low	Medium	High
Cyclicality	Low	Medium	High

* GNP – Gross National Product

Scoring segments (Step 11)

For each of the concluding segments arrived at in Steps 1 to 7, you can now establish how attractive each is to your business by using the attractiveness factors and their weightings relative to each other, scoring the segments individually against each factor, multiplying the percentage weighting by the score, and adding the resulting figures together in order to arrive at a total. A worked example of this quantitative approach to evaluation is given in Table 9.6.

Table 9.6 Segment attractiveness evaluation (for Year 0)

		Market: ABC					
		Segment 1		*Segment 2*		*Segment 3*	
Attractiveness	*Weight (%)*	*Score*	*Total*	*Score*	*Total*	*Score*	*Total*
Growth	25	10	2.5	7	1.75	8	2.0
Profitability	25	8	2.0	8	2.0	6	1.5
Size	15	5	0.75	7	1.05	6	0.9
Vulnerability	15	6	0.9	4	0.6	7	1.05
Competition	10	6	0.6	7	0.7	5	0.5
Cyclicality	10	2.5	0.25	3	0.3	2.5	0.25
Total	**100%**		**7.0**		**6.4**		**6.2**

In this example, an overall score of 7 out of 10 places Segment 1 in the highly attractive category for Year 0.

It should be noted that if, in carrying out Steps 1 to 7, you concluded your market had less than five segments, there is little point in using the DPM.

Plotting the position of segments on the portfolio matrix

Transpose the results of your segment attractiveness evaluation on to the matrix, writing the segments on the left of the matrix. Still using the matrix, draw a dotted line horizontally across from each segment, as shown in Figure 9.7.

A worksheet for plotting segments on the portfolio matrix appears in Chapter 10.

In considering the position of each segment on the 'attractiveness' axis at some time in the future, it is important to remember that they can only move vertically *if* the matrix also shows their current level of attractiveness. This implies carrying out one set of calculations for the present time using the agreed segment attractiveness factors, in order to locate segments on the vertical axis for Year 0, then carrying out another set of calculations for a future period (say, in three years' time) based on your forecasts using the same segment attractiveness factors. A reworked Table 9.6 illustrating the position of each segment in Year 3 appears in Table 9.7.

Year 3 sees a change in the attractiveness of the three segments, with Segment 1 being toppled from its leading position into second place and Segment 3 replacing it. These new positions can now be transposed on to the matrix, as in Figure 9.8.

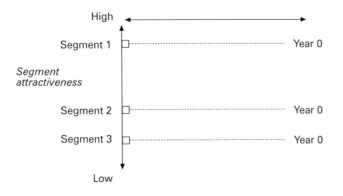

Figure 9.7   Plotting segments on the portfolio matrix according to their attractiveness

It has to be said that, in practice, it is quicker and easier to carry out only the calculations for the final year of the planning period, in which case the circles on the DPM can only move horizontally with changes to your company's relative strength in each segment.

It is worth repeating that, once agreed, under no circumstances should segment attractiveness factors be changed, otherwise the attractiveness of your segments is not being evaluated against common criteria and the matrix becomes meaningless. Scores, however, are specific to each segment.

Table 9.7   Segment attractiveness evaluation (for Year 3)

		Market: ABC					
		Segment 1		Segment 2		Segment 3	
Attractiveness	*Weight (%)*	*Score*	*Total*	*Score*	*Total*	*Score*	*Total*
Growth	25	6	1.5	5	1.25	10	2.5
Profitability	25	9	2.25	8	2.0	7	1.75
Size	15	6	0.9	5	0.75	8	1.2
Vulnerability	15	5	0.75	6	0.9	6	0.9
Competition	10	8	0.8	8	0.8	4	0.4
Cyclicality	10	2.5	0.25	3	0.3	2.5	0.25
Total	**100%**		**6.45**		**6.0**		**7.0**

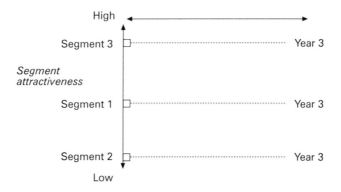

Figure 9.8   Replotting segments on the portfolio matrix according to their attractiveness at the end of the planning period

It is also worth stressing that segments positioned in the lower half of the matrix should *not* be treated as unattractive. All this means is that they are relatively less attractive than segments positioned in the top half of the matrix. In addition, it should not be forgotten that the cash generated from those segments in the lower half of the matrix (particularly the lower left quadrant) will be an important contribution to the investment required in those segments appearing in the top half of the matrix.

In the examples shown in Tables 9.6 and 9.7, it can be seen that the weighted scores for all three segments is above 5.0. If the vertical axis was scaled from 0 to 10, this would put all three segments in the 'highly attractive' quadrant. Should you have only three segments, which is unlikely, this would obviously be a nonsense. To overcome this problem in cases such as this, where all weighted scores are above 5.0, it is suggested that the scale on the vertical axis be amended so that 4.0 becomes the point of origin and, in the example given, 8.0 becomes the highest point. This will always ensure a spread, which is, of course, the whole point of using the device in the first place. Table 9.8 shows a more likely spread of weighted attractiveness scores.

When the final result is not what you expected

The first time managers try using the DPM, they frequently find that the points of intersection from the two axes for their individual segments do not come out where expected. One possible reason for this is a misunderstanding concerning the use of market attractiveness factors. Please remember, you will be most concerned about the *potential for growth in*

Table 9.8   The range of weighted attractiveness scores in a market with nine segments

		Segment 1		Segment 2		Segment 3	
		Market: DEF					
Attractiveness	*Weight (%)*	*Score*	*Total*	*Score*	*Total*	*Score*	*Total*
Profitability	35	8	2.8	9	3.15	10	2.1
Growth	30	3	0.9	4	1.2	7	1.2
Size	15	9	1.35	5	0.75	8	1.05
Competition	20	3	0.6	5	1.0	4	1.0
Total	**100%**		**5.65**		**6.1**		**5.35**

		Segment 4		Segment 5		Segment 6	
Attractiveness	*Weight (%)*	*Score*	*Total*	*Score*	*Total*	*Score*	*Total*
Profitability	35	7	2.45	7	2.45	5	1.75
Growth	30	7	2.1	8	2.4	2	0.6
Size	15	8	1.2	7	1.05	5	0.75
Competition	20	4	0.8	6	1.2	2	0.4
Total	**100%**		**6.55**		**7.1**		**3.5**

		Segment 7		Segment 8		Segment 9	
Attractiveness	*Weight (%)*	*Score*	*Total*	*Score*	*Total*	*Score*	*Total*
Profitability	35	5	1.75	2	0.7	3	1.05
Growth	30	3	0.9	1	0.3	5	1.5
Size	15	2	0.3	2	0.3	8	1.2
Competition	20	9	1.8	2	0.4	2	0.4
Total	**100%**		**4.75**		**1.7**		**4.15**

volume, growth in profit, and so on for your company in each of your 'segments'. For example, even if a 'segment' is mature (or even in decline), if the *potential* is there for your company to grow in this mature segment, then it would obviously be more attractive than one in which there was little or no potential for you to grow. (As would be the case, for example, if you already had a high share in a segment.) Likewise, even if a 'segment' is currently very profitable for your company, if there were little or no *potential* for profit growth, this segment might be considered less attractive than one which was currently not so profitable to your company, but which offered good *potential* for profit growth.

Process check

A number of factors have been listed which you may wish to consider when comparing the attractiveness of the segments in your market. The relative importance of these factors to each other has been determined and high, medium and low parameters established for each factor. This information has then been used to establish how attractive each segment is to your business and the results transposed on to a portfolio matrix.

A careful assessment now needs to be made of your company's competitive strength in each segment, relative to the competition.

10 Company Competitiveness and the Portfolio Matrix (Step 12)

It can now be very tempting to simply focus on those segments obtaining the highest attractiveness ratings (despite the cautionary comments towards the end of Chapter 9), which could also be the chosen strategy of your competitors. This, however, fails to acknowledge that your company's ability to be successful in each segment will differ according to how strong you are in it *relative to the competition*. This chapter therefore presents a format for you to follow which can be used to determine where your relative competitive strengths lie. It is the final stage of the segmentation process which is summarised in Figure 10.1.

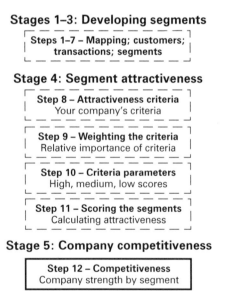

Figure 10.1   The process of segmentation – Step 12

Your company's ability to deliver the CPIs for each segment needs to be weighed up against your competitors' ability to deliver these very same CPIs. The results can then be plotted on the portfolio matrix to determine the point of intersection with the attractiveness weightings.

To complete the matrix, a circle is drawn at the point of intersection, the size of which represents either the volume/value of that segment or your company's volume/value within it.

Definition

Company competitiveness is a measure of an organisation's actual strengths in each segment (in other words, the degree to which it can take advantage of an opportunity). Thus, it is an *objective* assessment of an organisation's ability to satisfy the needs of each segment, relative to competitors.

Competitiveness factors

These factors will be principally a combination of an organisation's relative strengths versus competitors in connection with customer-facing needs in each segment, namely those that are required by the customer. These were identified in Chapter 6 as CPIs, with each concluding segment having its own rank order and relative value of the market CPIs. To win the business in any particular segment, therefore, the company has to be relatively more *successful* than its competitors in putting together an offer which matches up to the segment's CPIs. In constructing a portfolio matrix, the constituents of the offer required to deliver the CPIs are therefore often referred to as *Critical Success Factors* (CSFs); this is the term most often found in marketing text books and papers when describing this technique.

The CSFs can often be summarised under the following headings:

- Product/service requirements;
- Price requirements;
- Promotion requirements;
- Place (distribution and service) requirements.

In your review of how well your company can meet the requirements of each segment, you may well need to consider questions such as:

- Are we big enough?
- Can we grow?
- How large is our market share?

- Do we have the right products?
- How well are we known in this market?
- What image do we have?
- Do we have the right technical skills?
- Can we adapt to changes?
- Do we have enough capacity?
- How close are we to this market?

It should be stressed, however, that the answers to these questions should not be confused with customer-facing CSFs. They will only tell you in what ways you have to change to satisfy your customer's needs.

It will be clear that a company's relative strengths in meeting customer-facing needs will be a function of its capabilities in connection with the CSFs relative to the capabilities of the best competitor. For example, if a depot is necessary in each major town/city for any organisation to succeed in any segment, and the company carrying out the analysis doesn't have this, yet the competition does, then it is likely that this will account for its poor performance under 'customer service'. Likewise, if a major component of 'price' is the cost of feedstock, and it is necessary in some segments to have low prices in order to succeed, any company carrying out the analysis which doesn't have low feedstock costs, while competitors do, will find that it is this which accounts for its poor performance under 'price'.

Clearly, this type of assessment of a company's capabilities in respect of CSFs could be made in order to understand what has to be done in the organisation in order to satisfy customer needs better. This assessment, however, is quite separate from the quantification of the business strengths/position axis, and its purpose is to translate the analysis into actionable propositions for other functions within the organisation, such as purchasing, production, distribution and so on.

It is worth emphasising that for the purposes of the portfolio matrix, it is usually only necessary to work with the top three to five CSFs in your analysis of relative company competitiveness.

Weighting the factors

The weightings allocated to the factors appearing under the heading 'critical success factors' will, of course, be specific to each segment and will reflect their relative values to each other as observed for their respective CPIs in Chapter 6. An example is shown in Table 10.1.

Table 10.1   Weighting CSFs

Critical Success Factors	Weight (%)
Market: ABC Segment: A	
1. Price	50
2. Product technical performance	25
3. Service (delivery reliability)	15
4. Image (leading edge/forefront)	10
Total	**100%**

Scoring your company and your competitors

The parameters for each CSF are very straightforward, as they are common to all the CSFs. They consist of:

- highly competitive (which has a score range of 10 down to 7),
- competitive (with a score range of 6 down to 4),
- uncompetitive (scoring from 3 down to zero).

For each individual segment, score your own company and each of your main competitors out of 10 on each of the CSFs, then multiply the score by the weight as shown in Table 10.2. This calculation should first be carried out for the start of the planning period, namely Year 0. This enables you to establish a fixed position on the portfolio matrix for your company in each segment against which the forecast outcome of alternative strategies and assumptions for the planning period can be seen when plotted on to the DPM.

Table 10.2   Competitive strength evaluation (Year 0)

CSFs	Weight (%)	Your Company		Competitor A		Competitor B	
		Score	*Total*	*Score*	*Total*	*Score*	*Total*
Market: ABC Segment: A							
1. Price	50	5	2.5	6	3.0	4	2.0
2. Product	25	6	1.5	8	2.0	10	2.5
3. Service	15	8	1.2	8	1.2	6	0.9
4. Image	10	6	0.6	5	0.5	3	0.3
Total	**100%**		**5.8**		**6.7**		**5.7**

From this table it can be seen that:

- this company is not the segment leader;
- all competitors score above 5.0.

The problem with this and many similar calculations is that rarely will this method discriminate sufficiently well to indicate the relative strengths of a number of segments in a particular company's market portfolio, and many of the SBU's segments would appear on the left of the matrix.

Some method is required to prevent all segments appearing on the left of the matrix. This can be achieved by using a ratio, as in the Boston Matrix. This will indicate a company's position relative to the best in the segment.

In the example provided, Competitor A has most strengths in the segment so our organisation needs to make some improvements. To reflect this, our weighted score should be expressed as a ratio of Competitor A (the highest weighted score). Thus,

$$5.8 : 6.7 = 0.87 : 1$$

If we were to plot this on a logarithmic scale on the horizontal axis, this would place our organisation to the right of the dividing line as shown in Figure 10.2 (we should make the left-hand extreme point '3×' and start the scale on the right at '0.3×').

Figure 10.2   Plotting a relative competitive score of 0.87

A scale of '3×' to '0.3×' has been chosen because such a band is likely to encapsulate most extremes of competitive advantage. If it doesn't, just change it to suit your own circumstances (for example, 10× to 0.1×).

A worksheet which can be used for these various calculations appears in Table 10.3.

Table 10.3   Worksheet – relative company competitiveness

Market:							
Segment:			Your company		Competitor:		Competitor:
CSFs		Weight	Score	Total	Score	Total	Score	Total
Total		100%	Total		Total		Total	

Your company's relative competitive strength: _ _ _ _ : 1.0

Market:							
Segment:			Your company		Competitor:		Competitor:
CSFs		Weight	Score	Total	Score	Total	Score	Total
Total		100%	Total		Total		Total	

Your company's relative competitive strength: _ _ _ _ : 1.0

Producing the portfolio matrix

Once you have completed the competitive evaluation for Year 0, you can plot your position for each segment by drawing a vertical line from the relevant point on the horizontal scale, as shown on Figure 10.3, so that it intersects with the appropriate segment's horizontal line (initially from the Year 3 calculations).

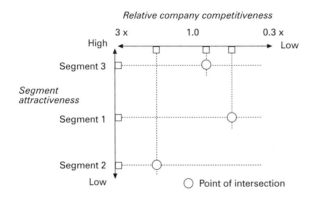

Figure 10.3   Plotting business positions on the portfolio matrix for each segment according to their relative competitive strength

A worksheet for plotting segments on the portfolio matrix appears in Table 10.4.

Table 10.4   Worksheet – portfolio matrix

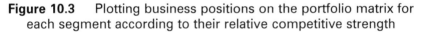

By plotting for each segment the intersection of their scores for both axes, initially using the segment attractiveness ratings for Year 3, along with the relative competitive strength assessment for the current year (Year 0), circles can be drawn with their area proportional to the forecast size of the segment, as defined in the previous chapter (the radius of the circle, therefore, being the square root of the area: that is, segment size, divided by pi). This can then be transferred on to a four-box matrix with your company's segment share put as a 'cheese' in each circle, as on Figure 10.4. It is, of course, the proportion of the circle taken up by the 'cheese' that contributes to the position of the circle on the horizontal axis (assuming segment share has contributed to your company's ability to compete in some of the segments). It is the size of the whole circle that contributes to the position of the circle on the vertical axis (assuming segment size has contributed to the attractiveness of segments).

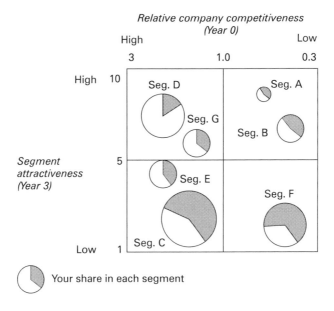

Figure 10.4   The initial segment portfolio matrix

Alternatively, your company's own sales into each segment can be used to determine the size of the circle. This can be seen on Figure 10.5 which is the segment portfolio matrix for the case study, Agrofertiliser Supplies. In practice, however, it is advisable to do both and compare them in order to see how closely actual sales match the opportunities.

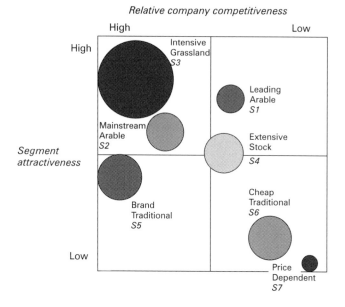

Figure 10.5   The segment portfolio matrix for the case study

The purpose of the portfolio matrix is to see how the segments in a market relate to each other in the context of the criteria used. This analysis should indicate whether the portfolio is well balanced or not, and should give a clear indication of any problems.

The DPM

It is now possible to start being creative in your use of the matrix and redraw your portfolio along a number of alternative lines by, for example:

- rescoring your relative business strength for each segment assuming the company continues with the strategies already in place;
- rescoring your relative business strength for each segment based on some realistic assumptions about your competitors, but assuming your company just stood still;
- a combination of the above.

By including these new locations of the segments on the original portfolio matrix, the resulting matrix will indicate whether your own position is getting worse or better. If this matrix then also includes the position of the segments in Year 0, you now have a very comprehensive picture of your market, as shown in Figure 10.6.

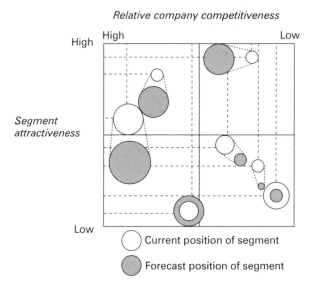

Figure 10.6   The DPM

Process check

Prioritising and selecting the segments in your market is now complete.

With this picture of the market in place, consideration should be given to marketing objectives and strategies which are now appropriate to the attractiveness of a segment and the extent to which such opportunities match your capabilities. For the objectives, this involves changing the volumes/values and/or share along with the scores on the horizontal axis (relative strength in a segment) in order to achieved the desired volumes/values. Conceptually, you are picking up the circle and moving it without specifying how this is to be achieved. This is encapsulated in the defined marketing strategies which will change the individual CSF scores.

As the setting of marketing objectives and strategies is obviously the whole point of all the previous diagnosis, the next chapter describes this process in some detail.

PART II

Segment Objectives and Strategies

11 *Setting Marketing Objectives and Strategies for Identified Segments*

Chapter 11 defines what marketing objectives are and explains how to set them. The relationship between marketing objectives and corporate objectives is also shown. To assist in the setting of marketing objectives, there is a section on competitive strategies. This chapter also begins to provide the link between segmentation and marketing planning and describes where and how to start the process of marketing planning, using the method known as 'gap analysis', and discusses new product development as a growth strategy. Finally, there is an explanation of what marketing strategies are and how to set them.

Briefly, *objectives* are what the business unit wants to achieve. They should be *quantitative*, and should be expressed where possible in terms of *values*, *volumes* and *segment shares*. General directional terms such as 'maximise', 'minimise' and 'penetrate' should be avoided unless quantification is included. On the other hand, *strategies* are how you plan to achieve the objectives. Thus, there are objectives and strategies at all levels in marketing – such as advertising objectives and strategies, pricing objectives and strategies, and so on.

Without doubt, setting objectives is the key step in the marketing planning process, for it will by now be clear that, following the analysis that takes place as part of the segmentation process, realistic and achievable objectives should be set for each of the company's major segments. Unless this step is carried out well, everything that follows will lack focus and cohesion. In previous chapters, you have gone to a lot of trouble to select the right targets. The purpose of this chapter is to ensure that you score a bull's-eye on your selected targets!

Marketing objectives: what they are and how they relate to corporate objectives

There are no works on marketing which do not include at least one paragraph on the need for setting objectives. Setting objectives is a mandatory step in the planning process. The literature on the subject, though, is not very explicit, which is surprising when it is considered how vital the setting of marketing objectives is.

An objective will ensure that a company knows what its strategies are expected to accomplish and when a particular strategy has accomplished its purpose. In other words, without objectives, strategy decisions and all that follows will take place in a vacuum.

Following the identification of opportunities and the explicit statement of assumptions about conditions affecting the business, the process of setting objectives should, in theory, be comparatively easy, the actual objectives themselves being a realistic statement of what the company desires to achieve as a result of market-centred analysis, rather than generalised statements born of top management's desire to 'do better next year'. However, objective setting is more complex than at first it would appear.

Most experts agree that the logical approach to the difficult task of setting marketing objectives is to proceed from the broad to the specific. Thus, the starting point would be a statement of the nature of the business, from which would flow the broad company objectives. Next, the broad company objectives would be translated into key result areas, which would be those areas in which success is vital to the firm. At one level, key result areas would include, for example, market penetration and the overall growth rate of sales. At a lower level, 'market penetration' could well be stepped down to 'segment penetration'. The third step would be creation of the sub-objectives necessary to accomplish the broad objectives, such as sales volume goals, geographical expansion, segment extension, product line extension, and so on.

The end result of this process should be objectives which are consistent with the strategic plan, attainable within budget limitations, and compatible with the strengths, limitations and economics of other functions within the organisation.

At the top level, management is concerned with long-run profitability which may well extend into market related objectives; at the next level in the management hierarchy, the concern is for objectives that are defined more specifically and in greater detail, such as increasing sales and segment share, moving into new segments, and so on. These objectives are merely a part of the hierarchy of objectives, in that corporate objectives will only be accomplished if these and other objectives are achieved. At the next level, management is concerned with objectives that are defined even more tightly, such as creating awareness among a specific target segment about a new product, changing a particular customer attitude, and so on. Again, the general marketing objectives will only be accomplished if these and other sub-objectives are achieved. It is clear that sub-objectives *per se*, unless they are an integral part of a broader framework of objectives, are likely to lead to a wasteful misdirection of resources.

For example, a sales increase in itself may be possible, but only at an undue cost. Such a marketing objective is, therefore, only appropriate within the framework of corporate objectives. In such a case, it may well be that an increase in sales in a particular segment will entail additional capital expenditure ahead of the time for which it is planned. If this is the case, it may make more sense to allocate available production capacity to more profitable segments in the short term, allowing sales to decline in another segment. Decisions such as this are likely to be more easily made against a backcloth of explicitly stated broad company objectives relating to all the major disciplines.

Likewise, objectives should be set for advertising, for example, which are wholly consistent with the wider marketing objectives. Objectives set in this way integrate the advertising effort with the other elements in the marketing mix and this leads to a consistent, logical marketing plan.

What is a corporate objective and what is a marketing objective?

A business starts at some time with resources and wants to use those resources to achieve something. What the business wants to achieve is a corporate objective, which describes a desired destination or result. How it is to be achieved is a strategy. In a sense, this means that the only true objective of a company is, by definition, what is stated in the corporate plan as being the principal purpose of its existence. Most often this is expressed in terms of profit, since profit is the means of satisfying shareholders or owners, and because it is the one universally accepted criterion by which efficiency can be evaluated, which will, in turn, lead to efficient resource allocation, economic and technological progressiveness and stability.

This means that stated desires, such as to expand segment share, to create a new image, to achieve an *x* per cent increase in sales, and so on, are in fact *strategies* at the corporate level, since they are the means by which a company will achieve its profit objectives. In practice, however, companies tend to operate by means of functional divisions, each with a separate identity, so that what is a strategy in the corporate plan becomes an objective within each department. For example, marketing strategies within the corporate plan become operating objectives within the marketing department, and strategies at the general level within the marketing department themselves become operating objectives at the next level down, so that an intricate web of interrelated objectives and strategies is built up at all levels within the framework of the overall company plan.

The really important point, however, apart from clarifying the difference between objectives and strategies, is that the further down the hierarchical chain one goes, the less likely it is that a stated objective will make a cost-effective contribution to company profits, unless it derives logically and directly from an objective at a higher level.

Corporate objectives and strategies can be simplified in the following way:

Corporate objective   Desired level of profitability.
Corporate strategies   Which segments and which products (marketing).
                         What kind of facilities (production and distribution).
                         Size and character of the staff/labour force (personnel).
                         Funding (finance).
                         Other corporate strategies such as social responsibility, corporate image, stock market image, employee image and so on.

It is now clear that at the next level down in the organisation (in other words, at the functional level) what products are to be sold into what segments, become *marketing objectives*, while the means of achieving these objectives using the marketing mix are *marketing strategies*. At the next level down there would be, say, *advertising objectives* and *advertising strategies*, with the subsequent *programmes* and *budgets* for achieving the objectives. In this way, a hierarchy of objectives and strategies can be traced back to the initial corporate objective. Figure 11.1 illustrates this point.

How to set marketing objectives

The Ansoff matrix (H.I. Ansoff, 'Strategies for diversification', *Harvard Business Review*, September–October 1957, 113–24) can be introduced here as a useful tool for thinking about marketing objectives. It is a concept normally written in terms of 'markets', but for the purposes of this book we will substitute (where appropriate) 'segment' for 'market'.

A firm's competitive situation can be simplified to two dimensions only, products and segments. To put it even more simply, Ansoff's framework is about what is sold (the 'product') and to whom it is sold (the 'segment'). Within this framework, Ansoff identifies four possible courses of action for the firm:

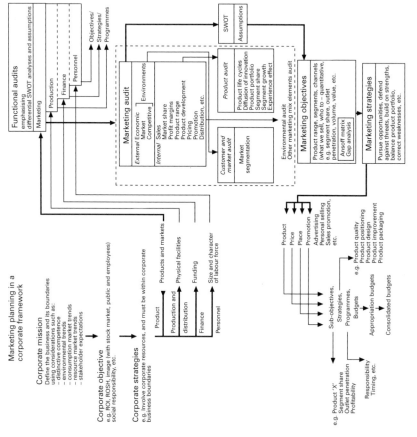

Figure 11.1 Objectives and strategies in a corporate framework

Source: Malcolm McDonald, *Marketing Plans – How to Prepare Them: How to Use Them,* (4th edn) Oxford, Heinemann, 1998.

- selling existing products to existing segments;
- extending existing products to new segments;
- developing new products for existing segments;
- developing new products for new segments.

The matrix in Figure 11.2 depicts these concepts.

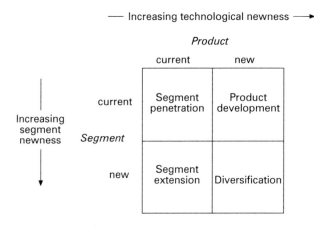

Figure 11.2   The Ansoff matrix

It is clear that the range of possible marketing objectives is very wide, since there will be degrees of technological newness and degrees of segment newness. Nevertheless, Ansoff's matrix provides a logical framework in which marketing objectives can be developed under each of the four main headings above. In other words, *marketing objectives are about products and segments only.* Common sense will confirm that it is only by selling something to someone that the company's financial goals can be achieved, and that advertising, pricing, service levels and so on, are the means (or strategies) by which it might succeed in doing this. Thus, pricing objectives, sales promotion objectives, advertising objectives and so on should not be confused with marketing objectives.

Marketing objectives are generally accepted as being quantitative commitments, usually stated either in standards of performance for a given operating period, or conditions to be achieved by given dates. Performance standards are usually stated in terms of sales volume and various measures of profitability. The conditions to be attained are usually a percentage of segment share and various other commitments, such as a percentage of the total number of a given type of retail outlet.

There is also broad agreement that objectives must be specific enough to enable subordinates to derive from them the general character of action required and the yardstick by which performance is to be judged. Objectives are the core of managerial action, providing direction to the plans. By asking where the operation should be at some future date, objectives are determined. Vague objectives, however emotionally appealing, are counter-productive to sensible planning, and are usually the result of the human propensity for wishful thinking, which often smacks more of cheerleading than of serious marketing leadership. What this really means is that while it is arguable whether directional terms such as 'decrease', 'optimise' or 'minimise' should be used as objectives, it seems logical that, unless there is some measure or yardstick against which to measure a sense of locomotion towards achieving them, they do not serve any useful purpose.

Ansoff defines an objective as 'a measure of the efficiency of the resource-conversion process. An objective contains three elements:

- the particular attribute that is chosen as a measure of efficiency;
- the yardstick or scale by which the attribute is measured;
- the particular value on the scale which the firm seeks to attain'.

Marketing objectives, then, are about each of the four main categories of the Ansoff matrix:

- Existing products in existing segments. (These may be many and varied and will certainly need to be set for all existing major segments and products.)
- New products in existing segments.
- Existing products in new segments.
- New products in new segments.

Thus, in the long run, it is only by selling something (a 'product') to someone (a 'segment') that any firm can succeed in staying in business profitably. Simply defined, product/segment strategy means the route chosen to achieve company goals through the range of products it offers to its chosen segments. Thus, the product/segment strategy represents a commitment to a future direction for the firm. Marketing objectives, then, are concerned solely with segments and products.

The general marketing *directions* which lead to the above objectives flow, of course, from product/market life cycle and portfolio analysis. However, when drawing up the objectives, we must concern ourselves with both the life cycles and portfolio analysis of our segments *and* the life cycles and portfolio analysis of our products in our chosen segments. The link between these two concepts is illustrated in Figure 11.3. For a full explanation, please refer to Malcolm McDonald's book, *Marketing Plans – How to Prepare Them: How to Use Them*, (4th edn) Oxford, Heinemann, 1998.

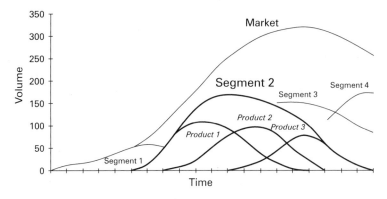

Figure 11.3 Product life cycles within segments

The marketing directions which come out of life cycle and portfolio analysis revolve around the following logical decisions (with a brief guide to the appropriate strategies also listed). Please note that, although we refer to the labels invented by the Boston Consulting Group (for example, 'cash cow'), such labels should not generally be used in connection with the DPM and are used here only for the purpose of explanation. We have suggested more appropriate labels for the DPM in Figure 11.4 and Table 11.1 below.

Maintain   This usually refers to the 'cash cow' type of segment/product (segments that fall in the bottom left-hand box of Figure 9.2) in which the company enjoys a competitive position, and reflects the desire to maintain a competitive and profitable position, even though it is acknowledged that these segments/products are not as attractive as other segments/products in terms of achieving the organisation's objectives.

   The emphasis will be on maintaining present earnings in the most profitable segments/products, rather than aggressive growth, while activity in those that are less profitable should be considered for cutting back. Marketing effort should be focused on differentiating products to maintain share of key segments. Discretionary marketing expenditure should be limited, especially when unchallenged by competitors, or when products have matured. Comparative prices should be stabilised, except when a temporary aggressive stance is necessary to defend segment share.

Improve   This usually refers to the 'star' type of segment/product (segments that appear in the top left-hand box) and reflects the desire to improve the competitive position in attractive segments which look as if their attractiveness will continue, or even improve. The obvious objective for such segments is to maintain your sales/volume growth rates at least at the segment growth rate, thus maintaining segment share, or to grow faster than the segment, thus increasing segment share.

Three principal factors should be considered:

- possible geographic expansion;
- possible product line expansion;
- possible product line differentiation.

These could be achieved by internal development, joint venture or acquisition.

The main point is that, in attractive segments, an *aggressive marketing posture is required*, together with a very tight budgeting and control process to ensure that capital resources are efficiently utilised.

Harvest   This usually refers to a particular category of 'dog' type segment/product (segments that appear in the bottom right-hand box, but towards the mid-point vertical line of the matrix) where the company has a moderately good to poor position (as opposed to an unquestionably poor position) and reflects the desire to relinquish competitive position in favour of short-term profit and cash flow, but not necessarily at the risk of losing the business in the short term. These are sometimes referred to as 'cash dogs'.

The reality of low growth should be acknowledged and the temptation to grow sales into these segments or grow sales of those products at the previous high rates of growth should be resisted. They should not be regarded as a 'marketing problem', which will be likely to lead to high advertising, promotion, product development and inventory costs, and therefore to lower profitability. Some of the 'maintain' policies may still be appropriate, but with more of an eye on profit and cash flow.

Finally, the attention of talented managers should be focused on these 'cash dogs'.

Exit   This usually refers to the genuine 'dog' type of segment/ product (segments that appear in the bottom right-hand box, but well to the right of the mid-point vertical axis), also sometimes to the 'question mark', and reflects a desire to divest because of a weak competitive position or because the cost of staying in it is prohibitive and the risk associated with

	improving its position is too high. Generally, immediate divestment is the preferred course of action, unless there is still the opportunity to generate some cash with minimal marketing expenditure.
Enter	This usually refers to the new and most promising emerging segments/products where it has been decided to invest for future segment/product leadership (selected segments that appear in the top right-hand box).

As already stated, however, great care should be taken not to follow slavishly any set of 'rules'. There can be no *automatic* policy for a particular segment or product, and SBU managers should consider three or more options before deciding on 'the best' for recommendation. Above all, SBU managers must evaluate the most attractive opportunities and assess the chances of success in the most realistic manner possible. This applies particularly to new business opportunities. New business opportunities would normally be expected to build on existing strengths, particularly in marketing, which can be subsequently expanded or supplemented.

As already stated, it can help the process if derogatory labels like 'dog', 'cash cow' and so on are avoided, if possible.

A full list of marketing guidelines as a precursor to objective setting is given in Figure 11.4. Table 11.1 sets out a fuller list which includes guidelines for functions other than marketing. One word of warning, however: such general guidelines should not be followed unquestioningly. They are included more as checklists of questions that should be asked about each major product in each major segment before setting marketing objectives and strategies.

It is at this stage that the circles in the DPM can be moved to show their relative size and position in three years' time. You can do this to show, first, where they will be if the company takes no action and, second, where you would ideally prefer them to be. These latter positions will, of course, become the marketing objectives. Precisely how this is done was shown in Chapter 10. It is, however, the key stage in the marketing planning process.

Competitive strategies

At this stage of the planning process, it would be helpful to explain recent developments in the field of competitive strategies, since an understanding of the subject is an essential prerequisite to setting appropriate marketing objectives.

Relative company competitiveness

High	Low
High		
Invest for growth	*Opportunistic*
Defend leadership, gain if possible.	The options are:
Accept moderate short-term profits and negative cash flow.	(i) move it to the left if resources are available to invest in it;
Consider geographic expansion, product line expansion, product differentiation.	(ii) keep a low profile until funds are available;
Upgrade production introduction effort.	(iii) divest to a buyer able to exploit the opportunity.
Aggressive marketing posture, viz. selling, advertising, pricing, sales promotion, service levels, as appropriate.	

Relative market attractiveness

Maintain market position, manage for sustained earnings	*'Selective' * *	*Cash*
Maintain segment position in most successful product lines.	Acknowledge low growth.	Prune product line aggressively.
Prune less successful product lines.	Do not view as a 'marketing' problem.	Maximise cash flow.
Differentiate products to maintain share of key segments.	Identify and exploit growth segments.	Minimise marketing expenditure.
Limit discretionary marketing expenditure.	Emphasise product quality to avoid 'commodity' competition.	Maintain or raise prices at the expense of volume.
Stabilise prices, except where a temporary aggressive stance is necessary to maintain segment share.	Systematically improve productivity.	
	Assign talented managers.	

Low

Figure 11.4   Strategies suggested by portfolio matrix analysis

* The term 'selective' refers to those segments or products which fall on or near the vertical dividing line in a DPM.

Table 11.1   Other functional guidelines suggested by portfolio matrix analysis

	Invest	Maintain	Selective	Cash	Opportunistic
Main thrust	Invest for growth	Maintain segment position, manage for earnings	Maintain selectively	Manage for cash	Opportunistic development
Segment share	Maintain or increase dominance	Maintain or slightly milk for earnings	Maintain selectively	Forgo share for profit	Invest selectively in share
Products	Differentiate, line expansion	Prune less successful, differentiate for key segments	Emphasise product quality. Differentiate	Aggressively prune	Differentiation, line expansion
Price	Lead. Aggressive pricing for share	Stabilise prices/raise	Maintain or raise	Raise	Aggressive, price for share
Promotion	Aggressive activity	Limit	Maintain selectively	Minimise	Aggressive activity
Distribution	Broaden distribution	Hold wide distribution pattern	Maintain selectively according to segment	Gradually withdraw distribution	Limited coverage
Cost control	Tight control. Go for scale economies	Emphasise cost reduction, viz. variable costs	Tight control	Aggressively reduce both fixed and variable	Tight, but not at expense of entrepreneurship
Production	Expand, invest (organic, acquisition, joint venture)	Maximise capacity utilisation	Increase productivity, for example, specialisation/ automation	Free up capacity	Invest
R&D	Expand, invest	Focus on specific projects	Invest selectively	None	Invest
Personnel	Upgrade management in key functional areas	Maintain. Reward efficiency, tighten organisation	Allocate key managers	Cut back organisation	Invest
Investment	Fund growth	Limit fixed investment	Invest selectively	Minimise and divest opportunistically	Fund growth
Working capital	Reduce in process, extend credit	Tighten credit, reduce accounts receivable, increase inventory turn	Reduce	Aggressively reduce	Invest

One of the principal purposes of marketing strategy is for you to be able to choose the customers, hence the segments, you wish to deal with. In this respect, the DPM discussed in Chapter 9 is particularly useful. The main components of competitive strategy are:

- the company;
- customers;
- competitors.

Clearly, if we are to succeed, we need to work hard at developing a sustainable competitive advantage. The important word here is 'sustainable', as temporary advantages can be gained in numerous ways, such as from a price reduction or from a clever sales promotion.

Most business people would agree that as segments mature, the only way to grow the business without diversifying is at the expense of competitors, which implies the need to understand in depth the characteristics of each important segment to the company and of the main competitors in it. We briefly referred to the leading thinker in this field in Chapter 9, namely Michael E. Porter of the Harvard Business School, and any reader wishing to explore this vital subject in more depth should refer to his book, *Competitive Strategy: Techniques for Analysing Industries and Competitors*, New York, The Free Press, 1980.

Perhaps the best way to summarise this complex subject would be to tell a story. Imagine three tribes on a small island fighting each other because resources are scarce. One tribe decides to move to a larger adjacent island, sets up camp, and is followed eventually by the other two, who also set up their own separate camps. At first it is a struggle to establish themselves, but gradually they begin to occupy increasing parts of the island; eventually, many years later, they begin to fight again over adjacent land. The more innovative tribal chief – that is, the one who was first to move to the new island – sits down with his senior warriors and ponders what to do, since none are very keen to move to yet another island. They decide that the only two options are:

- attack and go relentlessly for the enemy's territory;
- settle for a smaller part of the island and build in it an impregnable fortress.

These two options, namely terrain or impregnable fortress, are, in fact, the same options that face business people as they contemplate competitive strategy. Let's look in turn at each of these options, continuing for a moment longer with the military analogy, and starting with terrain.

Imagine two armies facing each other on a field of battle. One army has fifteen soldiers in it, the other twelve (depicted by circles). Imagine also that they face each other with rifles and all fire one shot at the other at the same time, but they don't all aim at the same soldier! Figure 11.5 depicts the progress of each side in disposing of the other. It will be seen that after only three volleys, the army on the right has only one soldier remaining, while the army on the left, with eight soldiers remaining, is still a viable fighting unit.

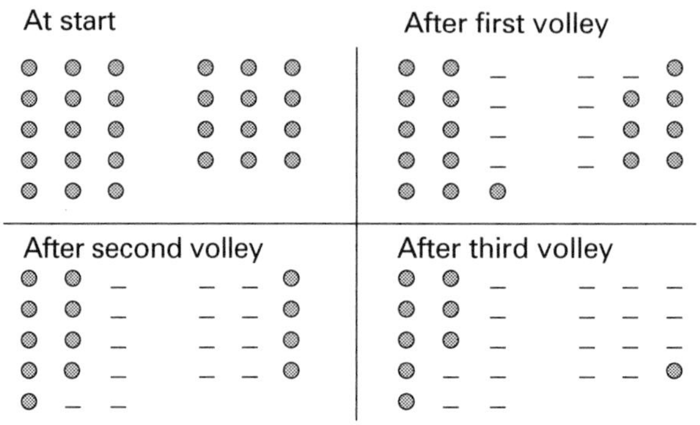

Figure 11.5   The importance of market share

One interesting fact about this story is that the effect observed here is *geometric* rather than *arithmetic*, and is a perfect demonstration of the effect of size and what happens when all things are equal, except size. The parallel in industry, of course, is segment share. Just look at what used to happen in the computer industry when GE, Rank Xerox, RCA, ICL and others attacked the giant (and once totally impregnable) IBM in its core segments. The larger competitor was able to win the battle. So, all things being equal, a company with a larger segment share than another should win in the long term over a smaller competitor. Or *should* they? Clearly, this is not inevitable, providing the smaller companies take evasive action. Staying with the computer industry, just look at how successful AT&T Global Information Systems have been with their 'global fortress' strategy (for example, Automatic Teller Machines (ATMs) for the financial market), Control Data with their scientific controls and, more recently, Dell Computers, each of whom focused on particular segments in the overall market *not* dominated by the likes of IBM.

Put yet another way, let us look for a moment at the economists' model of supply and demand shown in Figure 11.6.

Here, we see that when supply is greater than demand, price will fall, and that when demand exceeds supply, the price will tend to rise. The equilibrium point is when supply matches demand. The only way a competitor can avoid the worst effects of such a situation is by taking one of the following actions:

- being the lowest cost supplier;
- differentiating the product in some way so as to be able to command a higher price.

Supply
Price
Demand
Volume

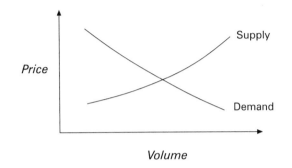

Figure 11.6 Supply and demand curves

Michael Porter combined these two options into a simple matrix, as shown in Figure 11.7.

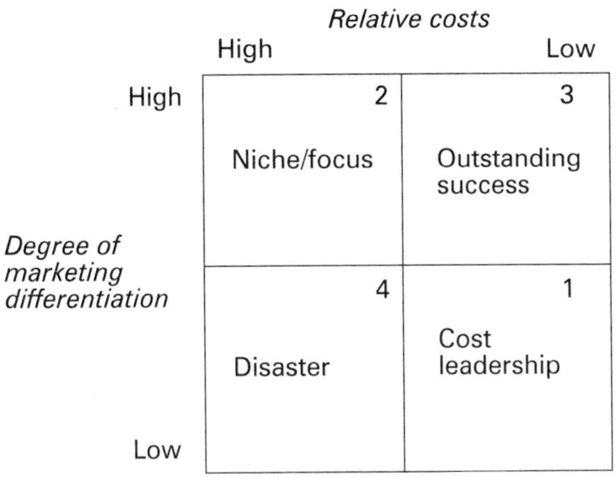

Relative costs
High
Low
High
2
Niche/focus
3
Outstanding success
Degree of marketing differentiation
4
Disaster
1
Cost leadership
Low

Figure 11.7 Cost versus differentiation matrix

Source: M. E. Porter, *Competitive Advantage – Creating and Sustaining Superior Performance*, New York, The Free Press, 1985.

It can be seen that Box 1 represents a sound strategy, particularly in commodity-type markets such as bulk chemicals, where differentiation is harder to achieve because of the identical nature of the chemical make-up of the product. In such cases, it is wise to recognise the reality and adopt a productive corporate drive towards being the corporate leader. It is here that the *'experience effect'* becomes especially important.

Very briefly, the experience effect, which also includes the 'learning curve', is a recognition of the fact that the more we do something, the better we are at doing it. Included in the experience effect are such items as better productivity from plant and equipment, product design improvements, process innovations, labour efficiency, work specialisation, and so on. In addition to the experience effect, and not necessarily mutually exclusive, are *economies of scale* that come with growth. For example, capital costs do not increase in direct proportion to capacity, which results in lower depreciation charges per unit of output, lower operating costs in the form of the number of operatives, lower marketing, sales, administration and R&D costs, and lower raw materials and shipping costs. It is generally recognised, however, that cost decline applies more to the value-added elements of cost than to bought-in supplies. In fact, the Boston Consulting Group discovered that costs declined by up to 30 per cent for every cumulative doubling of output. This phenomenon is shown in Figure 11.8.

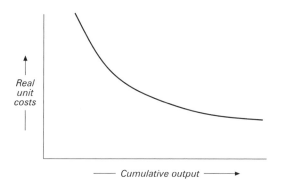

Figure 11.8   The impact on unit costs of the learning curve

There is an overwhelming body of evidence to show that this real cost reduction actually occurs, in which case it follows that the greater your volume, the lower your unit costs should be. Thus, irrespective of what happens to the price of your product, providing you have the highest segment share (hence the biggest volume), you should always be relatively more profitable than your competitors.

Many companies, however, such as Jaguar and BMW, could not hope to be low cost producers. Consequently, their whole corporate philosophy is geared to differentiation and what we have called 'added value'. Clearly, this represents a sensible strategy for any company that cannot hope to be a world cost beater and, indeed, many of the world's great companies succeed by means of such a focus and locate themselves in Box 2 (in Figure 11.7). Many of these companies also succeed in pushing themselves into Box 3, the outstanding success box, by occupying what can be called 'global fortresses'. A good example of this is AT&T Global Information Systems who dominate the world's banking and retail markets with their focused technological and marketing approach.

Companies like McDonalds and GE, however, typify Box 3, where low costs, differentiation and world leadership are combined in their corporate strategies.

Only Box 4 remains. Here we can see that a combination of commodity-type markets and high relative costs will result in disaster sooner or later. A position here is tenable only while demand exceeds supply. When, however, segments in these markets mature, there is little hope for companies who find themselves in this unenviable position.

An important point to remember when thinking about differentiation as a strategy is that you must still be *cost effective*. It is a myth to assume that sloppy management and high costs are acceptable as long as the product has a good image and lots of added value. Also, in thinking about differentiation, please refer back to the section on benefit analysis in Chapter 6, for it is here that the route to differentiation will be found. It is also clear that there is not much point in offering benefits that are costly for you to provide but which are not highly regarded by customers: in other words, benefits which are not their important CPIs. So consider using a matrix like the one given in Figure 11.9 to classify your benefits. Clearly, you will succeed best by providing as many benefits as possible that fall into the top right-hand box.

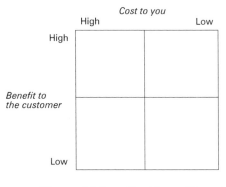

Figure 11.9   Cost/benefit matrix

ICI is a good example of a company that is proactively changing its global strategy by systematically moving away from bulk chemicals in Box 1 (in Figure 11.7) towards speciality chemicals in Box 2 and then going on to occupy a 'global fortress' position in these specialities (Box 3).

The main point here, however, is that when setting marketing objectives, it is essential for you to have a sound grasp of the position in your segments of yourself and your competitors and to adopt appropriate postures for the several elements of your business, all of which may be different. It may be necessary, for example, to accept that part of your product portfolio is in the 'Disaster' box (Box 4). You may well be forced to have some products here: for example, to complete your product range to enable you to offer your more profitable products into your chosen segment(s). The point is that you must adopt an appropriate stance towards these products and set your marketing objectives accordingly, using, where appropriate, the guidelines given in Figure 11.4 and Table 11.1.

Finally, here are some very general guidelines to help you think about competitive strategies:

- know the terrain on which you are fighting (the market and its segments);
- know the resources of your enemies (competitive analysis);
- do something with determination that the enemy isn't expecting.

Where to start (gap analysis)

Figure 11.10 illustrates what is commonly referred to as 'gap analysis'. Essentially, what it says is that if the corporate sales and financial objectives are greater than the current long-range forecasts, there is a gap which has to be filled.

The 'operations gap' can be filled in two ways:

- improved productivity (for example, reduce costs, improve the sales mix, increase price);
- segment penetration (for example, increase usage, increase segment share).

The 'new strategies gap' can be filled in three ways:

- segment extension (for example, find new user groups, enter new segments, geographical expansion);
- product development;
- diversification (for example, selling new products to new segments).

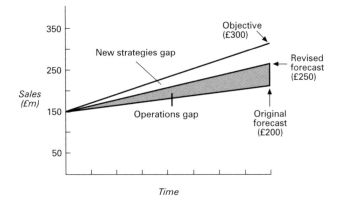

Figure 11.10   Gap analysis

A fourth option, of course, is to reduce the objectives!

If improved productivity is one method by which the operations gap is to be filled, care must be taken not to use measures such as reducing marketing costs by 20 per cent overall. The portfolio analysis undertaken earlier will indicate that this would be totally inappropriate for some segments (although it may be applicable to some of the products at the later stages of their life cycle sold into these segments) for which increased marketing expenditure may be needed, while for others a 20 per cent reduction in marketing costs may not be sufficient.

As for the other options, it is clear that segment penetration should always be a company's first option, since it makes far more sense to attempt to increase profits and cash flow from *existing* segments and products initially, because this is usually the least costly and the least risky. This is so because, for its present segments and products, a company has developed knowledge and skills which it can use competitively.

For the same reason, it makes more sense in many cases to move along the horizontal axis of the Ansoff matrix for further growth before attempting to find new segments. The reason for this is that it normally takes many years for a company to get to know its segments and to build up a reputation. That reputation and trust, embodied in either the company's name or in its brands, is rarely transferable to new segments, where other companies are already entrenched.

It is essential that you ensure that the method chosen to fill the gap is consistent with the company's capabilities and builds on its strengths. For example, it would normally prove far less profitable for a dry goods grocery manufacturer to introduce frozen foods than to add another dry foods product. Likewise, if a product could be sold through existing channels using the existing salesforce, this is far less risky than introducing a new product that requires new channels and new selling skills.

Exactly the same applies to the company's production, distribution and people. Whatever new products are developed should be as consistent as possible with the company's known strengths and capabilities. Clearly, the use of existing plant capacity is generally preferable to new processes. Also, the amount of additional investment is important. Technical personnel are highly trained and specialised, and whether this competence can be transferred to a new field must be considered. A product requiring new raw materials may also require new handling and storage techniques, which could prove expensive.

It can now be appreciated why going into new segments with new products (diversification) is the riskiest strategy of all, because *new* resources and *new* management skills have to be developed. This is why the history of commerce is replete with examples of companies that went bankrupt through moving into areas where they had little or no distinctive competence. This is also why many companies that diversified through acquisition during periods of high economic growth have since divested themselves of businesses that were not basically compatible with their own distinctive competence.

The Ansoff matrix, of course, is not a simple four-box matrix, for it will be obvious that there are degrees of technological newness, as well as degrees of segment newness. Figure 11.11 illustrates the point. It also demonstrates more easily why any movement should generally aim to keep a company as close as possible to its present position, rather than moving it to a totally unrelated position, except in the most unusual circumstances.

Nevertheless, the life cycle phenomenon will inevitably *force* companies to move along one or more of the Ansoff matrix axes if they are to continue to increase their sales and profits. A key question to be asked, then, is *how* this important decision is to be taken, given the risks involved.

A full list of the possible methods involved in the process of gap analysis is given in Figure 11.12. From this, it will be seen that there is nothing an executive can do to fill the gap that is not included in the list. The precise methodology to implement this concept can be found in Malcolm McDonald, *Marketing Plans – How to Prepare Them: How to Use Them*, (4th edn) Oxford, Heinemann, 1998.

At this point, it is important to stress that the 'objectives' point in gap analysis should *not* be an extrapolation, but your own view of what revenue would make this into an excellent business. The word 'excellent' must, of course, be relative only to comparable businesses. If all the executives in a company responsible for SBUs were to do this, and then work out what needed to be done to fill any gaps, it is easy to understand why this would result in an excellent overall business performance.

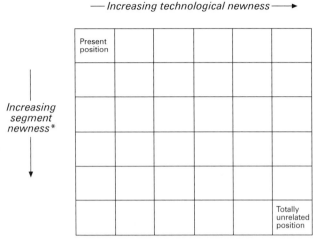

*Which eventually could become new segments in new markets

Figure 11.11   Technological and segment newness

Marketing strategies

What a company wants to accomplish, then, in terms of such things as segment share and volume is a 'marketing objective'. How the company intends to go about achieving its objectives is 'strategy'. Strategy is the overall route to the achievement of specific objectives and should describe the means by which objectives are to be reached, the time programme and the allocation of resources. It does not delineate the individual courses the resulting activity will follow.

There is a clear distinction between strategy and detailed implementation, or tactics. Marketing strategy reflects the company's best opinion as to how it can most profitably apply its skills and resources to the marketplace. Inevitably, it is broad in scope. The plan which stems from it will spell out action and timings and will contain the detailed contribution expected from each department.

There is a similarity between strategy in business and strategic military development. One looks at the enemy, the terrain, the resources under command, and then decides whether to attack the whole front, an area of enemy weakness, to feint in one direction while attacking in another, or to attempt an encirclement of the enemy's position. The policy and mix, the ways in which they are to be used, and the criteria for judging success, all come under the heading of strategy. The action steps are tactics.

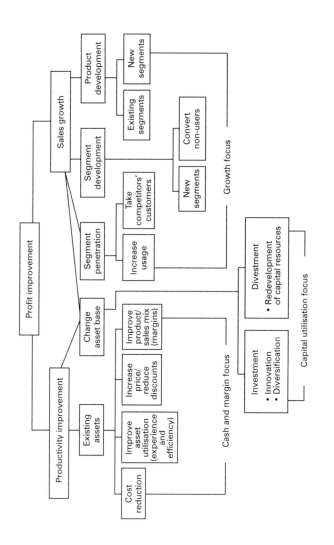

Figure 11.12 Profit/division profit improvement option (adapted from John Saunders, Loughborough University, used with his kind permission)

Similarly, in marketing, the commitment, mix and type of resources as well as guidelines and criteria that must be met, all come under the heading of strategy. For example, the decision to use distributors in all but the three largest segments, in which company salespeople will be used, is a strategic decision. The selection of particular distributors is a tactical decision.

The following headings indicate the general content of strategy statements in the area of marketing which emerge from marketing literature:

- policies and procedures relating to the products to be offered, such as range, additions, deletions, quality, technical specification, design, positioning, branding, packaging and labelling and so on;
- pricing levels to be adopted, margins and discount policies for product groups in particular segments;
- the policies for non-personal communication using advertising, direct mail and sales promotion (the creative approach, the type of media, type of displays, the amount to spend and so on);
- what emphasis is to be placed on personal selling, the sales approach, sales training and so on;
- the distributive channels to be used and the relative importance of each;
- warehousing, transportation, inventories, service levels and so on, in relation to distribution.

Thus, marketing strategies are the means by which marketing objectives will be achieved and are generally concerned with the four major elements of the marketing mix as follows:

Product The general policies for product deletions, modifications, additions, design, packaging and so on.

Price The general pricing policies to be followed for product groups in market segments.

Promotion The general policies for communicating with customers under the relevant headings, such as: advertising, salesforce, sales promotion, public relations, exhibitions, direct mail and so on.

Place The general policies for channels and customer service levels.

The following list of marketing strategies (in summary form) covers the majority of options open under the headings of the four Ps:

- *Product* expand the line;
  acquire new lines/production facilities;
  change performance, quality or features;
  consolidate the line;
  change design;
  standardise design;

positioning;
change the product portfolio;
branding;
● *Price*   change unit price, terms or conditions;
skimming policies;
penetration policies;
● *Promotion* change advertising or promotion;
change selling;
● *Place*   change delivery or distribution;
consolidate distribution;
change service levels;
change channels;
change the degree of forward integration.

You should refer to Chapters 7 to 10 of Malcolm McDonald's *Marketing Plans – How to Prepare Them: How to Use Them* (4th edn), Oxford, Heinemann, 1998, for a much more detailed consideration of promotion, price and place. These chapters describe what should appear in advertising, sales, pricing and distribution plans. This detail is intended for those whose principal concern is the preparation of a detailed one-year operational or tactical plan. The relationship between this detail and the strategic plan is in the provision of information to enable the planner to delineate broad strategies under the headings outlined above. In Chapter 5 of the same book, all the product options are covered.

Formulating marketing strategies is one of the most critical and difficult parts of the entire marketing process. It sets the limit of success. Communicated to all management levels, it indicates what strengths are to be developed, what weaknesses are to be remedied, and in what manner. Marketing strategies enable operating decisions to bring the company into the right relationship with the emerging pattern of market opportunities, which previous analysis has shown to offer the highest prospect of success.

It is worth stressing again that the vital phase of setting objectives and strategies is a highly complex process which, if done badly, will probably result in the considerable misdirection of resources.

Process check

This chapter has confirmed the need for setting clear, definitive objectives for all aspects of the marketing programme, and demonstrated that marketing objectives themselves have to derive logically from corporate objectives. The advantages of this practice are that it allows all concerned with marketing activities to concentrate their particular contribution on achieving the overall marketing objectives, as well as facilitating meaningful and constructive evaluation of all marketing activity.

For the practical purpose of marketing planning, it will be apparent from the observations above (concerning what was referred to as a 'hierarchy of objectives') that overall marketing objectives have to be broken down into sub-objectives which, taken all together, will achieve the overall objectives. By breaking down the overall objectives, the problem of strategy development becomes more manageable, hence easier.

A two-year study of 35 top industrial companies by McKinsey and Company revealed that leader companies agreed that market/product strategy is the key to the task of keeping shareholders' equity rising. Clearly, then, setting objectives and strategies in relation to market segments and products is a most important step in the marketing planning process.

Once agreement has been reached on the broad marketing objectives and strategies, those responsible for programmes can now proceed to the detailed planning stage, developing the appropriate overall strategy statements into sub-objectives.

Plans constitute the vehicle for getting to the destination along the chosen route, or the detailed execution of the strategy. The term 'plan' is often used synonymously in marketing literature with the terms 'programme' and 'schedule'. A plan containing detailed lists of tasks to be completed, together with responsibilities, timing and cost, is sometimes referred to as an appropriation budget, which is merely a detailing of the actions to be carried out and the expected sterling results in carrying them out. More about this can be read in Chapters 7 to 10 of *Marketing Plans – How to Prepare Them: How to use Them* which looks at advertising, sales promotion, the sales plan, pricing and distribution plan.

PART III

Segmentation and Organisations

12 *Organisational Issues in Market Segmentation*

The structuring of markets into clearly defined segments is undoubtedly a key input for the company's marketing plan. Segmentation not only identifies the customer groups your company should focus its resources into, but also (through the detailed analysis required in a professionally conducted segmentation process) identifies vitally important elements of a successful marketing strategy. Having an organisation which is both supportive of the process and supportive of carrying through the findings into the market place is therefore crucial.

The organisational issues associated with segmentation can best be grouped under two distinct headings:

- the company's approach to addressing segmentation; and
- the company's approach to implementing the conclusion.

These two areas are, however, closely linked as the degree of commitment to implementation is directly related to the extent of an organisation's commitment to, and involvement in, its segmentation review. For example, if the review is put into the hands of an 'elite group' who are required to look at segmentation as a 'closed' and confidential study, the implementation of their findings will, at best, be slow and tortuous or, at worst, simply fail.

Segmentation as a company exercise

Marketing's contribution to business success in manufacturing, the provision of services, distribution or retailing activities lies in its commitment to detailed analysis of future opportunities to meet customer needs and a wholly professional approach to selling to well-defined market segments those products or services that deliver the sought-after benefits. Achieving revenue budgets and sales forecasts are a function of how good our intelligence services are, how well suited our strategies are, and how well we are led.

Support from the chief executive and senior management

There can be no doubt that unless the chief executive sees the need for a segmentation review, understands the process and shows an active interest in it, it is virtually impossible for a senior marketing executive to implement the conclusions in a meaningful way.

This is particularly so in companies that are organised on the basis of divisional management, for which the marketing executive has no profit responsibility and in which he has no line management authority. In such cases, it is comparatively easy for senior operational managers to create 'political' difficulties, the most serious of which is just to ignore the new segments and their requirements entirely.

The vital role that the chief executive and senior management *must* play in segmentation underlines one of the key points in this chapter: that it is *people* who make systems work, and that system design and implementation have to take account of the 'personality' of both the organisation and the people involved, and that these are different in all organisations. A most striking feature is the difference in 'personality' between companies, and the fact that within any one company there is a marked similarity between the attitudes of executives. These attitudes vary from the impersonal, autocratic kind at one extreme to the highly personal, participative kind at the other.

Any system, therefore, has to be designed around the people who have to make it work, and has to take account of the prevailing conditions, attitudes, skills, resource availability and organisational constraints. Since the chief executive and senior management are the key influencers of these factors, without their active support and participation any formalised approach to segmentation is unlikely to work. The worst outcome can be a chief executive and senior management ignoring the plans built out of the segmentation review and continuing to make decisions which appear illogical to those who have participated in the segmentation process and in producing the resulting marketing plan. This quickly destroys any credibility that the emerging plans might have had, leading to the demise of the procedures and to serious levels of frustration throughout the organisation.

Indeed, there is some evidence leading to the belief that chief executives who fail, first, to understand the essential role of marketing in generating profitable revenue in a business and, second, to understand how marketing can be integrated into the other functional areas of the business through marketing planning procedures, are a key contributory factor to poor economic performance. There is a depressing preponderance of managers with an 'accounting' mentality who live by the rule of 'the bottom line' and who apply universal financial criteria indiscriminately to all products and segments, irrespective of the long-term consequences. There is a similar preponderance of managers with an 'engineering' mentality who see marketing as an unworthy activity that is something to do with activities such as television advertising, and who think of their products only in terms of their technical features and functional characteristics, in spite of the overwhelming body of evidence that exists that these are only a part of what a customer buys. Not surprisingly, in companies headed by people like this, market-based segmentation reviews and marketing planning are either non-existent, or where they are tried, they fail. This is the most frequently encountered barrier to effective marketing.

Size and diversity

In a large diversified company operating in many markets, a complex combination of market, segment, product and financial plans is possible. For example, what is required at the individual segment level will be different from what is required at headquarters level, while it is clear that the total corporate plan has to be constructed from the individual building blocks. Furthermore, the function of marketing itself may be further functionalised for the purpose of planning, such as market research, market management, segment management, product management, advertising, selling, distribution and so on.

Clearly, in a large diversified group, irrespective of any organisational issues, anything other than a systematic approach to the issues addressed in marketing is unlikely to enable the necessary control to be exercised over the public 'face' of the corporation. As size and diversity grow, so the degree of formalisation in its marketing processes must also increase. This can be simplified in the form of a matrix as shown in Figure 12.1.

Size is without doubt the biggest determinant of the two in the type of marketing systems required.

In small companies, there is rarely much diversity of markets, and top management has an in-depth knowledge of the key determinants of success and failure. While in such companies the central control mechanism is the sales forecast and budget, top managers are able to explain the rationale lying behind the numbers; they have a very clear view of their comparative strengths and weaknesses; and they are able to explain the company's marketing strategy without difficulty. This understanding and familiarity with the strategy is shared with key operating subordinates by means of personal, face-to-face dialogue throughout the year. Subordinates are operating within a logical framework of ideas, which they understand. There is a shared understanding between top and middle management of the industry and prevailing business conditions. In such cases, since either the owner or a director is usually also deeply involved in the day-to-day management of the business, the need to rely on informational inputs from subordinates is considerably less than in larger companies. Consequently, there is less need for written procedures about understanding markets, SWOT analyses, marketing objectives and strategies, as these are carried out by senior management, often informally at meetings and in face-to-face discussions with subordinates, the results of which are the basis of forecasts and budgets. Written documents in respect of the target segments and their price, advertising and selling strategies, for example, are very brief, but those managers responsible for those aspects of the business know what part they are expected to play in achieving the company's objectives. Such companies are, therefore, operating according to a set of structured procedures, but in a relatively informal way.

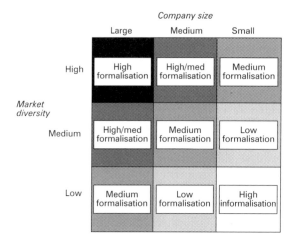

Figure 12.1 The influence of size and diversity on the need for formalisation in marketing

On the other hand, many small companies that have a poor understanding of the marketing concept and in which the top manager leaves his or her strategy implicit, suffer many serious operational problems.

These operational problems become progressively worse as the size of company increases. As the number and levels of management increase, it becomes progressively more difficult for top management to enjoy an in-depth knowledge of industry and business conditions by informal, face-to-face means. In the absence of written procedures and a structured framework, the different levels of operating management become increasingly less able to react in a rational way to day-to-day pressures.

From the point of view of management control, the least complex environment in which to work is an undiversified company. For the purposes of this discussion, 'undiversified' is taken to mean companies with homogeneous customer groups or limited product lines. For example, a diverse range of products could be sold into only one market such as, say, the motor industry, with this being the only 'market' in which segmentation is required. Alternatively, hydraulic hoses could be sold to many diverse markets, but it is only the benefits being sought from hydraulic hoses the segmentation work is required to consider. However, the need for institutionalised marketing processes will still increase with size and the resulting complexity of the management task. For example, an oil company will operate in many diverse markets around the world, through many different kinds of marketing systems, and with varying levels of segment share and segment growth. In most respects, therefore, the control function for headquarters management is just as difficult and complex as that in a major diversified conglomerate. The major difference is the greater level of in-depth knowledge which top management has about the key determinants of success and failure underlying the market or product world-wide, because of its homogeneity.

As a result of this homogeneity of market or product, it is usually possible for headquarters to impose world-wide policies on operating units in respect of things such as certain aspects of advertising, public relations, packaging, pricing, trade marks, product development and so on, whereas in the headquarters of a diversified conglomerate, overall policies of this kind tend to be impracticable and meaningless.

The view is often expressed that common marketing processes in companies comprising many heterogeneous units is less helpful and confuses rather than improves understanding between operating units and headquarters. However, the truth is that conglomerates often consist of several smaller multinationals, some diversified and some not, and that the actual task of marketing rests on the lowest level in an organisation at which there is general management profit responsibility. Forecasting and budgeting systems by themselves rarely encourage anything but a short-term, parochial view of the business at these levels, and in the absence of the kind of procedures described in this book, and found in books devoted to the process of marketing planning, higher levels of management do not have a sufficiently rational basis on which to set long-term marketing objectives.

Exactly the same principles apply at the several levels of control in a diversified multinational conglomerate, in that at the highest level of control there has to be some rational basis on which to make decisions about the portfolio of investments, and research has shown that the most successful companies are those with standard marketing procedures to aid this process. In such companies there is a hierarchy of audits, segments, SWOT analyses, assumptions, objectives, strategies and marketing programmes, with increasingly more detail required in the procedures at the lowest levels in the organisation. The precise details of each step vary according to circumstances, but the eventual output of the process is in a universally consistent form.

The basis on which the whole system rests is the information input requirements at the highest level of command. The marketing objectives and strategies necessary to exploit the chosen segments are frequently synthesised into a multi-disciplinary corporate plan at the next general management profit-responsible level, until at the highest level of command the corporate plan consists largely of financial information and summaries of the major operational activities. This is an important point, for there is rarely a consolidated operational marketing plan at conglomerate headquarters. This often exists only at the lowest level of general management profit responsibility, and even here it is sometimes incorporated into the corporate plan, particularly in capital goods companies, where engineering, manufacturing and technical services are major factors in commercial success.

To summarise, the smaller the company, the more informal and personal the procedures for segmentation and marketing planning. As company size and diversity increase, so the need for institutionalised procedures increases.

The really important issue in any system is the degree to which it enables *control* to be exercised over the key determinants of success and failure. A formally designed system seeks to find the right balance between the flexibility of operating units to react to changes in local market conditions and centralised control. The main role of headquarters is to harness the company's strengths on a world-wide basis and to ensure that lower-level decisions do not cause problems in other areas and lead to wasteful duplication. At the same time, however, it must not stifle creativity.

There would be little disagreement that in today's abrasive, turbulent and highly competitive environment, it is those firms that succeed in extracting entrepreneurial ideas and creative marketing programmes from systems that are necessarily yet acceptably formalised, that will succeed in the long run. Much innovative flair can so easily get stifled by systems.

Injecting new enthusiasm into the periodic reviews of the market is often best achieved by the involvement of senior managers, from the chief executive down through the hierarchy. Essentially what takes place is a personalised presentation of the findings in the review of the market and its segments, together with the proposed marketing objectives and strategies and outline budgets for the strategic planning period. These are discussed, and amended where necessary, and agreed in various synthesised formats at the hierarchical levels in the organisation *before* any detailed operational planning takes place. It is at such meetings that managers are called upon to justify their views, which tends to force them to be bolder and more creative than they would have been had they been allowed merely to send in their proposals. Obviously, much depends even here on the degree to which managers take a critical stance, and this will be much greater when the chief executive himself takes an active part in the process. *Every hour of time devoted at this stage by the chief executive has a multiplier effect throughout the remainder of the process.* And let it be remembered we are not, repeat not, talking about budgets at this juncture in anything other than outline form.

Although the segmentation task and the development of the findings into marketing objectives and strategies is less complicated in small, undiversified companies, and there is less need for formalised procedures than in large, diversified companies, experience has shown that exactly the same framework should be used in all circumstances, and that this approach brings similar benefits to all.

In a multinational conglomerate, headquarters management is able to assess major trends in markets and products around the world, and is thus able to develop strategies for investment, expansion, diversification and divestment on a global basis. For their part, subsidiary management can develop appropriate strategies with a sense of locomotion towards the achievement of coherent overall goals.

This is achieved by means of synthesised information flows from the bottom upwards, which facilitates useful comparison of performance around the world, and the diffusion of valuable information, skills, experiences and systems from the top downwards. The procedures which facilitate the provision of such information and knowledge transfers also encourage operational management to think strategically about their own areas of responsibility, instead of managing only for the short term.

It is abundantly clear that it is through the complete process of segmentation, marketing planning and planning skills that such benefits are achieved, and that discussions such as those about the standardisation process are largely irrelevant. Any standardisation that may be possible will become clear only if a company can successfully develop a system for identifying the needs of each market and each segment in which it operates, and for organising resources to satisfy those needs in such a way that it results in the best utilisation of resources world wide.

Planning for the segmentation process

A recipe for failure in segmentation is to assume that the process appearing in this book can be implemented immediately and taken all the way through to its conclusions in a matter of days, or even weeks. If the outcome of the review is best put into effect by incorporating it into a complete marketing planning system, then we are talking about years, with research indicating that a period of around three years is required in a major company before a complete marketing planning system can be implemented according to its design.

Failure, or partial failure, then, is often the result of not developing a timetable for introducing a new system, to take account of the following:

- the need to communicate why segmentation and reviews of segmentation are necessary;
- the need to recruit top management support and participation;
- the need to test the process out on a limited basis to demonstrate its effectiveness and value;
- the need for training programmes, or workshops, to train line management in its use;
- complete lack of data and information in some parts of the world, or data and information built either around products or around past 'segments';
- shortage of resources.

Above all, a resolute sense of purpose and dedication is required, tempered by patience and a willingness to appreciate the inevitable problems which will be encountered in implementing the conclusions.

This is all closely linked to the next issue companies need to get right in the segmentation process: line management support.

Line management support

Hostility, lack of skills, lack of data and information, lack of resources, and an inadequate organisational structure, all add up to a failure to obtain the willing participation of operational managers.

New processes inevitably require considerable explanation of the procedures involved and the accompanying pro-formas, flow charts and so on. Often these devices arrive on the desk of a busy line manager in the form of a book or a manual, without any previous explanation or discussion. The immediate reaction often appears to be fear of failing to understand it, let alone comply with it, followed by anger and finally rejection. Headquarters becomes the remote 'ivory tower', divorced from the reality of the market place.

This is often exacerbated by line management's absorption in the present operating and reward system, which is geared to the achievement of *current* results, while the segmentation process, and its translation into operational requirements through the marketing planning process, is geared towards establishing the future revenue sources for the company. Also, because of the trend in recent years towards the frequent movement of executives around organisations, there is less interest in spending time on future business gains from which someone else is likely to benefit.

The solutions to the problems which could stand in the way of line management support require a good deal of patience, common sense, ingenuity and flexibility on the part of both headquarters and operating management. This is closely connected with the need to consider resource availability and the prevailing organisation structure. The problem of lack of reliable data and information can only be solved by devoting time and money to its solution and, where available resources are scarce, it is unlikely that the information demands of headquarters can be met.

It is for this reason that some kind of appropriate headquarters organisation has to be found for the collection and dissemination of valuable information, and that training has to be provided on ways of solving this problem.

Again, these issues are complicated by the varying degrees of size and complexity of companies. It is surprising to see the extent to which organisational structures cater inadequately for marketing as a function. In small companies, there is often no-one other than the sales manager, who spends all his time engaged either in personal selling or in managing the salesforce. Unless the chief executive is marketing orientated, detailed extensive studies of markets to determine the most appropriate segments for the business will just not be done.

In medium-sized and large companies, particularly those that are divisionalised, there is rarely any provision at board level for marketing as a discipline. Sometimes there is a commercial director with line management responsibility for the operating divisions, but apart from sales managers at divisional level, or a marketing manager at head office level, marketing as a function is not particularly well catered for. Where there is a marketing manager, that person tends to be somewhat isolated from the mainstream activities.

The most successful organisations are those with a fully integrated marketing function, whether it is line management responsible for sales, or a staff function, with operating units being a microcosm of the head office organisation.

Integrating the segmentation process into a marketing planning system and into a total corporate planning system

Segmentation as a stand-alone process will end up being an intellectually challenging, but theoretical, exercise if the process and conclusions are not incorporated into a marketing planning system.

In turn, it is difficult to initiate an effective marketing planning system in the absence of a parallel corporate planning system. This is yet another facet of the separation of operational planning from strategic planning for, unless similar processes and time scales to those being used in the marketing planning system are also being used by other major functions (such as distribution, production, finance and personnel), the sort of trade-offs and compromises that have to be made in any company between what is wanted and what is practicable and affordable will not take place in a rational way. These trade-offs have to be made on the basis of the fullest possible understanding of the reality of the company's multifunctional strengths and weaknesses, and opportunities and threats.

One of the problems of systems in which there is either a separation of the strategic corporate planning process, or in which marketing planning is the only formalised system, is the lack of participation by key functions of the company, such as engineering or production. Where these are key determinants of success, as in capital goods companies, a separate marketing planning system is virtually ineffective.

Where marketing, however, is a major activity, as in fast-moving industrial goods companies, it is possible to initiate a separate marketing planning system. The indications are that when this happens successfully, similar systems for other functional areas of the business quickly follow suit because of the benefits which are observed by the chief executive.

Cross-functional involvement

The very nature of the segmentation process brings with it the temptation to delegate the process in its entirety to the market research manager, or to the marketing planning manager or, in the absence of a marketing planning manager, to the corporate planning function. This divorcing of the process from operations is likely to result in a strong reluctance by line management to accept the conclusions, especially if they represent a change from current thinking, as well as a resentment of the rigorous process it involves and of the people who follow it.

It also has to be said that such an approach is unlikely to produce the best results. Those staff in contact with the marketplace bring practical experience to the process. Staff from other areas of the company bring a different perspective to the issues addressed in the process, as well as a further resource for creative thinking.

The detailed work required for segmentation does not, however, suit a committee environment. As suggested in our opening chapter, a core team of two or three individuals needs to be established, whose job it is to carry out the detailed work, commission externally contracted agencies as required or agree such briefs with the relevant section of the company, use the cross-functional steering group as a sounding board, and raise topics with other members of staff as appropriate.

This raises the question again of the key role of the chief executive in both the segmentation process and marketing planning as a whole. Without both the chief executive's support and understanding of the very serious implications of initiating an effective segmentation review, everyone else's efforts will largely be ineffective.

Successful implementation of segmented marketing

As was pointed out at the beginning of this chapter, it is impossible to divorce implementation from the process of arriving at the concluding segments. Of critical importance here are:

- the support of the chief executive and senior management;
- a feeling of 'ownership' of the conclusions by the company's key operating units generated by their involvement in the process;
- an institutionalised marketing planning process which can take the results of the segmentation review and develop it into both a strategic three-year plan and a one-year marketing programme.

In addition, to operate effectively in the selected segments, the company's activities should be organised around them. If this cannot be achieved, the company's market share goals and financial objectives are unlikely to be reached.

This consideration of 'internal compatibility' is so important that it should be borne in mind whilst following the segmentation process. It is also one of the criteria used to assess the suitability of a concluding segment, along with size, differentiation and reachability.

Marketing departments can, of course, operate within the new segmentation structure on their own and develop advertising and promotional programmes accordingly (an implementation strategy referred to as 'bolt-on segmentation' (see Chapter 1) because of its high level of customer focus but low level of organisational integration). This approach will not, however, be as successful as one which has both a high level of customer focus *and* a high level of organisational integration, or 'strategic segmentation' as it is called by Jenkins and McDonald (see Chapter 1).

Organisational integration can be looked at on three levels, the strategic, the managerial and the tactical.

Strategic integration through the mission statement

Many organisations find their different departments, and sometimes even different groups in the same department, pulling in different directions. This often has disastrous results, simply because the organisation has not defined the boundaries of the business and the way it wishes to do business in its mission or purpose statement.

Take the example of a high-technology company. One group of directors felt the company should be emphasising technology, while another group felt technology was less important than marketing. With such confusion at the top of the company, it is not hard to imagine the chaos further down.

A different example concerns a hosiery buyer for a department store group. She believed her mission was to maximise profit, whereas research showed that women shopped in department stores for items other than hosiery. They did, however, expect hosiery to be on sale, even though that was rarely the purpose of their visit. This buyer, in trying to maximise profit, limited the number of brands, colours and sizes on sale, with the result that many women visitors to the store were disappointed and did not return. So it can be seen that in this case, by maximising her own profit, she was sub-optimising the total profit of the group. In this case, the role of her section was more of a *service* role than a profit-maximising role.

Here we can see two levels of mission. One is a *corporate* mission statement, the other is a lower level, or *purpose*, statement. But there is yet another level, as shown in the following summary.

Type 1   'Motherhood', usually found inside annual reports designed to 'stroke' shareholders. Otherwise no practical use.

Type 2   The real thing. A meaningful statement, unique to the organisation concerned, which 'impacts' on the behaviour of the executives at all levels.

Type 3   This is a 'purpose' statement (or lower-level mission statement). It is appropriate at the strategic business unit, departmental or product group level of the organisation.

The mission statement should in itself consist of brief statements which cover the following points:

- *Role or contribution of the unit*
  For example, profit generator, service department, opportunity seeker.

- *Definition of business*
  Preferably in terms of the *benefits* you provide or the *needs* you satisfy. Do not be too specific (for example, 'we sell milking machinery') or too general (for example, 'we are in the engineering business').

- *Distinctive competence*
  These are the essential skills/capabilities/resources that underpin whatever success has been achieved to date. This statement should be brief, consisting of one particular item or the possession of a number of skills that apply only to your organisation or specific SBU. A statement that could equally apply to any competitor cannot, by definition, be a *distinctive* competence and is therefore unsatisfactory.

- *Indications for future direction*
  A brief statement of the principal things you will do, and those you would give serious consideration to (for example, move into a new segment). In some instances it may also be appropriate to cover what you will *never* do.

It is particularly in the 'business definition' and 'indications for the future' areas that the conclusions drawn from the segmentation review will have an influence.

Managerial integration

In addition to adopting an organisational structure built around the segmentation structure, as discussed earlier, it will be necessary to provide management information in a form that supports the new segmentation focus. It has to be said, however, that changing organisational structures and management information systems are not tasks that can be achieved overnight. Both will take time, and it may take a great deal of determination to prevent the difficulties that will be encountered becoming a justification for throwing out the segmentation conclusions. Evolution, as opposed to revolution, may need to be the order of the day, and the process of evolution will be slower the more the 'new order' challenges the status quo and the distribution of power.

Tactical integration

Here we are concerned with the ability of the organisation at the operational level to be effective in the segment.

The advertising and promotions department needs to be able to target their activities into the selected segments. Single approach solutions will have to be dropped in favour of differentiated solutions, some of which may need to employ techniques currently unfamiliar to the department.

The salesforce will need to be trained both in distinguishing between the different segments, and in the appropriate benefits to be highlighted during sales meetings. Alternatively, of course, it may be possible to reorganise the sales group around the segments.

Differential pricing will need to be supported and understood within the organisation, as the days of the single pricing policy will most likely have disappeared. This will be particularly difficult for the salesforce, but they will be helped by being given carefully targeted products/services, supported by clear and distinctive promotional campaigns.

Distribution will also need to adapt, both in terms of the availability levels and channels required by the segments.

The human face in segmentation

The personal dimension in segmentation is clearly very important: without the belief and commitment of the employees to this method of looking at the market, the segmentation process is all but sunk. But the 'personal' side of the segments themselves can help win the support and enthusiasm of staff and, in doing so, encourage them to change any previously entrenched ways.

A number of companies have turned to cartoonists in order to give a human face to their segments and put their segments on first name terms. This has the additional advantage of emphasising that each segment is, in fact, a collection of living, breathing human beings who, just like the company's employees, look for the offer that best meets their needs. If in doing this they find themselves having to switch brands, then that is exactly what the segments will do.

This 'personalising' of segments was certainly put to good effect in ICI Fertilizers when a new marketing plan was rolled out at the end of their extensive segmentation project. After internally researching the needs of the target market (the company's employees) and testing alternative 'offers', the seven segments which emerged from the project were named, Martin, David, Oliver, Brian, George, Arthur and Joe. All seven of them were captured as cartoon characters, with each drawing carefully tested amongst the target market in terms of its ability to portray the profile of the segment it was meant to represent. The cartoon depictions of Brian, George and Joe appear below.

Drawings by Arthur Shell

PART IV

The Epilogue

13 *The Contribution of Segmentation to Business Planning: A Case Study of the Rise, Fall and Recovery of ICI Fertilizers*

For this final chapter, we look at the important contribution made by segmentation to a business plan that proved to be a critical turning point for a UK manufacturing company, which had enjoyed enormous success and prosperity but, within a very short time, found itself fighting for survival.

To ensure the part played by segmentation is seen in context, the case study starts well before the segmentation project was even commissioned.

Background

ICI Fertilizers (ICIF), formerly part of ICI Agricultural Division, was, until the end of 1997, an operating company in ICI plc. ICIF's business is best described as 'commercial crop nutrients', its main product lines supplementing the principal soil nutrients used up by today's intensive agricultural practices.

The elements most likely to be depleted in the soil are nitrogen (N), phosphate (P) and potash (K), collectively known as NPK. While, of course, there are other nutrients which occasionally become deficient in certain soils or for special crops, production of fertilisers containing just one element or various combinations of nitrogen, phosphate and potash has been the main function of the fertiliser industry.

'Chemical fertilisers' have an advantage over 'organic manures' because they are much more concentrated and thereby more efficient. In addition, they can be 'tailor made' to suit specific soil conditions.

At ICIF, the manufacturing processes for nitrogen, phosphate and potash are as follows:

- *Phosphate fertilisers:* phosphate rock is imported, mainly from Senegal, where it is mined on a large scale. In this raw state it is insoluble in water, even if finely ground. By treating it with sulphuric acid, it finishes up as superphosphate, which is soluble and can be produced in granular form.
- *Potash:* originally potash was imported, but now most of it is mined at Boulby near Whitby in North Yorkshire. This material is ready to use and can be incorporated into compound fertilisers without any further treatment.
- *Nitrogen:* although 80 per cent of the air around us is nitrogen, most crops cannot take advantage of it until it has been converted into nitrate either by bacteria or a chemical process.

   The chemical process involves combining nitrogen and hydrogen under high pressure and temperature in the presence of a catalyst. This produces ammonia, a gas, which, under pressure, becomes a liquid.

   The source of hydrogen, a key raw material, can be from any fossil fuel such as suitably treated coal, naphtha or from natural gas. Ammonia is the first stage in the production of nitrogen fertiliser. In the second production process ammonia is reacted with nitric acid to produce ammonium nitrate.

   Finally, ammonium nitrate is solidified into prills (small pellets), containing 34.5 per cent nitrogen, in which form it is sold as a straight nitrogen fertiliser. It may also be granulated along with phosphate and potash to produce the required compound ratio.

Therefore, taking the production of NPK as a whole, phosphate and potash present little in the way of manufacturing problems, any technology involved being low level. On the other hand, the nitrogen production, needing as it does the ammonia plant, represents high levels of investment and technical competence.

It should be pointed out that, during the manufacture of ammonia, there are several useful by-products which are subsequently sold. They include nitrous oxide (anaesthetics) and carbon dioxide (in liquefied form used in soft drinks, beer and as a heat exchange medium for nuclear reactors, in solid form used in refrigerated transport and food processing). In addition, a number of other products are also sold which, although not by-products, are closely associated with the technology of ammonia production. Among these are methanol (plastics and synthetic resins) nitrate of soda (glass, explosives and flares) nitric acid, sulphuric acid, urea (resins, adhesives, plastics and as a fertiliser in its own right) pentaerythritol (resins for paints, varnishes and printing inks) and sodium nitrite (dyestuffs, heat treatment, pharmaceutical products, anti-corrosion, meat preservation).

However, the production of these products cannot be described as the company's main mission. They are only mentioned here for completeness.

1917–87

In 1917, the government bought a site in Billingham on the north bank of the River Tees for a factory to make synthetic ammonia, 'Synthonia', as a first stage for producing the chemicals for munitions. After the war, in 1919, Brunner Mond and Company took over the site to make fertiliser from ammonia using the same process as originally intended in the government plan.

It wasn't until 1923 that the first ammonia plant started production, and by the following year the first 'straight' nitrogen fertiliser (that is, containing no phosphate or potash), sulphate of ammonia, was manufactured.

In 1928, another straight nitrogen fertiliser, 'Nitrochalk', was produced especially for grassland.

By 1930, the first concentrated complete fertiliser (CCF) was produced. This was the first compound of nitrogen, phosphate and potash. During the next three decades, the company experienced steady growth and accumulated considerable expertise; indeed, it led the way in the process, design and control of ammonia plants. In addition, its knowledge about catalysts and their manufacture became extensive.

The interruption of the war years, 1939–45, saw the company's expertise being applied to producing aviation spirit from coal. In order to reduce the risks of bomb damage threatening output, the company was directed to disperse production. As a result, relatively small factories were set up at Heysham, Dowlais, Prudhoe and Mossend. These additional facilities were converted to fertiliser production after the war, but have now all closed.

This enforced foray into new technology was a determining factor in ICI developing its post-war interests in plastics, petrochemicals and agrochemicals (plant protection). All of these fields of work were eventually harnessed into substantial operating divisions within the group.

Until the 1960s, the hydrogen essential to the production process was obtained by 'gasifying' local coal from the Durham coalfield. However, there was a vociferous and increasing concern about environmental pollution which arose from using coal. This, coupled with the run-down of the Durham mines, was instrumental in causing the company to switch its hydrocarbon fuel source from coal to naphtha. The company developed a commanding lead in the new technology associated with using naphtha and licensed the process all around the world. Finally, the company converted to its present source of hydrogen, North Sea gas. This took place in the early 1970s and, although not recognised at the time, this step was to prove to be one of the most significant steps in the company's history (for reasons that became clear later).

The 1960s was an expansionist period for the company. The goal was to be really big in ammonia, both in the UK and export markets.

Three very large ammonia plants of revolutionary design were bought from the USA, and new fertiliser production capacity was also built at Billingham. In addition the company built a manufacturing unit at Severn-side (Bristol), which contained two ammonia plants and ancillary fertiliser equipment. Offshoots were also being sponsored in India, Malaysia, Australia, South Africa and Canada, all eventually becoming autonomous operations.

Yet, even with this increased level of activity, the 1960s decade was not a particularly profitable one, mainly because of overcapacity in the industry and the relatively poor profitability of UK farming. The UK agricultural and international fertiliser markets were depressed for much of the period. In addition, the company had a protracted and expensive struggle to make the new ammonia plants work. During 1969–71, profits were close to zero.

A profound upturn in company fortunes followed the 1973 oil crisis, which had such a disastrous effect on most of the rest of manufacturing industry. As the price of oil soared, so did the production costs of ICI's competitors who used this as the source of hydrogen in their production processes.

In comparison, the virtually fixed-price gas contract negotiated earlier by ICI began to yield rich dividends, and effectively gave the company a tremendous cost advantage for this essential processing ingredient throughout the 1970s and into the 1980s. Not surprisingly, safeguarding the gas contract from political attack became a cornerstone of policy.

This advantage in manufacturing costs was exploited in the marketplace and the company became increasingly dominant. By 1980 it had 80–90 per cent of ammonia production in the UK (there was competition from only one other ammonia plant) and was certainly the largest producer in Europe, outside what was then referred to as the Eastern bloc. From this position of strength, the company pursued a policy of holding prices high and maximising profits, rather than seeking increased market share, and dictating how much, and when, its distributors and farmer customers could take product.

Even so, in nitrogen fertiliser terms, the company had the lion's share of the UK market: some 60 per cent, compared with the 25 per cent share of Fisons, the nearest competitor.

All of this contributed towards the fertiliser business becoming the veritable jewel in the crown of ICI. In 1981, ICIF contributed over a third of group profits and its future looked very bright.

Such was the level of confidence within the company that it dictated to the industry on prices and increasingly geared its output to what constituted the most economic production runs at the plants. The company's perspective had become very inward looking, and its over-confidence began to generate complacency. A discerning eye might have spotted some warning signals, nothing too obvious at first, but nevertheless worthy of attention. The danger was not from within the company, *but from outside in the marketplace.*

The fertiliser market

To describe the UK fertiliser market over the years to 1980 is tantamount to chronicling the fortunes of two companies, ICIF and Fisons.

Fisons was a long-established company and highly respected in the trade. The company was reputed to have a marketing ear 'close to the ground' and, as a result, carried a wider range of fertilisers than ICIF. A significant difference in their history, however, compared with ICIF, was that in the early 1960s a corporate decision was made not to be involved in basic ammonia production. Instead, Fisons chose to buy ammonia from other suppliers. This decision was coincident with ICIF's expansionist phase and it was seen to be mutually acceptable for ICIF to build and commission an ammonia plant dedicated to supplying the Fisons main site at Immingham, near Grimsby on Humberside.

From this time onwards, the two companies' destinies were somewhat interlinked. Whenever ICIF chose to increase prices, Fisons invariably followed. It was a strategy that suited the two fertiliser giants, and their growing dominance had the effect of removing some twenty or so small fertiliser manufacturers from the competitive arena. The smaller companies just did not have the advantage of the economies of scale of production and distribution afforded to the market leaders.

Thus by 1980, as mentioned above, ICIF had some 60 per cent share of the UK market and Fisons 25 per cent, the remainder being met by a number of small manufacturers, or by imports.

Imports

Just as it suited ICIF to have the number two competitor in the home market partially dependent upon it for basic raw materials and operating very much in ICIF's shadow, so it suited the company to keep imports to a minimum: not an easy task.

However, their major competitors on mainland Europe were just as concerned to protect their own home markets. Thus, the European market operated under an uneasy truce, and major producers did not see it as in their interest to disturb the status quo. The risk of massive retaliation for violating the unspoken code of conduct was too high a price to pay. There was some economic logic in this, since fertilisers are low cost, bulky products and therefore expensive to transport.

Changes in the market place

Traditionally, fertiliser had been supplied in 50kg bags, and for a long time these suited the needs of the marketplace. However, as farms became more mechanised and less dependent on muscle power, a demand for fertiliser bags to be palletised started to emerge.

At first, only minor suppliers responded to this need. There was a reluctance on the part of the major producers to switch to this form of packaging because of the additional costs which would be incurred at their plants. Not surprisingly, therefore, ICIF turned its back on this particular concept, and Fisons followed suit.

Another innovation in packaging was the introduction of 'shrink-wrapping' of pallets. Again, while this seemed to strike a chord in the market place, the two giants still resisted making any response to this development until forced to do so because of the lead given by small manufacturers.

Clearly, farmers were now becoming interested in semi-bulk packaging.

It was Fisons and some other small producers who eventually took the initiative by introducing a half-tonne 'Top Lift' bag, a tough but floppy plastic bag with a sturdy loop for lifting at the top. It was ideal for many farmers, who could use any tractor with a front-end loading arm to position it over the hopper of the spreading vehicle. The unloading could be accomplished by pulling a draw cord and allowing its contents to fall into the hopper. So popular was this packaging that Fisons soon brought out a larger one-tonne Top Lift bag to add to its range.

ICIF had to respond to the threat that Fisons and other smaller companies now posed. Its hitherto seemingly unassailable market share was now under threat. At first sight another form of Top Lift bag might have sufficed to restore the differential between the two companies, but there were snags.

The rather shapeless and bulky Top Lift bags could not be stacked more than two high. Above this height, the bags became very unstable. This was no worry for a farmer who would not be holding very much stock, but for ICIF (with its throughput of some 2 million tonnes per annum of fertiliser) the overall effect would be to reduce the warehouse storage capacity several fold. The prospect of investing in new storage, and its subsequent impact on production costs, turned the company against the Top Lift bag, yet it somehow had to respond to the new and increasing demand in the market for bulk deliveries.

When it came, in 1984, ICIF's response was in keeping with its production engineering traditions. It was called the 'Dumpy' bag, and it held 750kg. More sophisticated than the Top Lift bag, the Dumpy was basically a squat cylindrical bag sitting in a wooden cradle, not unlike a simplified form of the pallet idea that had been rejected earlier. The cradle and bag shape ensured that the Dumpy met its main design criteria: it could be stacked high enough to make good use of the existing storage facilities at ICIF and it lent itself to transportation by lorry. The cradle was also designed to accommodate the arms of a fork-lift truck and was cheap enough to be considered disposable.

However, using a fork-lift truck in a warehouse is a different proposition from using one on a farm, and the advantages of the Dumpy could only be exploited to the full by farmers with good pallet handling facilities. Unfortunately, such farmers were in the minority.

For these reasons, the Dumpy never completely matched the competitive advantage of the Top Lift bag, and ICIF failed to keep pace with the growth in this semi-bulk delivery market. Although initial sales were promising, repeat business fell short of expectation and eventually the company was forced to introduce an additional range of top lift products in 1986.

Despite Fisons' success with Top Lift, it had been progressively weakened by its lack of ammonia capacity and its poor production assets had been debilitated by the need to supply cash to Fisons' growing pharmaceutical business. By 1980, it was clear that the end was in sight, but for monopoly reasons ICI's hands were tied. In 1982, Fisons' fertiliser interest was bought for some £40 million by Norsk Hydro, a Norwegian state-owned company which had grown rich from North Sea oil, reputedly earning a surplus of approximately £400 million per year, and £80 million was earmarked for updating and improving the former Fisons' production facilities.

It was soon evident that Norsk Hydro was buying its position in the European fertiliser market. In addition to its investment in the UK, Norsk Hydro acquired the premier fertiliser producer in Sweden (Supra) and the second largest in Germany (Brunsbuttle), France (Cofaz) and Holland (NSM).

In contrast, ICIF appeared to have no European strategy. Indeed, it could even have pre-empted the purchase of NSM, since as a 25 per cent shareholder it had first refusal. It chose, instead, to turn its back on continental involvement.

Meanwhile, UKF (which had bought the Shell Fertilisers' complex at Ince, Cheshire, in 1975) became increasingly competitive in the market-place. By a combined strategy of increasing capacity and enterprising marketing, they quietly acquired something like a 20 per cent market share in straight nitrogen fertilisers and about 15 per cent in compounds, while ICIF's attentions were directed towards Norsk Hydro. In addition to Norsk Hydro and UKF buying into the UK market, Kemira Oy, the Finnish state-owned fertiliser company, acquired a 4 per cent market share by purchasing in 1982 a small company, L&K Fertilisers; they embarked upon an expansionist strategy aiming to give them national coverage and a stated 10 per cent market share objective.

As if this were not enough, substantial imports reappeared on the UK fertiliser scene. Since most of these imports originated from the Eastern bloc, the pricing was not subject to conventional economic rationale and, in effect, the material was being dumped at prices with which ICIF could not compete.

Not all the pressure came purely from competitors, however. The problems surrounding surplus production of many agricultural products in the European Union resulted in lower prices and a decline in farm incomes. The hitherto buoyant European fertiliser market went into decline. There was again considerable overcapacity of fertiliser production in Europe.

The delicate, gentlemanly restraints regarding exporting to a competitor's country were now severely tested by a new economic reality and were found to be wanting.

From ICIF's viewpoint, this was something of a disaster, because their earlier strategy of dominating the market and keeping prices high made the UK an extremely attractive market for continental producers with surplus capacity, and indeed for manufacturers from even further afield.

To put this new development into perspective, between 1982 and 1987 ICIF lost something like 15 per cent of their market share in straight nitrogen fertilisers as follows:

- Norsk Hydro: 1 per cent;
- UKF: 3 per cent;
- imports: 11 per cent.

All of the above factors, uncomfortable as they were, might have been weathered because ICIF had such a tremendous advantage over its competitors due to the 'cost plus' gas contract that had been negotiated in the early 1970s; however, in 1983, this contract was renegotiated in advance of the old contract reaching completion.

New gas contract

The basis of the initial contract was for ICIF to be provided with gas on a 'cost plus' formula. A key determinant in the contract price was the fact that the gas could be extracted relatively easily from the accessible Lincolnshire gas field, which was just off shore.

As this reservoir of natural energy became depleted, a new source had to be found. This proved to be the Ninian field, well out in the North Sea, with all the attendant costs. Gas at 1970s prices was now out of the question.

Despite hard renegotiations, ICIF ended up paying a series of annual stepped increases for gas over a five-year period. Each increase was equivalent to adding £20 million to the company's raw materials costs, though this was far better than having to pay the increase in one horrendous jump.

At the very time that ICIF's main advantage was being eroded in this way, the vagaries of world economics led to a fall in oil prices, which in turn benefited competitors who used that source of hydrogen for their ammonia plants. Although such a benefit might be a transitory phenomenon only, lasting perhaps one or two years, it can be quite significant in terms of providing a launch pad for winning a few points' market share. Inevitably, a proportion of customers will remain loyal to their new supplier and so the transition can have repercussions in the longer term.

Indeed, so critical is the hydrocarbon 'raw material' to fertiliser production that, unlike the UK, many governments subsidise the energy prices that their domestic manufacturers pay. Again, this is an important factor when taking into account a company's competitive position, since the majority of ICIF's competitors are state companies.

The impact of local blenders

The rich, flat landscape of East Anglia lent itself to mechanised farming. Field sizes could be optimised without any interfering topographical features, and farmers were quick to seize the economic advantages that larger field sizes and mechanisation gave them. In turn, the demand for fertilisers increased dramatically in this area as crop yields improved.

As in any market with a record of growth, it does not take long before the entrepreneur, with ears tuned in to the customers' wavelength, discovers unmet needs and new opportunities in the marketplace. So it was with fertilisers.

The relatively low technology for producing phosphate and potash fertilisers meant that someone with very little capital could set up a small 'manufacturing' plant. The raw materials, phosphates and potash, could be imported by the shipload to the East Anglian ports. All that remained for the manufacturer to do was to blend these raw materials in proportions sought by the marketplace and 'bag' them up. The equipment required for doing this was not sophisticated, being rather like a cement mixer, and even second-hand production facilities were easy to obtain. The unskilled, often casual, labour necessary for this work and all the ancillary jobs could be readily found. Thus, start up costs were negligible.

Not surprisingly, a number of 'blenders' (as they are called) set up small businesses in old barns, converted hangars and similar readily available buildings. Typically, the blenders only distributed on a local basis, probably within a 50-mile radius of the plant. To exceed this distance would cause the small company considerable logistical problems.

However, the blender's modest scale of operation, with its low fixed costs, meant that they could make a tonne of compound for some £30 less than ICIF.

The impact of blenders was easy to see. Nationally, ICIF's share of the compound fertiliser market was about 22 per cent. In East Anglia it was only 8–10 per cent and in Essex it was even less, at around 5 per cent. In these two localities, it was estimated that blenders had something like 50 per cent of the market.

While blenders were only involved in phosphate and potash fertilisers, ICIF were not over-concerned. The company did not see this as a real threat; it was just a locally irritating, but explainable phenomenon.

However, the activities of the small local suppliers did have the effect of stimulating the already very price-conscious farmers of the region to be on the look out for ever better bargains.

The more enterprising blenders were also quick to latch on to the over-capacity for nitrogen fertilisers in Europe. They found it an easy process to import straight nitrogen from mainland Europe, primarily through Antwerp. Without having to invest in new equipment, these blenders now had the capacity to offer nitrogen, phosphate and potash compound fertilisers as well as straight nitrogen. Thus, collectively, blenders had become significant competitors to ICIF, albeit on a confined, local basis.

The lower prices offered by blenders, combined with the weakening international market, put so much pressure on ICIF's pricing structure that eventually, in mid-1986, it was found to be impossible for the company to stick to its previous policy of umbrella pricing. Prices were lowered to a level necessary to compete with imports. This step, combined with the higher gas contract, had the effect of transforming the company into a loss-maker once more.

Seasonal demand and discounts

The use of fertilisers is highly seasonal. Thus the need to equate monthly sales with monthly output from fertiliser plants has made it necessary for manufacturers to offer seasonal prices to encourage an even off-take of production.

However, with the international market becoming increasingly volatile, during the 1980s the out-of-season purchaser was frequently penalised, rather than rewarded, for planning ahead. This being the case, farmers began to delay making commitments on future purchases and instead bought at the time of usage in order to take advantage of the best 'bargains' available at that moment.

As would be expected, this shift in the purchasing pattern caused something of a logistics problem at the production end. 'A nightmare' was how one company spokesman described this particular development.

ICIF's marketing organisation

Historically, sales and marketing were seen as two separate functions and this was embodied in the original organisation structure, which had the respective heads of the two groups reporting directly to the board.

Increasingly, this separation was proving to be unhelpful and was often a weakness when the company needed to respond to new circumstances. For example, responsibility for pricing policy tended to fluctuate between marketing, sales (effectively the regional sales managers) and the board.

The board would insist on the need to have sales at a 'cost-plus' recovery or not at all. Yet, whenever stocks accumulated at the plants, they had to be moved. The regional sales managers duly obliged by taking large orders at low prices.

Within this 'stop–go' situation, the marketing department was somewhere in the middle. The market was confused, and sometimes felt betrayed.

In late 1985, the organisation structure was changed with the objective of getting a much better integration of the sales and marketing functions within the fertiliser business: they now reported to one general manager. In addition, the new structure addressed itself to the problem of establishing better co-ordination with the autonomous distribution channels.

Distribution channels

Sales to the ultimate consumer, the farmer, are made via a wholesale route using agricultural merchants as distributors. In all, there were approximately 400 distributors in the mid-1980s.

These distributors range from large private companies, operating nationally, down to individual traders. In between are a number of small and medium-sized companies (some of which are co-operatives) whose sales are essentially regional in nature.

To maintain a service to its wholesalers, ICIF had 70 local depots throughout the UK. The company's salesforce (of approximately 100 technical representatives at that time) were responsible for maintaining contact with distributors and influencing them to stock ICIF products. They also provided a technical service to farmers and encouraged them to use the local ICIF distributor.

However, large individual farmers and many local groups of farmers were seeking to bypass the traditional wholesale system and deal direct with the manufacturers.

An added complication came from the Pareto 80/20 rule when distributors were measured against throughput. In fact, one distributor accounted for nearly 20 per cent of ICIF's sales. So, increasingly, the bargaining position of major distributors was becoming more powerful, with the net effect being a downward pressure on wholesale prices.

In an attempt to counter 'distributor power', as well as retaining as much of the available margin in-house as possible, the company had two separate retail sales organisations, selling direct to farmers under their own brand names. Both were secured through previous acquisitions, with 'Britag' selling solid fertilisers and 'Chafer' selling liquids. Some 100 sales representatives were employed in this part of the organisation.

However, the only way the direct sales operations can take business away from major distributors, and keep them in their place, is to be more competitive on pricing. This also had the effect of pushing down prices or reducing sales of ICIF's leading branded products.

Missed opportunities

In addition to ICIF being slow to recognise opportunities for palletising and semi-bulk delivery systems, opportunities were missed in special compound fertilisers. The company, mainly for reasons of its technology and the relative advantage this gave over its competitors, had always been mainly concerned with nitrogen fertilisers. Phosphate and potash compounds were something like poor relations, and treated as accessories to improve the range of use (and thus production throughput) of the nitrogen fertilisers.

Perhaps the company was right to adopt this philosophy. Certainly, the straight nitrogen market showed the more spectacular growth pattern, growing by roughly 7 per cent per annum until 1983–84, as shown in Figure 13.1.

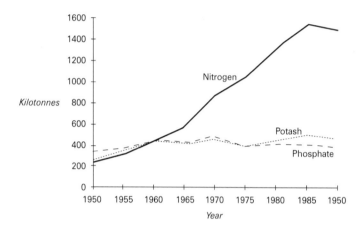

Figure 13.1   Annual use of NPK fertilisers in the UK

Source: The Fertiliser Manufacturers Association, *UK Consumption of Inorganic Fertilisers* (1952–92).

However, while the market for compounds overall was growing at perhaps a modest 0–2 per cent per annum, within this sector the demand for some individual compounds was growing quite rapidly. For example, a compound of 25 per cent nitrogen, 5 per cent phosphate and 5 per cent potash, used extensively on grassland, became very popular.

Both UKF and Norsk Hydro/Fisons spotted this opportunity, while ICIF did not. By 1987 the total market for this compound was estimated at 350 000 tonnes and the relative sales of the three companies tell their own story: UKF 120 000 tonnes; Norsk Hydro 100 000 tonnes; ICIF 25 000 tonnes.

Another growth sector was for zero nitrogen fertilisers which are used with autumn sown winter wheat. Typically, the formula for these will be 0–5 per cent nitrogen, 24 per cent phosphate and 24 per cent potash. These are low margin products to ICIF, but not to the blenders referred to earlier. ICIF's position in this market fluctuated, although towards the end of this period it decided to become more competitive in this sector, believing that lost sales in compounds also resulted in lost sales in straight nitrogen fertilisers.

Summary

ICIF had a long and largely distinguished history, in which it had been in the forefront of technological and production engineering developments. It was this impetus and striving for excellence which carried it to a leading position in the fertiliser industry.

The somewhat fortuitous gas contract initially negotiated only served to embellish the company's prospects and standing in the marketplace.

In recent years, it had to cope with pressures coming from a number of different directions:

- changes in the marketplace in terms of customer needs;
- more flexible, customer orientated competitors;
- a new, giant, pan-European competitor with investment capital;
- a local challenge from small entrepreneurial 'blenders';
- adjustment to a zero-growth market;
- an increase in imports;
- a large price increase in its key raw material, gas, which did not affect competitors in the same way.

All of these factors had their effect on the company's profits:

1981: £120 million;
1985: £72 million (£55 million of which was made in the first six months);
1986: Break-even.

Notwithstanding this, the company was still the market leader in terms of share and had considerable assets in terms of facilities, expertise and staff. Coupled with this was a determination to fight back and recover much of the lost ground.

1987–89

ICIF fought back on a number of fronts: in its manufacturing technology and capacity, through its organisational structure, and in its sales and marketing strategies. This enabled the company to retain its market leadership in the UK fertiliser market, though its share in straight nitrogen fertilisers, its primary product, had fallen from a high of 50 per cent down to 30 per cent. Norsk Hydro was the number two supplier and Kemira Oy was in third position (assisted by its acquisition of UKF), having retained their combined straight nitrogen market share at 32 per cent. Blenders were collectively still an effective competitor. No major producer had the flexibility and closeness to customers that characterised these small 'producers'. However, blenders also exhibited other characteristics of small firms, in that many started up only to end in failure. Even so, as one failed another started up elsewhere. The picture was, therefore, fragmented and transitory but, overall, the aggregate effect of blenders – while not increasing – still made an impact on the company's sales, particularly in East Anglia.

In the European fertiliser market, Norsk Hydro retained its market leadership, with Kemira Oy effectively number two. ICIF remained some way down the European 'league table'.

Manufacturing facilities

Production capacity at ICIF was trimmed to get it more in line with demand, which had declined quite significantly since the mid-1980s. As a result, plants were closed at Barton and Beverley, calcium ammonium nitrate production at Billingham was closed and the compound production facility at Severnside was closed in the summer of 1989. In addition, old ammonia-producing equipment at Severnside was replaced by a new, more energy efficient ammonia plant commissioned in early 1989. Nitrate production at Leith also ceased, but the nitric acid and compound plants continued to function there.

At the same time, however, Norsk Hydro had built a new ammonium nitrate facility at Immingham. The commissioning of the new plant was celebrated by the launch of a new branded fertiliser called 'ExtraN'. With its 34.5 per cent nitrogen concentration, ExtraN became a direct competitor for ICIF's 'Nitram', a product which had remained virtually unchanged for over 25 years. The only perceptible difference between the products was the prill size. To be strictly accurate, ExtraN is made as granules. ExtraN's larger size was claimed to be more acceptable to users and was marketed as having 'extra spread width'. ICIF claimed that the larger granule was technically inferior and was not so conducive to even distribution. Despite this technical counter-attack, farmers claimed to prefer the larger size.

A particular success at the close of this period was the turnaround in the company's profits slide. After approximately two years in the 'red', the company returned to the 'black' in 1989, achieved essentially by reducing costs, improving efficiency and increasing market prices, rather than by increasing sales volume.

This turnaround was no small achievement, taking into account the volatile industry conditions in which the company had to perform.

The gas contract

The once highly favourable gas contract became history. Gas became purchased at commercial rates through negotiated, short-term contracts. Even so, the volatility of relative gas prices in the UK and mainland Europe could still be significant. For example, a £0.01p per therm difference could make an impact on the bottom line by as much as £3.5 million, and during 1989 the company was at a significant disadvantage compared with the Dutch tariff.

Imports

In this second period of the company's history, fertiliser prices tended to be higher in the UK than in much of mainland Europe. This meant that, although fertiliser is bulky and costly to transport over great distances, sales margins achievable in the UK made it a viable proposition for some foreign producers to export. As a result, imports had been gradually increasing and now accounted for well over one-third of the UK straight nitrogen market. It is interesting to note that most imports were in the form of urea, a technically inferior nitrogen fertiliser according to ICIF, but one which was becoming increasingly popular with the final users. Of more particular concern to ICIF was the more recent arrival in the UK of quality ammonium nitrate.

The marketing initiative

One of the board directors took an interest in marketing and attended a public course at one of the UK's leading business schools, Cranfield University School of Management. The most immediate result of this was the adoption of a company-specific education and training programme run by the Marketing faculty at Cranfield for all the key staff of ICIF and its subsidiaries. This was quickly followed by the commissioning of some preliminary market research amongst both the distributors (agricultural merchants) and final users (farmers), and the recruitment of someone totally new to the chemical business, but with a strong background in marketing. This appointment precipitated a complete re-assessment of the UK market, starting at its very roots, the final user. In 1988 ICIF began to relearn its business.

Despite initial pressure from senior management to move straight to a product strategy, distribution strategy and advertising strategy for the company, it soon agreed that to arrive at any effective marketing strategies a structure for the market first needed to be developed and accepted. Target customer groups would then need to be identified and accepted, along with an assessment of the resources required to become successful in the target groups. A 'segmentation' project got underway.

Segmentation

In the past, the traditional way the company segmented the market was by splitting it between the products used (Nitram or compounds), further split (at times) between arable and grass. In some cases, the company's view of segmentation further broke the market down by the crop being grown in the arable market or by the type of stock being kept in the grassland market.

By the autumn of 1988, an initial structure for the final users of fertilisers had been put together solely from taking account of *their* approach and attitudes towards the purchase of fertilisers along with *their* farming style. This initial structure was tested in the market and a final picture arrived at in early 1989. No account was taken of how the company viewed the market.

The key stages of the process gone through to reach this segmentation were as follows:

- Group discussions with farmer groups from around the country, across farming practice and with different manufacturing loyalties, were conducted by an independent consultant with the sponsoring company (ICIF) kept confidential.
- The important issues were identified and a questionnaire developed, then tested with farmers to ensure it would cover the areas required. The questionnaire was then amended and the final questionnaire completed using face-to-face interviews. Again, these were conducted by an independent group of field researchers, with the sponsoring company's name not revealed.
- Data were analysed and an initial view of segmentation made based on farmer attitudes to fertilisers and their farming style. Four segments were identified, but some farmers fell into 'grey' areas and weren't satisfactorily categorised in the four-segment structure. The two major features accounting for this uncertainty were price and brand.
- The first segmentation structure was tested in the market with farmers and the grey areas explored by repeating the whole process again, but this

time with a more detailed look at price sensitivity and the components of brand. To enable this more detailed discussion to take place, members of each group were recruited from the same initial segment.

- Final analysis was undertaken, which led to a seven-segment structure being made. Then, for each segment, a typology (attitudes, motivations and needs), SWOT analysis, critical success factors and offer (product, price, promotion, place) was drawn up *without* any reference to ICIF's offers available in the market.
- A preliminary marketing plan for ICIF was drawn up matching ICIF's capabilities with the needs of each segment.

Segmentation summary

A summary of the segments appears in Figure 13.2 and in Table 13.1.

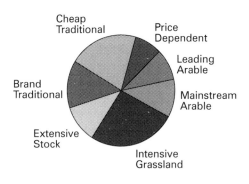

Figure 13.2   Segments in the UK fertiliser market

Note: Output from *Market Segment Master* PC support package, modified for monochrome printing.

Table 13.1   A brief summary of the segments in the UK fertiliser market

Farmer Segment	Profile	Trend
Leading Arable	Profit driven. Innovative. Produces for a market (as opposed to impressing the neighbouring farmers). Has the latest equipment. Prefers complicated approaches (because what is being done is not simple!). Sources product from anywhere. Can handle a range of qualities.	Growing in number and affected by the first environmental legislation. This had yet to reflect in demand.
Mainstream Arable	Prefers branded products. Adopts proven approaches. Requires quality. Becoming increasingly confident in their merchant's recommendations. Attracted to practical approaches.	Declining in number and buying straight nitrogen products increasingly on recommendation from merchants. Environment becoming an issue.
Intensive Grassland	Focus is on intensive dairy farming. Looks for quality practical approaches. Local technical support. Merchant orientated. Requires product development. Will spend money to impress his neighbours (show off).	Static/slightly declining in numbers. Tending to see straight nitrogen as a commodity, therefore increasingly price sensitive. Milk quota restrictions and the impact of 'mad cow' disease (BSE – Bovine Spongiform Encephalitis) on sales becoming concerns.
Extensive Stock	Quality practical approaches. Local technical support. Local proof required on new ideas. Paced product development. Right merchant the key to a sale.	Stable segment, but could be affected by tightening of subsidies. Could also be affected by BSE.
Mixed: Brand Traditional	Established approaches preferred (the good old ways). Doesn't want any changes to the current offers. Established brands give security. Prefers simple approaches. Local availability of product required.	Slowly declining in number.
Mixed: Cheap Traditional	Looks for low cost approaches. Established approaches preferred. Dislikes manufacturers' branded products. Simple approaches. Quality not important. Chooses the cheapest.	Growing at the expense of Brand Traditional
Grassland and Arable: Price Dependent	Price. Price. Price. Price.	Growing. The only option left, particularly for frustrated Leading Arable and Intensive Grassland farmers. Also some Mainstream Arable.

Segments in a portfolio matrix

When the requirements of each segment were matched up to the capabilities of ICIF, and the attractiveness of each segment to ICIF was determined, a segment portfolio matrix was arrived at as shown in Figure 13.3.

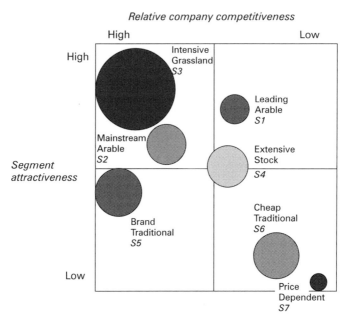

Figure 13.3 ICIF's segment portfolio matrix

Note: The codes S1 to S7 link the segments to Table 7.10 and Figures 7.2, 7.3 and 7.4 in Chapter 7.

For segments in which the company believed it was strong, the opposite had proved to be the case. One segment was also waiting for specific offers to be made to it and was ripe for development.

Marketing strategy: the first changes

New products

With the exception of ExtraN, mentioned earlier, the only heavily promoted new products to come on to the fertiliser market during this period were from ICIF.

In the autumn of 1988, its first new heavily promoted fertiliser products since 1975 were launched. These were designed for a newly identified market segment, the 'intensive grassland' farmer. This segment had, of course existed for some time: only its recognition by ICIF can be said to be new, especially in a marketing sense. These new products were given brand names, 'Turn Out' and 'First Cut'. As well as providing the obvious benefits, these products were, in addition, characterised by their efficient use of ammonium nitrate. Thus, these fertilisers were more environmentally 'friendly' because they reduced the risk of polluting rivers and other water supplies.

The most interesting fact about these new products was that this was the first time products had been given names reflecting their usage (after market research) rather than reflecting their chemical analysis. The specific design and subsequent targeting on a clearly defined market segment made both of these products immediate successes with, at that time, no obvious rivals. Sales of these products in the launch season were in excess of £8 million.

As might be expected, the company's expertise in new product launches was somewhat 'rusty' after such a long period. Nevertheless, Turn Out and First Cut rapidly became established and produced considerable 'on-the-job' learning for all those who were involved in the project.

This was quickly followed by the launch of a new arable range of compounds (strictly speaking, an old range repackaged) which, for the first time, were presented as a flexible range under the brand name 'Crop Start'. These fertilisers were just phosphate and potash fertilisers for use in the autumn; the deliberate omission of nitrogen again has an environmental story and recognises that nitrogen is usually readily available in the soil in autumn from natural processes.

However, the linkage which had been assumed to exist between the purchase of Nitram and compounds had proved to be unfounded in a number of segments.

Packaging

The market continued to show a preference for semi-bulk packaging and so the trend for larger pack sizes continued.

Although the original Dumpy bag had its faults, it did prove to be popular with those users who had bottom loading equipment.

Its successor, 'Dumpy 2', also a 750kg container, had the facility of top or bottom lifting; that is, using the front-end loading arm of a tractor or forklift truck. It was, therefore, extremely versatile and competed favourably with competitor alternatives. Its 'squatter' profile also improved its storage ability on the farm (which had been a problem with Dumpy 1).

The 50kg bags remained a popular size and were palletised and 'shrink-wrapped'. A recent innovation in this field was the use of coloured shrink film on which was printed the product's name. It is interesting to note that the market still prefers 50kg bags.

Advertising

Advertising had been very much a 'committee' affair, with the committee being made up of ICIF representatives from sales and marketing. Visuals and copy were approved by the committee, with no reference to the consumer. Each product also had its own campaign, often changed each year, and there was no overall ICIF campaign for its products.

In 1988, a proposed advertising campaign for the company's mainline product, Nitram, was tested opposite the consumer along with some alternative advertisements. The proposed campaign failed badly, as it was seen as too clever and complicated, but by including alternative advertisements in the research, a more effective campaign was developed and used. No internal committee played any part in advertising for this campaign (and subsequent ones). This consumer-based approach was carried through to the advertising for the two new products (Turn Out and First Cut), and resulted in recall levels above 60 per cent during their first three months. Advertising for these products also had a similar look to the Nitram advertisements, thus forming the basis of an ICIF campaign.

Distribution

An activity which also occupied much of this period was that of rationalising the distributor network.

From something in the order of 400, a sharper and altogether more professional network of just 68 approved distributors was set up. Those chosen were selected with improved customer service in mind, so that the eternal 'trade-off' of service levels versus distribution costs could be better balanced. Britag remained as one of the distributors, as did SAI in Scotland.

It was expected that the number of distributors would continue to reduce, by about 5–10 per year, over the next few years. Such changes in the distribution network necessitated a rethink about the role of the sales organisation.

New sales organisation

Heading the field sales organisation was a national sales manager to whom reported seven business managers (six in England and Wales, one in Scotland).

Each business manager had a number of account managers reporting to him, along with technical representatives and distributor support representatives.

Each business manager also controlled a distributor training manager, who played a training and development role for the approved distributors.

The whole ethos of the new sales organisation was to generate sales by working with and through the chosen distributors and could be described as follows.

Business manager	Responsible for the business performance in a defined geographical area.
Account manager	Responsible for the business performance of specified distributors, being the distributor's first-line contact with ICIF.
Technical representatives	Provide the distribution sale representatives with the agronomic story behind the products and services ICIF provides. They also acted as technical trainers for the distributors in their area and went to farms with or on behalf of the distributor to sort out technical queries or to provide technical advice in support of a sale. A danger, however, was that ICIF's traditional agronomic expertise and approaches could well lead to overkill and few sales.

A summary of the sales organisation appears in Figure 13.4.

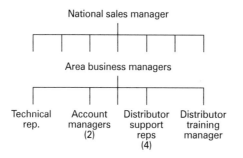

Figure 13.4   The sales organisation

This new sales organisation was achieved with an overall reduction of about 25 staff from the salesforce.

Organisational structure

In order to simplify the organisational structure, clarify jobs and responsibilities, and provide less 'top-down' management, on 1 December 1988 a new structure for the commercial section was introduced, as shown in Figure 13.5.

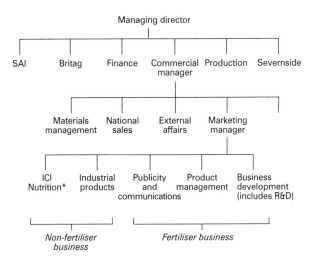

Figure 13.5   Structure of the commercial organisation

* *Note*:   The ICI Nutrition group were concerned with animal nutrition.

This new structure reduced confusion and improved communications within the group. There were, however, no specific responsibilities by segment, but the most appropriate way of tackling this omission with the resources available was a hot topic between the business development and product management groups.

Business teams

Even before the organisational changes, it had been recognised that there were benefits to be derived form setting up cross-functional teams charged with running distinctive product ranges as independent businesses, including the more effective exploitation of the products.

As a result, four business teams were set up to focus on ammonium nitrate, spring compounds, autumn compounds and calcium ammonium nitrate.

The leaders of each of these teams met with selected board members on a regular basis as the fertiliser business team, which made recommendations about policy and operational issues to the full board.

These business teams went some way towards improving cross-functional communication and tapping a broader range of the company's brain-power. Useful though this was, it might be concluded that the business teams were doing no more than might be expected from an integrated marketing function.

It is also interesting to note that the focus was on product, as opposed to market.

Concerns on the horizon in 1989

'1992: an opportunity or a threat?'

The European fertiliser market had always been susceptible to structural changes as individual governments changed their agricultural policies. The removal of trade barriers at the end of 1992 should, in theory, have made little difference to the 1989 situation because there were, in effect, already no barriers.

European legislation

Perhaps more worrying than the 'new order' of 1993 was the way that European Union legislation was already having an increasing influence in the member countries. There was a relentless inevitability that Euro-laws would gradually take over and set new and comprehensive standards, designed mainly to protect water supplies from nitrate contamination.

Although fertiliser manufacturers argued that nitrate levels in soils had risen mainly through natural processes (for example, because more grass-land had been converted to arable use, particularly during the last war), and from the burning and ploughing in of stubble, they were not winning the day. As a result, legislation was expected in several areas, such as:

- restrictions on the use of fertilisers within specified distances of rivers and boreholes, in order to prevent contamination of water supplies;

- restrictions on the number of cattle that can be kept per acre; (this can have implications about how land might be converted to other uses in the future);
- further tightening of milk quotas introduced earlier in the decade, which had led to rationalisation of production and, for the survivors, a very profitable dairy sector; the next move, in addition to the possible tightening of milk quotas, could be grain quotas.

On the whole, the UK had more relaxed standards than those being proposed in Europe, but the public interest in 'green' issues was seen as being a contributing factor which ensured the UK would fall into line with the new legislation.

Some farmers were already anticipating some of these changes and this, along with financial pressures in the arable sector, had resulted in a recent decline of the fertiliser market.

Phosphate and potash fertilisers

These were still very much also-rans when compared with nitrates and often only used when soil correction was required. Their relatively low usage in the UK had not put them under the 'microscope' of the environmental lobby in the same way as nitrates. This could be a factor which provided some commercial possibilities. However, phosphate and potash fertilisers do carry in-built environmental problems (for example, recent studies have shown a build up of phosphates in Dutch soil).

1990

Fully attuned to the marketplace, the ICIF board now required a full strategic business plan, based on utilising the company's current resources, to cover the period mid-1990 to mid-1993. This plan was quickly to prove a watershed in the affairs of the company, in a most unexpected way. What follows are some of the marketing issues which, in addition to the segmentation work, further contributed to the shape and nature of that plan.

Background analysis

Forecast of demand and supply

In Europe it was forecast that the demand for calcium ammonium nitrates and straight ammonium nitrates would fall by about 20 per cent by 1992.

This would be due to the combined influence of legislation, more efficient use of the product and its substitution by urea solutions (both forecast to grow).

Even though manufacturing capacity had been reduced, there was still a considerable excess. In addition, the relatively high fertiliser prices in Europe were attracting imports, mainly from the Eastern bloc (approximately 4 per cent of the market).

With respect to the UK, domestic nitrogen fertiliser capacity was below demand, but imports more than bridged the gap, making it difficult for manufacturers to maximise their output. Nitrogen fertiliser demand was forecast to fall by about 7 per cent by 1993.

Competitors' activity

Kemira seemed to have a strategy similar to ICIF, in that they were differentiating their products by quality and brand, having successfully adopted the higher-quality image of UKF. They also launched new products to compete directly with Turn Out and First Cut, but a delayed response had given ICIF the competitive advantage they had sought.

Norsk Hydro concentrated on improving the quality and branding of their straight nitrogen fertiliser. In compounds, they appeared to be rationalising their range and cutting out uneconomic production units or processes. Thus, they could still maintain their overall volume, but at lower cost.

Both Kemira Oy and Norsk Hydro priced below ICIF in order to support their strategies of maximising volume sales and hence filling their production capacities. In addition, both had established distributor networks which operated in a similar way to ICIF's. Blenders continued to concentrate on the arable market with phosphate/potash fertilisers, or phosphate/potash with a low level of nitrogen included, along with commodity compounds.

ICIF's products

The ICIF products which sold in the greatest volume were all in the later stages of their life cycles, either in the saturation or decline phase. Turn Out and First Cut (ICIF's two new brands) were at the beginning of the growth phase. A summary of the company's product portfolio appears in Figure 13.6.

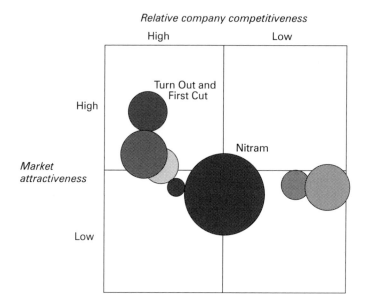

Figure 13.6   The fertiliser product portfolio of ICIF

Although not all of the products appear in the portfolio matrix, they all tended to fall within the same general area.

ICIF's strategy by market segment since 1989

Leading Arable	No new products or services had been developed for this segment.
Mainstream Arable	The salesforce had been withdrawn from calling on farmers. Contact was only through distributors, which would weaken loyalty in this segment to the ICIF brand.
Intensive Grassland	The withdrawal of the salesforce was expected to have the same impact as with Mainstream Arable. In the past no new products or services had been targeted at this segment. It was a growth area for Turn Out and First Cut.
Extensive Stock	ICIF had a good image in this segment, but withdrawal of the salesforce and the move to distributors might weaken it. There were no new products or services. There was a small but increasing use of Turn Out by sheep farmers.

Mixed: Brand Traditional	Withdrawal of farm visits by the salesforce was weakening this segment's loyalty to the ICIF brand.
Mixed: Cheap Traditional	Although sales were continuing to this segment, no special activity was targeted at it.
Grassland and Arable: Price Dependent	Sales also continued into this segment, but, again, no special activity was targeted at it.

Distribution

The current practice was for product to be available within 24 hours, and at 'farm gate' pricing. To achieve this, ICIF effectively took on the costs of distribution and storage. The latter was required because of uneven usage patterns and the need for constant production levels. This approach cost just under £28 million in the last operating year. No other major competitor had such an approach.

Marketing strategy

The overall mission for the company was to continue to generate a positive cash balance from its trading. Furthermore, it needed to establish a basis for ensuring that there would be sustained profitability in future years.

In line with this thinking, the mission of the fertiliser business in ICIF was stated as:

> To maximise the profit contribution to the group by selling our own manufactured high nitrogen fertilisers.

The strategy for achieving this involved a number of activities:

- focusing only on those UK segments where cost leadership was possible;
- developing a product range for those segments which not only met the farmers' needs, but also made good use of the existing production facilities and for which ICIF was a credible supplier;
- minimising the costs of distribution by effective development of trade channels;
- maintaining high plant utilisation by exporting to the rest of Europe those products which returned acceptable margins;
- eliminating the reselling of purchased products unless they were essential to providing a full product range to the targeted segments.

In short, this strategy was aimed at focusing on key segments in the home territory, developing strengths in new ones in order to retain overall sales volumes, and putting pressure on Norsk Hydro and Kemira Oy in Europe in an attempt to force some of the reduction in the UK market on to them.

However, at the heart of this strategy was the need for plant capacity to have a high utilisation. Unless this was achieved, it would be impossible for the company to achieve cost leadership as is clear in Figure 13.7.

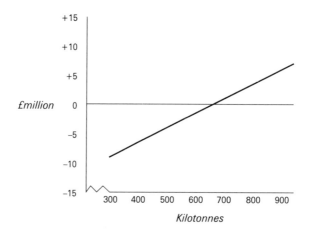

Figure 13.7 Relationship between plant utilisation and net margins

The break-even point was around 650 000 tonnes of production. The higher the volume above this level, the more advantageous the net margin became, and the better the company's scope for manoeuvre.

Product strategy

Straight nitrogen fertilisers

The objective was to maintain a 45 per cent share of the solids market available to Norsk Hydro, Kemira Oy and ICIF.

A larger Nitram prill needed to be developed to compete with Norsk Hydro's granulated ExtraN. The current 'prilled' version was not perceived as having the same quality. However, converting to a granulation plant would cost in the order of £10 million. An alternative, and less costly, development was pursued which would perceptibly increase the size of the prill, although not increase it to quite the size of the ExtraN granule.

Calcium ammonium nitrate sales could be maintained using the Nitrochalk brand. Bulk calcium ammonium nitrate sales to blenders were to be increased. This business produced good margins and gained ICIF a foothold in the blender market. However, only blenders supplying to the arable market were to be considered, otherwise this strategy would be tantamount to the company shooting itself in the foot by undermining its own markets.

Autumn compounds   The objective was to exit from this market. For ICIF, these were unprofitable and did not pull through other product sales. Local blenders were better placed to meet the needs of this market.

Spring compounds   The objective was to concentrate production capacity into compounds requiring high levels of nitrogen, as these produced the highest gross margins. The portfolio of compounds also needed to be such as to minimise production and distribution costs.

The manufacture of products for Scotland was to be based at Leith, whereas those for England and Wales would come from Billingham. This would rationalise aspects of production and improve the distribution logistics.

Research and product development was to focus on the intensive grassland segment. Three new products were to be launched in the autumn of 1991, including a development based on Nitram, plus a development of Turn Out.

Pricing strategy

The overall positioning of ICIF as a leading, quality manufacturer with value-for-money products meant that price levels could never be reduced to a level which made them appear cheap.

Even so, newly introduced products had to be aggressively priced in order to gain penetration and win market share quickly.

Those products at the mature end of the life cycle needed to be priced relative to competition, in order to maintain market share and production volume.

Where strong branding could be developed, prices were inclined to be less sensitive to competing formulae.

The pricing strategy for Europe needed to be geared to volume objectives. Here there were advantages, since ICIF was a relatively small player and there was little branding on the continent.

Packaging strategy

It was intended to drop the Dumpy and explore how to introduce inter-mediate bulk packaging more in line with market requirements.

Promotion strategy

The overall strategy was to re-open the dialogue with farmers via direct marketing, while also building up close ties with selected distributors.

It would also be necessary to train the farmer-contact personnel of distributors, especially in the segments where the relationship with the farmer was critical.

ICIF's own company farms were to be kept, because market research had confirmed that they played an important role in the image of the company, particularly in the practical testing of new products.

Service strategy

Services were only of value to ICIF if:

- they differentiated the product;
- they brought the 'product package' up to a level of competing products;
- they attracted extra margins for the product;
- they pulled through a greater sales volume of product;
- their costs could be recovered in product sales or from fees.

Of the main services on offer from ICIF, the soil nitrogen testing service certainly led to sales of Nitram and for this reason would be continued, free of charge, though it needed to be simplified and more suited to its users.

Additional margins generated by the soil-sampling service, a service expected from major suppliers of fertilisers, were tenuous. This service would therefore have to be self-financing.

Despite the focus on the grassland segment, the two specific services for this sector were dropped. They did not meet the required criteria.

The remaining ICIF services would be designed to help distributors differentiate themselves from their competitors. This was to be done by providing preferential terms, such as a lower fee or fast response.

Environmental strategy

An industry-wide strategy was essential, because the environmental issues were affecting all businesses adversely in terms of:

- the market size, which was reducing;
- the products which could be sold and the way in which they were sold;
- the image of the agricultural sector.

Notwithstanding this, ICIF still had to have environmentally responsible products and practices. Therefore, technical information needed to be provided with products so that they would be used correctly.

It was possible to turn environmentalism into an opportunity by insisting that nitrogen fertilisers should only be used after nitrogen testing of soil. Exporters of fertilisers to the UK would not be able to respond to such a requirement easily.

R&D strategy

The key R&D activities were to centre on new high nitrogen products for grassland, which could be economic and produce grass in greater quantity, or to a higher and more consistent quality, without damaging the environment.

Improvement in existing products would also be required, as would technical 'updating' of the remaining services on offer.

Distribution

It was intended to consolidate around the present distribution pattern, recognising that the channels used would vary according to geographic areas.

Segment strategy

This is summarised in Table 13.2.

Table 13.2 ICIF's segment strategy, 1990–93

Farmer Segment	Objective	Products	Price	Promotion	Place	Product Development
Leading Arable	Bottom out declining share to 7%	Mainly Nitram	Prevailing market price for quality nitrate product	Sales to work with selected distributors	Through selected distributors. Direct to buying groups	None for solid fertilisers. Some specialist liquids
Mainstream Arable	Hold share to 33% for Nitram	1. Nitram 2. Spring compounds	Nitram price to shadow Norsk Hydro and Kemira Oy. Compounds priced for volume sales	Retain brand awareness. Promote 'N-Sure'	Through limited number of specified distributors	As above
Intensive Grassland	Retain 30% share. Increase sales of compounds	1. Nitram 2. Turn Out 3. First Cut 4. Kaynitro	Nitram at market price. Compounds at highest price for volume sales	Full support. Develop 'umbrella' brand. Use ICI farms and soil sampling	Selected key distributors dealt with by account managers	Develop a specific straight nitrogen product. Enhance First Cut and Turn Out
Extensive Stock	Increase share of Nitram to 30%, and spring compounds to 30%	1. Nitram 2. Spring compounds 3. Launch version of Turn Out	Nitram and spring compounds to be priced in line with volume objectives	Full promotional support	As above	Grazing and cutting compounds including sulphur
Mixed: Brand Traditional	Maintain share – Nitram 40%, spring compounds 30%	1. Nitram 2. Spring compounds	As above	No specifically targeted activity	As above	None specifically
Mixed: Cheap Traditional	Hold share – Nitram 12%, spring compounds 20%	1. Nitram 2. Spring compounds	Nitram near market price to achieve volumes. Spring compounds at top end of range	As above	As above	None specifically
Price Dependent	Residual sales only					

Threats

Possible competitor response

It was likely that Norsk Hydro and Kemira Oy would respond to ICIF's UK strategy by putting pressure on prices. The extent of this pressure would depend on two issues:

- how much ICIF's European strategy convinced Norsk Hydro and Kemira Oy that ICIF would be a threat to their overall business; and
- how successful ICIF was in reducing its cost base, by filling its ammonium nitrate capacity with non-UK destined product.

Since it was in nobody's interest to get involved in a price war in a declining market, some sabre-rattling might be expected as an initial response from the major competitors. However, the more likely result would have been that UK straight nitrogen prices declined slightly or, at best, remained static.

In Europe, it was considered unlikely that home producers would drop their prices in response to ICIF's exports, since they would be selling at market price. However, they might strive to maintain their capacity volumes by exporting to the UK in retaliation. Even so, ICIF would be in a stronger position to resist imports in its key market segments. Also, a 'pre-emptive' push for sales on the continent should be successful in the short term, and could provide ICIF with a bridgehead on which to build.

The ICIF focus on the profitable grassland segment would not go unnoticed and would be likely to attract 'me-too' products from Norsk Hydro and from the blenders, in addition to the response already seen from Kemira Oy. However, ICIF had a lead in this segment and there was still growth potential, especially if ICIF could continue to develop new products ahead of the field.

Other possible threats

- The UK market might decline faster than predicted because of any of the following:

  - higher levels of imports than forecast;
  - legislation restricting the use of nitrogen;
  - other legislation with a 'knock-on' effect reducing the use of nitrogen (for example, limits on the number of cattle per acre of land).

If this were to happen, it might become necessary to adopt a fall-back strategy (see below).

- BSE leading to a slaughter programme to remove all possible links with the virus. This would have the effect of reducing demand for fertiliser while stocks were being rebuilt.
- Unseasonal weather conditions (which seemed to be becoming more frequent) could intervene to affect fertiliser use.

Other than the possible competitor response reaching damaging levels, none of these threats deterred ICIF from following their proposed strategy.

Alternative strategy

If Norsk Hydro and Kemira Oy continued to price their way into the UK straight nitrogen market, ICIF would have to switch from a strategy of holding market share and expanding in key segments to one of maximising its cash flow potential.

In effect, this would mean scaling down to a one-plant operation and achieving the massive cost reductions that would come from a smaller and much simpler business. Such a step would also lead to a dramatic reduction in what the company could offer, or indeed tackle. For example, it could mean pulling out of Europe and/or several market segments, or it could mean dropping Nitram sales for other compounds. Product development could be curtailed, and the distributor network would shrink.

ICIF could buy in fertilisers to make up some lost sales, but the logistics of doing this and the margins involved would need to be calculated carefully to ensure that this would be a profitable route.

In fact, it would not be possible to be specific about the one-plant option, except to say that its acceptance could produce a high return on investment in the short term, but in the long term ICIF would probably be too small a player to survive in an industry dominated by larger and literally more resourceful competitors.

A tempting Finnish

The glimpses that have been provided about the issues and the thinking that went into the strategic marketing plan for mid-1990 to mid-1993 demonstrate that the company's response to its situation was not taken lightly. Considerable effort went into this plan, as well as into the other areas covered by the business plan, which, in effect, was a plan to rescue the company's ailing fortunes and to build a foundation for continued success in the future.

For reasons of confidentiality, volume sales and profit margins have been omitted from this case study. Nevertheless, an interested reader will have understood the rationale and thrust behind this marketing plan.

The segmentation project of 1988–89 provided ICIF with a fresh insight into its market and enabled the company to arrive at an extremely realistic view of its prospects. When the resulting plan was put before the board of ICIF in May 1990, it was accepted as reflecting the best possible use of the resources the company had. All that remained was for the plan to gain the approval of the main board of ICI plc.

The strategic vision of the main board was of a company with a portfolio of businesses each of which was, or had the potential of becoming, a global force in its field (this is still the case today). For ICIF, decisions made at earlier stages in its development meant that the fertiliser business would find it extremely difficult to achieve this objective.

A key consideration in implementing the strategic vision was the requirement of the main board to deliver increasing shareholder value, both in terms of capital worth and in distributed profits. If a business could not deliver the strategic vision it would therefore remain of interest to the main board if it could deliver a specific level of return over the period of the corporate plan.

The new plan for ICIF dramatically improved the returns of the business, but it could not achieve the prescribed level. This shortfall was partially linked to the requirement that the business had to base its plan on utilising *all* its current asset base. Nevertheless, the new plan presented a business that was both profitable and delivering a positive cash flow. But something else was afoot. Recent successes in the market had attracted attention.

Unbeknown to the segmentation team at ICIF, the Finnish company Kemira Oy had been in touch with the main board of ICI plc and submitted an attractive bid for the fertiliser business.

At the main board meeting, held in July 1990, it was decided that ICIF's plan, although optimising assets and delivering greatly increased returns, did not stack up to the bid now lying on the table. As a consequence of this, it was agreed to sell the business to Kemira Oy. A public statement to this effect was issued by the company.

All that remained was to verify that such a business transaction did not fall foul of the legislation surrounding monopolies and mergers. Thus, the issue was tabled for a meeting of the Monopolies and Mergers Commission (MMC) in September 1990. The decision at this meeting was that the MMC would have to submit their deliberations on the sale in a written report to the Minister of Trade and Industry by the end of 1990.

In the event, ICI faced something of a setback when, in early 1991, the Minister for Trade and Industry refused to approve the £75 million sale of its fertiliser business to Kemira Oy. Had the sale gone ahead, it would have increased the Finnish state-owned group's share of the UK fertiliser market from something like 18 per cent to approximately 50 per cent. This factor, coupled with the Minister's avowed policy of preventing British companies from being controlled by foreign nationalised industries, no doubt weighed heavily in favour of this decision.

However, since the only other possible buyer would be Norsk Hydro (51 per cent owned by the Norwegian government), ICI's options in terms of pursuing the selling strategy were severely limited.

Postscript

After the rejection of the Kemira Oy bid, the board of ICIF proposed an alternative plan to the ICI board which slimmed the business down even further than had been proposed in the 1990/93 marketing plan, but at the same time increased the returns from the company. The requirement to utilise all of the current asset base was now no longer a condition.

This resulted in a very different ICIF re-emerging in the UK market: an ICIF focused on a very limited product range which included Turn Out and First Cut, and, not long afterwards, the Nitram successor for the grassland segment 'Graze More', along with some other solid stable mates, including Nitram. As a result, profitability not only returned, but was also maintained and in 1996, the latest year available, an operating profit of £60 million on a turnover of £220 million was reported. Although profit levels were much lower than those seen in the company's heyday, they were certainly at a level commensurate with its lower turnover. They were also generating outside interest in the company once again, but this time from a most unexpected quarter.

On 20 November 1997 ICI announced the sale of its fertiliser business to Terra Industries of Sioux City, Iowa, USA, subject to clearance by the regulatory authorities. By the end of 1997 the sale had been completed and ICI received an initial payment of £200 million with a further £50 million available if certain targets were met. ICI had achieved a profit of at least £140 million on the sale of its fertiliser business compared to a profit of around £25 million which would have come from the sale to Kemira Oy. ICI's veritable jewel in the crown of the early 1980s had certainly found its sparkle once again.

The legacy of ICIF, however, will remain long after its sale as the re-emergence of a successful ICIF in the early 1990s attracted a great deal of interest from other businesses within ICI plc. The clear benefits to be derived from a detailed understanding of a market, particularly the segments to be found within it, became a key business issue.

Senior management across ICI began to ask, 'If a business involved in fertilisers can do this, why can't we?'

They could, and they did!

Appendix I: Customer Classification Systems

Social grading

Source: D. Monk, extract from Interviewers' Guide on Social Grading, from JICNARS, *Social Grading on National Research Surveys*, 1978.

Guide to grade 'A' households (upper middle class)

Informants from Grade 'A' households constitute about 3 per cent of the total. The head of the household is a successful business or professional person, senior civil servant, or has considerable private means. A young person in some of these occupations who has not fully established himself or herself may still be found in Grade 'B' though he or she eventually should reach Grade 'A'.

In country or suburban areas, 'A' grade households usually live in large detached houses or in expensive flats. In towns, they may live in expensive flats or town houses in the better parts of town. Some examples, which are by no means exhaustive, are given below.

Examples of occupations of the head of the household

Professional and semi-professional
Church of England dignitaries (bishop and above) and those of other denominations.
Physician, surgeon, specialist.
Established doctor, dentist (if a principal or partner in a large practice).
Established solicitor, barrister (own practice or partner in a large practice).
Matron of a large teaching hospital.

Headmaster of a public or grammar school or of any large school or college (750 pupils or more).

Architect, chartered accountant, surveyor, actuary, fully qualified and either principal or partner in a large practice. Also if working as a very senior (at or near board level) executive in a very large (200+) organisation.

Senior civil servant, for example, Permanent Secretary, Deputy Secretary, Under Secretary, Assistant Secretary, Principal.

Local Government chief officers.

Senior Local Government Officer (for example, Town Clerk, County Planning Officer, Borough Surveyor).

University Professor.

Editor of a newspaper or magazine; senior journalist on national or very large provincial publication.

Commercial airline pilot (captain or first officer).

Captain of large merchant vessel (5 000 tons or more and/or 25+ crew).

Senior professional executives: that is, professionally qualified people working as very senior executives or administrators (at or near board level in very large (200+) establishments), for example, Chief Engineer, Company Surveyor, Chief Accountant, Curator, Artistic Director, Chief Designer and so on.

Librarian, qualified, in charge of a really major library.

Business and industry

Senior buyers for leading wholesale or retail establishments.

Self-employed owners of businesses with 25 or more employees.

Self-employed farmers with 10 or more employees.

Board (Directors) or near board level managers in large organisations (with 200 or more employees).

Managers in sole charge of branches or outlying establishments with 200 or more employees at the branch (for example, factory managers, managers of very large retail establishments, depots, hotels and so on).

Stockbroker or jobber (principal or partner in the firm).

Insurance underwriter.

Advertising, research, public relations executives (and others offering professional or semi-professional services in specialised agencies) if at board level or principals or partners in agencies or practices with 25 or more employees.

Bank branch managers; managers of branches of other financial institutions (for example, building society, insurance company, finance house) with 25 or more employees at the branch.

Police and Fire Brigade

Superintendent, Chief Constable.

CID Superintendent and Chief Superintendent.
Chief Fire Officer.

Armed Forces
Army: Lieutenant Colonel and above.
Navy: Commander and above.
RAF: Wing Commander and above.

Non-earners
People living in comfort on investments or private income.
Retired people where the head of the household before retirement would
    have been 'A' grade.

Guide to grade 'B' households (middle class)

Grade 'B' informants account for about 12 per cent of the total. In general,
the heads of 'B' Grade households will be quite senior people but not at the
very top of their profession or business. They are quite well-off, but their
style of life is generally respectable rather than rich or luxurious. Non-
earners will be living on private pensions or on fairly modest private means.

Examples of occupations of the head of the household

Professional and semi-professional
Vicars, rectors, parsons, parish priests and ministers; clergymen above these
    ranks but below bishop.
Headteachers of secondary, primary or preparatory schools with fewer than
    750 pupils; qualified teachers aged 28 and over in public, secondary or
    grammar schools.
Civil servant: higher and senior and Chief Executive Officers, Executive
    Officers. Recently qualified assistant principal.
Local government: senior officers (9 grades).
University lecturers, readers; technical college lecturers.
Established journalist for provincial and local papers, trade and technical
    publications; less senior journalist for national press.
Matron of a smaller hospital (non-teaching); sister tutor in large hospital or
    teaching hospital.
Qualified pharmacist.
Qualified accountants, surveyors, architects, solicitors and so on, who do
    not have their own practices but are employed as executives not senior
    enough to be graded 'A'.

Newly qualified professional men/women of all sorts who have not yet established themselves (that is less than 3 years from qualification).

Librarian, qualified, in charge of a library or branch library.

Business and industry

Self-employed owners of business with 5–24 employees in skilled or non-manual trades (for example, shopkeepers, plumbing contractors, electrical contractors and so on).

Self-employed farmers with 2–9 employees.

Managers of large farms, stewards, bailiffs and so on.

Bank clerks with special responsibilities (for example, chief clerk, teller and so on).

Insurance clerk with professional qualifications and/or special responsibilities in large branch or head office.

Manager of a retail or wholesale establishment with 25–199 employees at the establishment.

Some relatively senior managers or executives in commerce and industry.

General Foreman, Clerk of Works (that is, with other foremen under him or her).

Chief buyers for wholesale or retail establishments.

Area sales managers or senior representatives (especially if technically professionally qualified).

Executives with professional or technical qualifications who are not senior enough to be graded 'A' (for example, department managers).

Technicians with degree or equivalent qualifications, especially in high-technology industries such as electronics, computers, aircraft, chemicals, nuclear energy and so on.

Police and Fire Brigade

Chief Inspector, Inspector.

Assistant Chief Officer.

Divisional Officer.

Armed Forces

Army: Captain, Major.

Navy: Lieutenant, Lieutenant-Commander.

RAF: Flight Lieutenant, Squadron Leader.

Non-earners

People with private income living in a less luxurious way than 'A' grade people.

Retired people who, before retirement, would have been 'B' grade people.

Guide to grade 'C1' households (lower middle class)

Grade 'C1' constitutes about 23 per cent of total informants. In general it is made up of the families of small trades-people and non-manual workers who carry out less important administrative, supervisory and clerical jobs, namely those who are sometimes called 'white collar' workers.

Examples of occupations of the head of the household

Professional and semi-professional
Curates in the Church of England; ministers of 'fringe' free churches; monks and nuns of any denomination, except those with special responsibilities.
Teachers, other than those graded 'B'.
Student nurses; staff nurses; sisters in smaller hospitals; midwives; dispensers; radiographers.
Bank clerk, insurance clerk with no special qualifications or responsibilities.
Insurance agent (door to door collector).
Civil servant: clerical grades.
Local government: clerical, junior administrative, professional and technical grades.
Articled clerk.
Library assistant (not fully qualified).
Student (on grant).

Business and industry
Self-employed owners of small business (1–4 employees) in non-manual or skilled trades (for example, shopkeepers, electrical contractors, builders and so on).
Self-employed farmers with only one employee.
Manager of a retail or wholesale establishment with 1–24 employees.
Some relatively junior managers in industry and commerce.
Clerks, typists, office machine operators, punch operators.
Telephonists, telegraphists.
Buyers (except very senior buyers).
Representatives, salesmen (except those graded 'B').
Technicians/engineers and so on, with professional/technical qualifications below degree standard.
Foremen in charge of 25 or more employees, mainly supervisory work (other than a few very senior foremen coded 'B').
Draughtsman.
Driving instructor.

Police and Fire Brigade
Station Sergeant, Sergeant, Detective Sergeant.
Station Officer and Sub-Station Officer, Leading Fireman.

Armed Forces
Army: Sergeant, Sergeant Major, Warrant Officer, 2nd Lieutenant, Lieutenant.
Navy: Petty Officer, Chief Petty Officer, Sub-Lieutenant.
RAF: Sergeant, Flight Sergeant, Warrant Officer, Pilot Officer, Flying Officer.

Non-earners
Retired people who, before retirement, would have been 'C1' grade and have pensions other than state pensions or have private means of a very modest nature.

Guide to grade 'C2' households (the skilled working class)

Grade 'C2' consists in the main of skilled manual workers and their families. It constitutes about 32 per cent of informants. When in doubt as to whether the head of the household is skilled or unskilled, check whether that person has served an apprenticeship; this may be a guide, though not all skilled workers have served an apprenticeship.

Examples of occupations of the head of the household

General
Foreman (responsible for up to 24 employees), Deputy (mining) Charge Hand, Overlooker, Overseer, whose work is mainly manual (these may be found in nearly all trades and industries, including farming and agriculture).

Agriculture
Agricultural workers with special skill or responsibilities (for example, head cowman, chief shepherd).

Building industry (including construction and woodworkers)
Most adult male skilled workers or craftsmen including: bricklayer, carpenter, plasterer, glazier, plumber, painter.

Coal mining
Skilled underground workers, including: coal cutter, filler, getter, hewer, miner, putter.

Metal manufacturing, shipbuilding and repairing, engineering, furnace, forge, foundry and rolling mills
Most adult male workers including: furnaceman (except coal, gas and coke ovens), moulder, smelter, blacksmith, coppersmith.
Plater, riveter, shipwright.
Fitter, grinder, millwright, setter, toolmaker, turner.
Vehicle builder, welder.
Electrical fitter, electrician, lineman.
Skilled labourer (docks and Admiralty only).

Rubber
Most adult skilled workers.

Textiles, clothing and leather
Skilled workers in rayon or nylon production.
Skilled knitters (hosiery or other knitted goods), weaver, bleacher, dryer, drawer-in.
Boot and shoemaker.
Cutter and fitter (tailoring).

Furniture and upholstery
Most adult male skilled workers including carpenter, joiner, cabinet maker.

Paper and printing trades
Most adult male skilled workers including machine man, finisher (paper and board manufacturer).
Compositor, linotype operator, typesetter, electrotyper, stereotyper, process engraver.

Transport
A few only of the better paid workers such as: all heavy and long distance vehicle drivers, engine driver and fireman; bus drivers, bus inspectors, signalmen, train drivers, shunters; passenger and goods guards; AA patrolman, ambulance drivers; Post Office sorters and high grade postman; stevedore.

Distributive trades
Proprietors and managers of small shops with no employees.
Shop assistants with responsibilities.

Glass and ceramics
Most adult workers including: formers, finishers and decorators, furnacemen and kilnmen.

Electrical and electronics
Including radio and radar mechanics, telephone installers and linesmen, electrical and electronic fitters.

Agriculture: farming, forestry and fishing
Skilled and specialised workers.

Food and drink
Baker.
Pastrycook.
Brewer.
Maltster.

Police and Fire Brigade
Prison Officer.
Constable.
Fireman.
CID Detective Constable.

Security officers
For example, Securicor.

Miscellaneous
Self-employed unskilled workers with 1–4 employees: for example chimney sweep, window cleaner, taxi driver (London).
Self-employed skilled manual workers with no employees.
Coach builder, plumber.
Dental mechanic and technician.

Armed Forces
Army: Lance Corporal, Corporal.
Navy: AB Seaman, Leading Seaman.
RAF: Aircraftsman, Leading and Senior.

Non-earners
Retired people who before retirement would have been in 'C2' grade and have pensions other than state pensions or have private means.

Guide to grade 'D' households (the semi-skilled and unskilled working class)

Grade 'D' consists entirely of manual workers, generally semi-skilled or unskilled. This grade accounts for 21 per cent of families.

Examples of occupations of the head of the household

General
Most semi-skilled and unskilled workers.
Labourers and mates of the occupations listed in 'C2' grade.
All apprentices to skilled trades.

Agriculture: farming, forestry and fishing
The majority of male agricultural workers, other than those with special skills or responsibilities, including: tractor or other agricultural machine driver, ditcher, hedger, farm labourer; forestry worker, timber man; fisherman; gardeners and self-employed market gardeners with no employees.

Coal mining and quarrying
Surface workers except those with special responsibilities.
Unskilled underground workers.

Textiles and clothing manufacture
Most manual workers including the following: woolsorter, blender, carder, comber, spinner, doubler, twister, textile printer.
Machinist (clothing manufacturer).

Food, drink and tobacco
The majority of adult workers, including the following: dough mixer, oven man; bottler, opener; stripper, cutter (tobacco).

Transport
Bus conductor, railway porter (including leading porter).
Ticket collector (railway).
Cleaner.
Traffic warden.

Distributive trades
Shop assistant without special training or responsibility.

Gas, coke and chemical
Most adult workers including furnacemen and chemical production process workers.

Plastics
Most adult workers.

Glass and ceramics
Production process workers.

Electrical and electronics
Assemblers.

Miscellaneous
Caretaker, warehouseman, park keeper, storekeeper, postman, works policeman, domestic servant, woman factory worker, waitress, laundry worker.
All goods delivery including milk and bread roundsmen.
Meter readers.
Self-employed manual workers with no employees: for example, window cleaner, chimney sweep, taxi driver (provinces).

Armed Forces
Army: Private or equivalent.
Navy: Ordinary Seaman.
RAF: Aircraftsman.

Non-earners
Retired people who before retirement would have been in 'D' grade and have pensions other than state pensions, or have other private means.

Guide to grade 'E' households (those at lowest levels of subsistence)

Grade 'E' consists of old age pensioners, widows and their families, casual workers and those who, through sickness or unemployment, are dependent on social security schemes, or have very small private means. They constitute about 9 per cent of all informants. Individual income of the head of the household (disregarding additions such as supplementary benefits) will be only slightly, if at all, above the basic flat-rate social security benefit.

Only those informants will be graded as 'E' whose head of the households is 'E' and where no other member of the family is in fact the chief wage earner.

Examples of occupations of the head of the household

Earners
Casual labourers.
Part-time clerical and other workers.

Non-earners
Old age pensioners.
Widow (with state widow's pension).
Those dependent on sickness, unemployment and supplementary benefits
for over two months who are without benefits related to earnings.
Disabled pensioners.
Private means, private pension, disability pension compensation, and so on,
amounting to little, if any, above the basic flat-rate social security benefit.

Examples of occupations under industries

Social grade

I Farmers, Foresters, Fishermen

D	Agricultural workers, unskilled.
C2	Skilled agricultural workers.
D	Agricultural machinery drivers.
D	Gardeners with no qualifications.
D	Foresters and woodmen with no qualifications.
D	Fishermen (employed).
C1	Agricultural workers (junior technically qualified).
B	Grieve (Scotland only) farm manager, bailiff, steward (of large farms or estate).

II Miners and Quarrymen

C2	Coal mine: face workers.
C2	Coal mine: underground workers (skilled).
D	Coal mine: underground workers (unskilled).
D	Coal mine: majority of workers above ground.

III Gas, Coke and Chemicals Makers

D	Furnacemen, coal, gas and coke ovens.
D	Chemical production process workers.

IV Glass and Ceramics Makers

C2	Ceramic formers.
C2	Glass formers, finishers and decorators.
C2	Furnacemen, kilnmen, glass and ceramic.
C2	Ceramics' decorators and finishers.
C2	Ceramics' decorators doing hand painting.
D	Glass and ceramics production process workers.

V Furnace, Forge, Foundry, Rolling Mill Workers
C2   Furnacemen: metal.
C2   Rolling, tube mill operators, metal drawers.
C2   Moulders and coremakers (foundry).
C2   Smiths, forgemen.
D   Metal making and treating workers.
D   Fettlers, metal dressers.

VI Electrical and Electronic Workers
C2   Radio and radar mechanics.
C2   Installers and repairmen, telephone.
C2   Linesmen, cable jointers.
C2   Electricians.
C2   Electrical and electronic fitters.
D   Assemblers (electrical and electronic).
C2   Electrical engineers (manual).
D   Mates to above workers.

VII Engineering and Allied Trades Workers
C2   Sheet metal workers.
C2   Constructional engineers: riggers.
C2   Metal plate workers: riveters.
C2   Gas, electric welders, cutters: braziers.
C2   Machine tool setters, setter-operators.
D   Machine tool operators.
C2   Tool makers, tool room fitters.
C2   Fitters, machine erectors and so on.
C2   Engineers (manual).
C2   Electro-platers, dip platers and related workers.
C2   Plumbers, lead burners, pipe fitters.
D   Press workers and stampers.
C2   Metal workers (skilled).
C2   Watch and chronometer makers and repairers.
C2   Precision instrument makers and repairers.
C2   Goldsmiths, silversmiths, jewellery makers.
C2   Coach, carriage, wagon builders and repairers.
D   Other metal making, working; jewellery and electrical production process workers (unskilled).

VIII Woodworkers
C2   Carpenters and joiners.
C2   Cabinet makers.
C2   Sawyers and wood working machinists.

C2	Coopers, hoop makers and benders.
C2	Pattern makers.
C2	Woodworkers.
D	Mates to above workers.

IX Leather Workers

C2	Tanners: leather, fur dressers, fellmongers.
C2	Shoemakers.
C2	Shoe repairers.
C2	Cutters, lasters, sewers, footwear and related workers.
C2	Leather product makers.
D	Mates to above workers.

X Textile Workers

D	Fibre preparers
D	Spinners, doublers, winders, reelers.
C2	Warpers, sizers.
C2	Drawers-in.
C2	Weavers.
D	Weavers: jute, flax, hemp (Scotland only).
C2	Knitters.
C2	Bleachers and finishers of textiles.
C2	Dyers of textiles.
C2	Textile fabrics and related product makers and examiners.
D	Textile fabrics (and so on), production process workers.
D	Winders and reelers.
C2	Rope, twine and net makers.

XI Clothing Workers

C2	Tailors: cutters and fitters.
C2	Upholsterers and related workers.
D	Sewers and embroiderers, textile and light leather products.

XII Food, Drink and Tobacco Workers

C2	Bakers and pastry cooks.
C2	Butchers and meat cutters.
C2	Brewers, wine makers and related workers.
D	Food processors.
D	Tobacco preparers and product makers.

XIII Paper and Printing Workers

C2	Makers of paper and paperboard.
C2	Paper products makers.

C2	Compositors.
C2	Printing press operators.
C2	Printers (so described).
C2	Printing workers.
D	Mates to above workers.

XIV Makers of Other Products

C2	Workers in rubber.
D	Workers in plastics.
C2	Craftsmen.
D	Other production process workers.
D	Mates to above workers.

XV Construction Workers

C2	Bricklayers, tile setters.
C2	Masons, stone cutters, slate workers.
C2	Plasterers, cement finishers, terrazzo workers.
D	Mates to above workers.

XVI Painters and Decorators

D	Aerographers, paint sprayers.
C2	Painters, decorators.
D	Mates to above workers.

XVII Drivers of Stationary Engines, Cranes, and so on

D	Boiler firemen.
C2	Crane and hoist operators: slingers.
C2	Operators of earth moving and other construction machinery.
D	Stationary engine, materials handling plant operators: oilers and greasers.

XVIII Labourers

D	Railway lengthmen.
D	Labourers and unskilled workers.
D	Chemical and allied trades.
D	Engineering and allied trades.
D	Foundries in engineering and allied trades.
D	Textiles.
D	Coke ovens and gas works.
D	Glass and ceramics.
D	Building and contracting.
D	All other labourers.

XIX Transport and Communications Workers

B	Deck, engineering officers and pilots, ships.
D	Deck and engine room rating, barge and boatmen.
A	Aircraft pilots, navigators and flight engineers.
C2	Drivers, motormen, firemen, railway engine.
C2	Railway guards (passenger and goods).
C2	Drivers of buses, coaches, trams.
C2	Drivers of road goods vehicles (heavy or long distance).
D	Drivers of road goods vehicles (local and light).
C2	Shunters, pointmen.
C1	Telephone operators.
C1	Telegraph and radio operators.
D	Postmen.
C2	Sorters and higher grade postmen.
D	Messengers.
D	Bus and tram conductors.
D	Porters, railway.
D	Ticket collectors, railway.
C2	Bus Inspector.
C2	Stevedores.
D	Dock labourers.
C2	Skilled labourers (Dock and Admiralty only).
D	Lorry drivers' mates, van guards.
D	Unskilled workers in transport and communication occupations.

XX Warehousemen, Storekeepers, Packers, Bottlers

D	Warehousemen, storekeepers.
D	Assistant warehousemen, assistant storekeepers.
D	Packers, labellers, and related workers.

XXI Clerical Workers

C1	Typists.
C1	Shorthand writers, secretaries.
C1	Clerks, cashiers, office machine operators.

XXII Sales Workers

C1	Salesmen, representatives (unless professionally qualified).
C1	Shop assistants with qualifications and training.
C2	Shop assistants with special responsibilities.
D	Shop assistants without special responsibilities and training.
D	Roundsmen (bread, milk, laundry, soft drinks).
D	Street vendors, hawkers.

XXIII Service, Sport and Recreation Workers

C2	Security guards.
D	Barmen, barmaids.
D	Housekeepers.
D	Stewards.
D	Waiters, counter hands.
C2	Cooks.
D	Kitchen hands.
D	Maids, valets and related service workers.
D	Caretakers, office keepers.
D	Chimney sweeps (employed).
D	Charwomen, office cleaners.
D	Window cleaners (employed).
C2	Hairdressers, beauticians if apprenticeship served.
D	Hairdressers, beauticians if serving apprenticeship.
D	Hospital or ward orderlies.
D	Launderers, dry cleaners and pressers.
C2	Ambulance men.

XXIV Administrators and Managers

A	Ministers of the Crown; MPs: senior government officials.
A	Local authority senior officers.

XXV Professional, Technical Workers, Artists

A	Medical practitioners (qualified with own practice).
B	Junior medical practitioners (recently qualified).
A	Dental practitioners (qualified with own practice).
B	Junior practitioners.
A, B, C1	Authors, journalists and related workers. Stage managers, actors, entertainers, musicians. Painters, sculptors and related creative artists.

The grade of these and similar cases, for example sportsmen, obviously depends on their success and your grading must depend on this.

Classification of occupations

Source: J.H. Goldthorpe, D. Lockwood, F. Bechhofer and J. Platt, *The Affluent Worker: Industrial Attitudes and Behaviour*, Cambridge University Press, 1968.

The occupational classification set out below was constructed on the basis of previous efforts by British sociologists, notably that of Hall and Cardog Jones (and is sometimes referred to as the 'Hall-Jones' classification).

In allocating occupations to classes, we followed the general rule of choosing the 'lower' alternative in all bordering cases where our information was incomplete or ambiguous. The examples given below are selected in order to give some idea of the range of occupation included in particular categories as well as 'typical' occupations.

Occupational status level	Example	Registrar General's social class equivalent
1(a) Higher professional, managerial and other white-collar employees.	Chartered accountant, business executive, senior civil servant, graduate teacher.	I
1(b) Large industrial or commercial employers, landed proprietors.		
2(a) Intermediate professional, managerial and other white-collar employees.	Pharmacists, non-graduate teachers, departmental manager, bank cashier.	II
2(b) Medium industrial or commercial employers, substantial farmers.		
3(a) Lower professional, managerial and other white-collar employees.	Chiropodist, bar manager, commercial traveller, draughtsman, accounts or wages clerk.	III Non-manual
3(b) Small industrial or commercial employers, small farmers.	Jobbing builder, taxi owner-driver, tobacconist.	
4(a) Supervisory, inspectional, minor official and service employees.	Foreman, meter-reader, shop assistant, door-to-door salesman.	III Manual or non-manual
4(b) Self-employed men (no employees or expensive capital equipment).	Window cleaner, jobbing gardener.	
5 Skilled manual workers (with apprenticeship or equivalent).		III
6 Other relatively skilled manual workers.	Unapprenticed mechanics and fitters, skilled miners, painters and decorators, public service vehicle drivers.	III Manual or IV
7 Semi-skilled manual workers.	Machine operator, assembler, storeman.	IV
8 Unskilled manual workers.	Farm labourer, builder's labourer, dustmen.	V

Life cycle (an overview)

Source: G. Gubar and W.D. Wells, 'Life Cycle Concepts in Marketing Research', *Journal of Marketing Research*, November 1966.

Bachelor-stage young single people not living at home	*Newly married couples, young, no children*	*Full nest I (youngest child under six)*	*Full nest II (youngest child six or over six)*
Few financial burdens. Fashion opinion leaders. Recreation orientation BUY: basic kitchen equipment, basic furniture, cars, equipment for the mating game, vacation.	Better off financially than they will be in the near future. Highest purchase rate and highest average purchase of durables. BUY: cars, refrigerators, stoves, sensible and durable furniture, vacations.	Home purchases at peak, liquid assets low. Dissatisfied with financial position and amount of money saved. Interested in new products. Like advertised products. BUY: washers, dryers, television, baby food, chest rubs and cough medicine, vitamins, dolls, wagons, skates.	Financial position better. Some wives work. Less influenced by advertising. Buy larger sized packages, multi-unit deals. BUY: many foods, cleaning materials, bicycles, music lessons, pianos.

Full nest III (older married couples with dependent children)	*Empty nest I (older married couples, no children living with them, head in labour force)*	*Empty nest II (older married couples, no children living at home, head retired)*	*Solitary survivor, in labour force*	*Solitary survivor, retired*
Financial position still better. More wives work. Some children get jobs. Hard to influence with advertising. High average purchase of durables. BUY: new more tasteful furniture, autotravel, non-necessary appliances, boats, dental services, magazines.	Home ownership at peak. More satisfied with financial position and money saved. Interested in travel, recreation, self-education. Make gifts and contributions. Not interested in new products. BUY: vacations, luxuries, home improvements.	Drastic cut in income. Keep home. BUY: medical appliances, medical care, products which aid health, sleep and digestion.	Income still good but likely to sell home.	Same medical and products needs as other retired group, drastic cut in income. Special need for attention, affection and security.

Registrar General's 'Social Class'

Source: Classification of Occupations, and each year's Census Report of Great Britain, Office for National Statistics (Crown Copyright).

Occupied* males and females aged 16 and over	% of Total 1971[a]	1981	1991
Class I: Professional, Administrative Examples: company directors and secretaries, bankers, shipowners and managers, stockbrokers, insurance underwriters, clergymen, lawyers, doctors, scientists, administrative class of civil service, officers of armed forces, professional engineers (civil, electrical and so on).	3.7	3.9	4.7
Class II: Intermediate Owners and managers: farmers, land agents, dock and harbour officials, local authority, administration, commercial managers, hotel managers, proprietors of retail shops. Professional: teachers, trained nurses, medical auxiliaries, social welfare workers, artists, civil service executive class.	17.4	22.0	27.8
Class III: Skilled Workers (N = Non-manual, M = Manual). Four main sub-groups: (a) foreman, under managers and overlookers; (b) clerks, typists; (c) skilled craftsmen; (d) salesmen, shop assistants.	50.1 N=21.6 M=28.5	48.5[b] N=23.0 M=25.5	45.0 N=23.3 M=21.7
Class IV: Intermediate Semi-skilled machine minders, labourers assisting craftsmen (provided there is some degree of skill).	20.8	18.9	16.2
Class V: Unskilled Labour Railway porters, builders' labourers, dock labourers, lift attendants, watchmen, charwomen.	8.0	6.7	6.3

*   Excludes armed forces, those on government schemes and those whose occupation is inadequately described or not stated.

[a] The population sample appearing in the 1971 census included those aged 15 and over.

[b] For the 1980 'Social Class' changes, see list below:

Class I Professional occupations

General administrators: national government (Assistant Secretary and above). Judges, solicitors, accountants, management consultants, clergymen, doctors, dentists, opticians, vets, scientists, engineers, architects, town planners, mathematicians.

Class II Intermediate occupations
Personnel and industrial relations officers, authors, marketing, advertising, PR executives, sales managers, actors, entertainers, proprietors and managers of hotels, pubs and so on, company secretaries, brokers, taxation experts, computer programmers, teachers, nurses, farmers, police officers (inspectors and above), prison officers (chief officers and above). National government (HEO to Senior Principal level). Local government officers (administration and executive functions).

Class III (N) Skilled occupations: Non-manual
Market and street traders, typists, secretaries, driving instructors, hairdressers and barbers, managers and proprietors, restaurateurs, sales representatives, scrap dealers, supervisors of: clerks, telephone operators, tracers, shop assistants, police sergeants.

Class III (M) Skilled occupations: Manual
Repairers (shoes, watches, television, radio); production workers for various industries, plumbers, welders, fitter/mechanics, painters, building workers, gardeners, service workers, foremen/supervisors, bus inspectors.

Class IV Partly skilled occupations
Street traders and assistants, security guards, materials processing handlers. Sewers, making and repairing of plastics, other (excluding metal and electrical), machine tool operators, construction workers, waiters/waitresses, bar staff, domestic assistants, bus conductors.

Class V Unskilled occupations
Messengers, dustmen, cleaners, drivers mates, stevedores, dockers, railway stationmen, labourers and unskilled workers in textiles, gas works, chemicals and so on.

Appendix II: Standard Industrial Classifications

United Kingdom and Europe

Agriculture, Hunting and Forestry
0100 *Agriculture and Hunting*
0111 Grow cereals and other crops
0112 Grow vegetables and nursery products
0113 Grow fruits, nuts, beverage and spice crops
0121 Farming of cattle, dairy farming
0122 Farm sheep, goats, horses and so on
0123 Farming of swine
0124 Farming of poultry
0125 Other farming of animals
0130 Crops combined with animals, mixed farms
0141 Agricultural service activities
0150 Hunting and game rearing, including services

0200 *Forestry*
0201 Forestry and logging
0202 Forestry and logging related services

Fishing
0500 *Fishing*
0501 Fishing
0502 Operation of fish hatcheries and farms

Mining and Quarrying
1000 *Mining of coal and lignite; extraction of peat*
1010 Mining and agglomeration of hard coal
1020 Mining and agglomeration of lignite
1030 Extraction and agglomeration of peat

1100	*Extraction of oil, gas and incidental services*
1110	Extraction of crude petroleum and natural gas
1120	Services to oil and gas extraction

1200	*Mining of uranium and thorium ores*
1200	Mining of uranium and thorium ores

1300	*Mining of metal ores*
1310	Mining of iron ores
1320	Mining of non-ferrous metal ores

1400	*Other mining and quarrying*
1411	Quarrying of stone for construction
1412	Quarrying of limestone, gypsum and chalk
1413	Quarrying of slate
1421	Operation of gravel and sand pits
1422	Mining of clays and kaolin
1430	Mining of chemical and fertiliser minerals
1440	Production of salt
1450	Other mining and quarrying

Manufacturing

1500	*Manufacturing of food products and beverages*
1511	Production and preserving of meat
1512	Production and preserving of poultry meat
1513	Production of meat and poultry meat products
1520	Processing and preserving of fish and fish products
1531	Processing and preserving of potatoes
1532	Manufacture of fruit and vegetable juice
1533	Processing and preserving of fruit and vegetables
1541	Manufacture of crude oils and fats
1542	Manufacture of refined oils and fats
1543	Manufacture of margarine and similar edible fats
1551	Operation of dairies and cheese making
1552	Manufacture of ice cream
1561	Manufacture of grain mill products
1562	Manufacture of starches and starch products
1571	Manufacture of prepared feeds for farm animals
1572	Manufacture of prepared pet foods
1581	Manufacture of bread, fresh pastry and cakes
1582	Manufacture of biscuits, preserved pastry and so on
1583	Manufacture of sugar
1584	Manufacture of cocoa, chocolate and sugar confectionery
1585	Manufacture of macaroni and similar farinaceous products
1586	Processing of tea and coffee

1587   Manufacture of condiments and seasonings
1588   Manufacture of homogenised food preparations and dietetic food
1589   Manufacture of other food products
1591   Manufacture of distilled potato alcoholic drinks
1592   Production of ethyl alcohol from fermented materials
1593   Manufacture of wines
1594   Manufacture of cider and other fruit wines
1595   Manufacture of other non-distilled fermented drinks
1596   Manufacture of beer
1597   Manufacture of malt
1598   Production of mineral water and soft drinks

1600   *Manufacture of tobacco products*
1600   Manufacture of tobacco products

1700   *Manufacture of textiles and textile products*
1711   Preparation and spinning of cotton-type fibres
1712   Preparation and spinning of woollen-type products
1713   Preparation and spinning of worsted-type fibres
1714   Preparation and spinning of flax-type fibres
1715   Throwing and preparation of silk and synthetic fibres
1716   Manufacture of sewing threads
1717   Preparation and spinning of other textile fibres
1721   Cotton-type weaving
1722   Woollen-type weaving
1723   Worsted-type weaving
1724   Silk-type weaving
1725   Other textile weaving
1730   Finishing of textiles
1740   Manufacture of made-up textile articles except apparel
1751   Manufacture of carpets and rugs
1752   Manufacture of cordage, rope, twine and netting
1753   Manufacture of nonwovens and articles made from nonwovens
       except apparel
1754   Manufacture of other textiles
1760   Manufacture of knitted and crocheted fabrics
1771   Manufacture of knitted and crocheted hosiery
1772   Manufacture of knitted and crocheted pullovers

1800   *Manufacture of apparel and dyeing of fur*
1810   Manufacture of leather clothes
1821   Manufacture of workwear
1822   Manufacture of other outerwear
1823   Manufacture of underwear

1824 Manufacture of other wearing apparel and accessories
1830 Dressing and dyeing of fur; manufacture of fur articles

1900 *Manufacture of leather and leather products*
1910 Tanning and dressing of leather
1920 Manufacture of luggage, handbags and so on, saddlery
1930 Manufacture of footwear

2000 *Manufacture of wood and of wood products and cork*
2010 Sawmilling, planing and impregnating wood
2020 Manufacture of veneer sheets and plywood
2030 Manufacture of builders' carpentry and joinery
2040 Manufacture of wooden containers
2051 Manufacture of other products of wood
2052 Manufacture of articles of cork, straw and plaiting materials

2100 *Manufacture of pulp, paper and paper products*
2111 Manufacture of pulp
2112 Manufacture of paper and paperboard
2121 Manufacture of corrugated paper, paperboard and products
2122 Manufacture of household and sanitary goods
2123 Manufacture of paper stationery
2124 Manufacture of wallpaper
2125 Manufacture of other articles of paper and paperboard

2200 *Publishing, printing and reproduction*
2211 Publishing of books
2212 Publishing of newspapers
2213 Publishing of journals and periodicals
2214 Publishing of sound recordings
2215 Other publishing
2221 Printing of newspapers
2222 Printing not elsewhere classified
2223 Bookbinding and finishing
2224 Composition and plate making
2225 Other activities related to printing
2231 Reproduction of sound recording
2232 Reproduction of video recording
2233 Reproduction of computer media

2300 *Manufacture of coke, refined petroleum products and nuclear fuels*
2310 Manufacture of coke oven products
2320 Manufacture of refined petroleum products
2330 Processing of nuclear fuel

2400	*Manufacture of chemicals and chemical products*
2411	Manufacture of industrial gases
2412	Manufacture of dyes and pigments
2413	Manufacture of other inorganic basic chemicals
2414	Manufacture of other organic basic chemicals
2415	Manufacture of fertilisers and nitrogen compounds
2416	Manufacture of plastics in primary forms
2417	Manufacture of synthetic rubber in primary forms
2420	Manufacture of pesticides and other agrochemical products
2430	Manufacture of print ink, paints, varnishes and similar coatings
2441	Manufacture of basic pharmaceutical products
2442	Manufacture of pharmaceutical preparations
2451	Manufacture of soap, detergents and polishes
2452	Manufacture of perfumes and toilet preparations
2461	Manufacture of explosives
2462	Manufacture of glues and gelatines
2463	Manufacture of essential oils
2464	Manufacture of photographic chemical material
2465	Manufacture of prepared unrecorded media
2466	Manufacture of other chemical products
2470	Manufacture of man-made fibres
2500	*Manufacture of rubber and plastic products*
2511	Manufacture of rubber tyres and tubes
2512	Retreading and rebuilding rubber tyres
2513	Manufacture of other rubber products
2521	Manufacture of plastic plates, sheets, tubes and profiles
2522	Manufacture of plastic packing goods
2523	Manufacture of builders' ware of plastic
2524	Manufacture of other plastic products
2600	*Manufacture of other non-metallic mineral products*
2611	Manufacture of flat glass
2612	Shaping and processing of flat glass
2613	Manufacture of hollow glass
2614	Manufacture of glass fibres
2615	Manufacture of other glass including technical glassware
2621	Manufacture of ceramic household and ornamental articles
2622	Manufacture of ceramic sanitary fixtures
2623	Manufacture of ceramic insulators and insulating fittings
2624	Manufacture of other technical ceramic products
2625	Manufacture of other ceramic products
2626	Manufacture of refractory ceramic products
2630	Manufacture of ceramic tiles and flags

2640   Manufacture of bricks, tiles and construction products in baked clay
2651   Manufacture of cement
2652   Manufacture of lime
2653   Manufacture of plaster
2661   Manufacture of concrete products for construction purposes
2662   Manufacture of plaster products for construction purposes
2663   Manufacture of ready-mixed concrete
2664   Manufacture of mortars
2665   Manufacture of fibre cement
2666   Manufacture of other articles of concrete, plaster and cement
2670   Cutting, shaping and finishing stone
2681   Production of abrasive products
2682   Manufacture of other non-metallic mineral products

2700   *Manufacture of basic metals*
2710   Manufacture of basic iron and steel and of ferro-alloys
2721   Manufacture of cast iron tubes
2722   Manufacture of steel tubes
2731   Cold drawing
2732   Cold rolling of narrow strips
2733   Cold forming or folding
2734   Wire drawing
2735   Other first processing of iron and steel
2741   Precious metals production
2742   Aluminium production
2743   Lead, zinc and tin production
2744   Copper production
2745   Other non-ferrous metal production
2751   Casting of iron
2752   Casting of steel
2753   Casting of light metals
2754   Casting of other non-ferrous metals

2800   *Manufacture of fabricated metal products, not machines*
2811   Manufacture of metal structures and parts of structures
2812   Manufacture of builders' carpentry and joinery of metal
2821   Manufacture of tanks, reservoirs and containers of metal
2822   Manufacture of central heating radiators and boilers
2830   Manufacture of steam generators except hot water boilers
2840   Forging, pressing, stamping and roll forming metal
2851   Treatment and coating of metals
2852   General mechanical engineering
2861   Manufacture of cutlery
2862   Manufacture of tools

2863 Manufacture of locks and hinges
2871 Manufacture of steel drums and similar containers
2872 Manufacture of light metal packaging
2873 Manufacture of wire products
2874 Manufacture of fasteners, screw, chains, machine products
2875 Manufacture of other fabricated metal products

2900 *Manufacture of machinery and equipment*
2911 Manufacture of engines and turbines, not aircraft
2912 Manufacture of pumps and compressors
2913 Manufacture of taps and valves
2914 Manufacture of bearings, gears, gearing and driving elements
2921 Manufacture of furnaces and furnace burners
2922 Manufacture of lifting and handling equipment
2923 Manufacture of non-domestic cooling and ventilation equipment
2924 Manufacture of other general purpose machinery
2931 Manufacture of agricultural tractors
2932 Manufacture of other agricultural and forestry machinery
2940 Manufacture of machine tools
2951 Manufacture of machinery for metallurgy
2952 Manufacture of machinery for mining, quarrying and construction
2953 Manufacture of machinery for food, beverage and tobacco processing
2954 Manufacture of machinery for textile, apparel and leather production
2955 Manufacture of machinery for paper and paperboard production
2956 Manufacture of other special purpose machinery
2960 Manufacture of weapons and ammunition
2971 Manufacture of electric domestic appliances
2972 Manufacture of non-electric domestic appliances

3000 *Manufacture of office machinery and computers*
3001 Manufacture of office machinery
3002 Manufacture of computers and other information processing equipment

3100 *Manufacture of electrical machinery*
3110 Manufacture of electric motors, generators and transformers
3120 Manufacture of electricity distribution and control apparatus
3130 Manufacture of insulated wire and cable
3140 Manufacture of accumulators, primary cells and primary batteries
3150 Manufacture of lighting equipment and electric lamps
3161 Manufacture of electric equipment for engines and vehicles
3162 Manufacture of other electrical equipment

3200   *Manufacture of radio, television and communications equipment*
3210   Manufacture of electronic valves and tubes
3220   Manufacture of television, radio and telephony transmitters and apparatus
3230   Manufacture of television and radio receivers, sound or video recording equipment

3300   *Manufacture of medical, precision and optical instruments*
3310   Manufacture of medical and surgery equipment
3320   Manufacture of instruments for measuring, checking and testing
3330   Manufacture of industrial process control equipment
3340   Manufacture of optical instruments and photographic equipment
3350   Manufacture of watches and clocks

3400   *Manufacture of motor vehicles and trailers*
3410   Manufacture of motor vehicles
3420   Manufacture of motor vehicle bodies (coachwork)
3430   Manufacture of motor vehicle and engine parts and accessories

3500   *Manufacture of other transport equipment*
3511   Building and repairing of ships
3512   Building and repairing of pleasure and sporting boats
3520   Manufacture of railway locomotives and rolling stock
3530   Manufacture of aircraft and spacecraft
3541   Manufacture of motorcycles
3542   Manufacture of bicycles
3543   Manufacture of invalid carriages
3550   Manufacture of other transport equipment

3600   *Manufacture of furniture and manufacturing not elsewhere specified*
3611   Manufacture of chairs and seats
3612   Manufacture of other office and shop furniture
3613   Manufacture of other kitchen furniture
3614   Manufacture of other furniture
3615   Manufacture of mattresses
3621   Striking of coins and medals
3622   Manufacture of jewellery and related articles
3630   Manufacture of musical instruments
3640   Manufacture of sports goods
3650   Manufacture of games and toys
3661   Manufacture of imitation jewellery
3662   Manufacture of brooms and brushes
3663   Other manufacturing

3700   *Recycling*
3710   Recycling of metal waste and scrap
3720   Recycling of non-metal waste and scrap

Electricity, Gas and Water Supply
4000   *Electricity, gas, steam and hot water supply*
4010   Production and distribution of electricity
4020   Manufacture of gas; distribution of gaseous fuels
4030   Steam and hot water supply

4100   *Collection, purification and distribution of water*
4100   Collection, purification and distribution of water

Construction
4500   *Construction*
4511   Demolition and wrecking of buildings; earth moving
4512   Test drilling and boring
4521   General construction of buildings and civil engineering works
4522   Erection of roof covering and frames
4523   Construction of highways, roads, airfields and sports facilities
4524   Construction of water projects
4525   Other construction work involving special trades
4531   Installation of electrical wiring and fittings
4532   Insulation work activities
4533   Plumbing
4534   Other building installation
4541   Plastering
4542   Joinery installation
4543   Floor and wall covering
4544   Painting and glazing
4545   Other building completion
4550   Renting of construction or demolition equipment with operator

Wholesale, Retail and Certain Repairs
5000   *Sale, maintenance and repair of motor vehicles*
5010   Sale of motor vehicles
5020   Maintenance and repair of motor vehicles
5030   Sale of motor vehicle parts and accessories
5040   Sale, maintenance and repair of motorcycles and parts
5050   Retail sales of automotive fuel

5100   *Wholesale trade except of motor vehicles*
5111   Agents involved in the sale of agricultural and textile raw
         materials
5112   Agents involved in the sale of fuels, ores and metals

5113 Agents involved in the sale of timber and building materials
5114 Agents involved in the sale of machinery, industrial equipment and ships
5115 Agents involved in the sale of furniture and household goods
5116 Agents involved in the sale of textiles, clothing and footwear
5117 Agents involved in the sale of food, drink and tobacco
5118 Agents specialising in the sale of particular products
5119 Agents involved in the sale of a variety of goods
5121 Wholesale of grain, seeds and animal feeds
5122 Wholesale of flowers and plants
5123 Wholesale of live animals
5124 Wholesale of hides, skins and leather
5125 Wholesale of unmanufactured tobacco
5131 Wholesale of fruit and vegetables
5132 Wholesale of meat and meat products
5133 Wholesale of dairy produce, eggs, and edible oils and fats
5134 Wholesale of alcoholic and other drinks
5135 Wholesale of tobacco products
5136 Wholesale of sugar and chocolate and sugar confectionery
5137 Wholesale of coffee, tea, cocoa and spices
5138 Wholesale of other food, including fish
5139 Non-specialised wholesalers of food, drink and tobacco
5141 Wholesale of textiles
5142 Wholesale of clothing and footwear
5143 Wholesale of electrical household appliances
5144 Wholesale of china and glassware
5145 Wholesale of perfume and cosmetics
5146 Wholesale of pharmaceutical goods
5147 Wholesale of other household goods
5151 Wholesale of solid, liquid and gaseous fuels
5152 Wholesale of metal and metal ores
5153 Wholesale of wood, construction materials and sanitary equipment
5154 Wholesale of hardware, plumbing and heating equipment
5155 Wholesale of chemical products
5156 Wholesale of other intermediary products
5157 Wholesale of waste and scrap
5161 Wholesale of machine tools
5162 Wholesale of construction machinery
5163 Wholesale of machinery for the textile industry
5164 Wholesale of office machinery and equipment
5165 Wholesale of other machinery for use in industry and trade
5166 Wholesale of agricultural machines, tractors and accessories
5170 Other wholesale

5200	*Retail trade except of motor vehicles, and certain repairs*
5211	Retail non-specialised stores of food and so on
5212	Other retail non-specialised stores
5221	Retail sale of fruit and vegetables
5222	Retail sale of meat and meat products
5223	Retail sale of fish, crustaceans and so on
5224	Retail sale of bread, cakes and confectionery
5225	Retail sale of alcoholic and other drinks
5226	Retail sale of tobacco products
5227	Other retail sale of specialised foods and so on
5231	Dispensing chemists
5232	Retail sale of medical and orthopaedic goods
5233	Retail sale of cosmetic and toiletry articles
5241	Retail sale of textiles
5242	Retail sale of clothing
5243	Retail sale of footwear and leather goods
5244	Retail sale of furniture household goods
5245	Retail sale of electrical household goods
5246	Retail sale of hardware, paints and glass
5247	Retail sale of books, newspapers and so on
5248	Other retail specialised stores
5250	Retail sale of second hand goods in stores
5261	Retail sale via mail order houses
5262	Retail sale via stalls and markets
5263	Other non-store retail sale
5271	Repair of boots, shoes and leather goods
5272	Repair of electrical household goods
5273	Repair of clocks and jewellery
5274	Repair not elsewhere specified

Hotels and Restaurants

5500	*Hotels and restaurants*
5511	Hotels and motels with restaurants
5512	Hotels and motels without restaurants
5521	Youth hostels and mountain refuges
5522	Camp and caravan sites
5523	Other provision of lodgings
5530	Restaurants
5540	Bars
5551	Canteens
5552	Catering

Transport, Storage and Communications
6000	*Land transport and transport via pipelines*
6010	Transport via railways
6021	Other scheduled passenger land transport
6022	Taxi operation
6023	Other passenger land transport
6024	Freight transport by road
6030	Transport via pipelines
6100	*Water transport*
6110	Sea and coastal water transport
6120	Inland water transport
6200	*Air transport*
6210	Scheduled air transport
6220	Non-scheduled air transport
6230	Space transport
6300	*Supporting and auxiliary transport activities*
6311	Cargo handling
6312	Storage and warehousing
6321	Other supporting land transport activities
6322	Other supporting water transport activities
6323	Other supporting air transport activities
6330	Travel agencies, tourist offices and so on
6340	Activities of other transport agencies
6400	*Post and telecommunications*
6411	National post activities
6412	Courier activities other than national post activities
6420	Telecommunications

Financial Intermediation
6500	*Banking, leasing, credit and financial intermediation not specified elsewhere*
6511	Central banking
6512	Other monetary intermediation
6521	Financial leasing
6522	Other credit granting
6523	Other financial intermediation
6600	*Insurance and pension funding, not compulsory social security*
6601	Life insurance
6602	Pension funding
6603	Non-life insurance

6700   *Activities auxiliary to financial intermediation*
6711   Administration of financial markets
6712   Security broking and fund management
6713   Activities auxiliary to financial intermediation
6720   Activities auxiliary to insurance and pension funding

Real Estate, Renting and Other Business Activities
7000   *Real estate activities*
7011   Development and selling of real estate
7012   Buying and selling of own real estate
7020   Letting of own property
7031   Real estate agencies
7032   Management of real estate on a fee or contract basis

7100   *Renting of machinery and equipment without operator*
7110   Renting of automobiles
7121   Renting of other land transport equipment
7122   Renting of water transport equipment
7123   Renting of air transport equipment
7131   Renting of agricultural machinery and equipment
7132   Renting of civil engineering machinery and equipment
7133   Renting of office machinery and equipment, including computers
7134   Renting of other machinery and equipment
7140   Renting of personal and household goods

7200   *Computer and related activities*
7210   Hardware consultancy
7220   Software consultancy and supply
7230   Data processing
7240   Data base activities
7250   Maintenance and repair of office machinery
7260   Other computer related activities

7300   *Research and development*
7310   Research and development on natural sciences and engineering
7320   Research and development on social sciences and humanities

7400   *Other business activities*
7411   Legal activities
7412   Accounting, book-keeping and auditing activities
7413   Market research and public opinion polling
7414   Business and management consultancy activities
7415   Management activities of holding companies
7420   Architectural, technical and engineering consultancy activities
7430   Technical testing and analysis

7440	Advertising
7450	Labour recruitment and provision of personnel
7460	Investigation and security activities
7470	Industrial cleaning
7481	Photographic activities
7482	Packaging activities
7483	Secretarial and translation services
7484	Other business activities
7499	Non-trading company

Public Administration and Defence

7500	*Public administration and defence*
7511	General (overall) public service activities
7512	Regulation health, education and so on
7513	Regulation more efficient business
7514	Support services for government
7521	Foreign affairs
7522	Defence activities
7523	Justice and judicial activities
7524	Public security, law and order
7525	Fire service activities
7530	Compulsory social security

Education

8000	*Education including driving schools*
8010	Primary education
8021	General secondary education
8022	Technical and vocational secondary education
8030	Higher education
8041	Driving school activities
8042	Adult and other education not specified elsewhere

Health and Social Work

8500	*Health and social work including veterinary activities*
8511	Hospital activities
8512	Medical practice activities
8513	Dental practice activities
8514	Other human health activities
8520	Veterinary activities
8531	Social work with accommodation
8532	Social work without accommodation

Other Social and Personal Services

9000	*Sewage and refuse disposal*
9000	Sewage and refuse disposal, sanitation and similar activities

9100	*Activities of membership organisations*
9111	Activities of business and employers organisations
9112	Activities of professional organisations
9120	Activities of trade unions
9131	Activities of religious organisations
9132	Activities of political organisations
9133	Activities of other membership organisations
9200	*Recreational, cultural and sporting activities*
9211	Motion picture and video production
9212	Motion picture and video distribution
9213	Motion picture projection
9220	Radio and television activities
9231	Artistic and literary creation and interpretation
9232	Operation of arts facilities
9233	Fair and amusement park activities
9234	Other entertainment activities
9240	News agency activities
9251	Library and archive activities
9252	Museum and preservation of history
9253	Botanical, zoos and nature reserves
9261	Operation of sports arenas and stadiums
9262	Other sporting activities
9271	Gambling and betting activities
9272	Other recreational activities not specified elsewhere
9300	*Other service activities*
9301	Washing and dry cleaning of textiles and fur products
9302	Hairdressing and other beauty treatment
9303	Funeral and related activities
9304	Physical well-being activities
9305	Other service activities

Private Households with Employees and Miscellaneous

9500	*Private household with employees*
9500	Private household with employees
9600	*Residents property management*
9600	Residents property management

Extra-Territorial Organisations

9900	*Extra-territorial organisations*
9900	Extra-territorial organisations

United States of America

000   **Agriculture, Forestry and Fishing**
010   *Agricultural production – crops*
011   Cash grains including rice and soya beans
013   Field crops excluding cash grains
016   Vegetables
017   Fruits and tree nuts
018   Horticultural specialists including food crops grown under cover and floriculture
019   General farms, primarily crop

020   *Agricultural production – livestock*
021   Livestock, excluding dairy and poultry
024   Dairy farms
025   Poultry and eggs
027   Animal specialties not specified elsewhere
029   General farms, primarily livestock

070   *Agricultural services*
071   Soil preparation services
072   Crop services
074   Veterinary services
075   Livestock and animal specialty services, excluding veterinary
076   Farm labour and management services
078   Landscape, lawn, garden, ornamental shrub and tree services

080   *Forestry*
081   Timber tracts
082   Forest nurseries and gathering of forest products
084   Gathering of forest products not specified elsewhere
085   Forestry services

090   *Fishing, hunting and trapping*
091   Marine products
092   Fish hatcheries and reserves
097   Hunting, trapping and game propagation

100   **Mining**
100   *Metal mining*
101   Iron ores
102   Copper ores
103   Lead and zinc ores
104   Gold and silver ores
105   Bauxite and other aluminium ores
106   Ferroalloy ores, excluding vanadium

108 Metal mining services
109 Metal ores not specified elsewhere

110 Anthracite mining
111 Anthracite mining and services

120 Bituminous coal and lignite mining
121 Bituminous coal and lignite mining and services

130 Oil and gas extraction
131 Crude petroleum and natural gas
132 Natural gas liquids
138 Oil and gas drilling and field services

140 Mining, quarrying non-metallic minerals, excluding fuels
141 Dimension stone
142 Crushed and broken stone not specified elsewhere
144 Sand and gravel
145 Clay, ceramic and refractory minerals
147 Chemical and fertiliser minerals
148 Non-metallic mineral services excluding fuel
149 Non-metallic minerals, not specified elsewhere

150 Construction
150 Building construction – general contractors
152 Domestic house builders and residential construction – hotels, flats and so on
153 Operative builders
154 Industrial, municipal and service building contractors

160 Construction, excluding buildings, general contractors
161 Street and paving construction
162 Heavy construction and civil engineering

170 Construction – special trade contractors
171 Plumbing, heating and air conditioning
172 Painting and decorating
173 Electrical contracting
174 Masonry, stonework, plastering, marble, tile and mosaic work
175 Carpentry and floorlaying
176 Roofing contractors
177 Concrete work
178 Water well drilling
179 Special trade contractors not specified elsewhere

200 Manufacturing

200 Food and kindred products
201 Production of meat and meat products including poultry and egg processing
202 Dairy products
203 Canned, dried, dehydrated, pickled and frozen fruit and vegetable products; frozen specialities not specified elsewhere
204 Products from grain and rice milling; pet food and animal feeds
205 Bread and bakery products
206 Sugar, chocolate, confectionery and cocoa products
207 Cottonseed, soya bean and vegetable oil mills; animal and marine fats and oils
208 Malt and malt beverages, spirits, soft drinks, carbonated waters and flavourings
209 Food preparations, not specified elsewhere

210 Tobacco products
211 Cigarettes
212 Cigars
213 Tobacco (chewing and smoking) and snuff
214 Tobacco stemming and redrying

220 Textile mill products
221 Broad woven fabric mills, cotton
222 Broad woven fabric mills, man-made fibre, silk
223 Broad woven fabric mills, (including dyeing and finishing)
224 Narrow fabrics: cotton, wool, silk, and man-made fibre
225 Hosiery and knitting mills
226 Finishers of textiles
227 Carpets and rugs
228 Yarn spinning, texturising, throwing, twisting and winding mills; thread mills
229 Textile goods not specified elsewhere including processed waste and recovered fibres and flock; rope twine and net

230 Apparel and other finished fabric product manufacturers
231 Men's and boys' suits, coats and overcoats
232 Men's and boys' clothing not specified elsewhere
233 Women's and girls' outerwear
234 Women's, girls' and babies' underwear and nightwear; corsets and allied garments
235 Millinery, hats and caps
236 Girls' and babies' outerwear
237 Fur goods

238   Apparel and accessories not specified elsewhere
239   House furnishings, textile bags, canvas and related products; pleating, stitching and tucking for the trade; automotive trimmings, apparel findings and related products; fabricated textile products not specified elsewhere

240   *Timber and wood products, excluding furniture*
241   Forestry camps and forestry contractors
242   Sawmills, planing mills and flooring mills; special products sawmills not specified elsewhere
243   Millwork, wood kitchen cabinets, veneers, plywood and structural wood members not specified elsewhere
244   Wood boxes, pallets and containers not specified elsewhere
245   Mobile homes, prefabricated wood buildings and components
249   Wood preserving; particleboard; wood products not specified elsewhere

250   *Furniture and fixtures*
251   Wood and metal household furniture; mattresses and bedsprings; household furniture not specified elsewhere
252   Wood and metal office furniture
253   Public building and related furniture
254   Wood and metal partitions, office and store fixtures
259   Drapery hardware, window blinds and shades; furniture and fittings not specified elsewhere

260   *Paper and allied products*
261   Pulp mills
262   Paper mills
263   Paperboard mills
264   Pulp, paper, paperboard and cardboard products not specified elsewhere
265   Paperboard, corrugated and solid fibre boxes; sanitary food containers and fibre containers
266   Building paper and building board mills

270   *Printing, publishing and allied industries*
271   Newspaper publishing and printing
272   Periodical publishing and printing
273   Book publishing and printing
274   Miscellaneous publishing
275   Commercial printing; engraving and plate printing
276   Continuous and carbonised stationery
277   Greeting cards publishing

278 Pads and loose leaf binders; bookbinding and related works
279 Typesetting, photoengraving, electrotyping and stereotyping; lithographic platemaking and related services

280 *Chemical and allied products*
281 Alkalies, chlorine, industrial gases, inorganic pigments and industrial inorganic chemicals not specified elsewhere
282 Plastic materials, synthetic resins, cellulosic man-made fibres and synthetic organic fibres
283 Biological products, medicinal chemicals, botanical products and pharmaceutical preparations
284 Detergents, speciality cleaners, polishers, surface active and finishing agents, sulphonated oils; perfumes, cosmetics and other toilet preparations
285 Paints, varnishes, lacquers, enamels, and allied products
286 Gum and wood chemicals; cyclic organic crudes, organic dyes and pigments; industrial organic chemicals not specified elsewhere
287 Fertilisers, pesticides and agricultural chemicals not specified elsewhere
289 Chemicals and chemical preparations not specified elsewhere

290 *Petroleum refining and related industries*
291 Petroleum refining
295 Asphalt paving mixtures, blocks, felts and coatings
299 Products of petroleum and coal not specified elsewhere

300 *Rubber and miscellaneous plastic products*
301 Tyres and inner tubes
302 Rubber and plastic footwear
303 Reclaimed rubber
304 Rubber and plastic hose and belting
306 Fabricated rubber products not specified elsewhere
307 Miscellaneous plastic products

310 *Leather and leather product manufacturers*
311 Leather tanning and finishing
313 Leather boot, shoe soles, inner soles
314 Leather footwear, excluding athletic footwear
315 Leather gloves and mittens
316 Leather luggage
317 Personal leather goods
319 Leather goods not specified elsewhere

320 *Stone, clay, glass and concrete products*
321 Flat glass

322   Pressed and blown glass and glassware not specified elsewhere
323   Glass products made of purchased glass
324   Cement, hydraulic
325   Structural clay products and clay refractories
326   Pottery products including vitreous china, earthenware and porcelain
327   Concrete and concrete products; lime and gypsum products
328   Cut stone and stone products
329   Non-clay refractories and non-metallic mineral products not specified elsewhere

330   *Primary metal industries*
331   Blast furnaces, rolling mills, steel and electro-metallurgical products
332   Iron and steel foundries
333   Primary smelting and refining of non-ferrous metals
334   Secondary smelting and refining of non-ferrous metals
335   Rolling, drawing and extruding of non-ferrous metals; drawing and insulating of non-ferrous wire
336   Non-ferrous foundries
339   Metal heat treating and primary metal products not specified elsewhere

340   *Fabricated metal products, excluding machinery and transportation equipment*
341   Metal cans, shipping barrels, drums, kegs and buckets
342   Cutlery and hardware not specified elsewhere
343   Enamelled iron and metal sanitary ware; brass plumbing fixtures, fittings and trim; heating equipment, except electric and warm air furnaces
344   Metal work; fabricated metal work; prefabricated metal buildings and components
345   Screw machine products; bolts, nuts, screws, rivets and washers
346   Metal forgings, stampings, crowns and closures
347   Electroplating, plating, polishing, anodising, colouring, coating, engraving and allied metal services
348   Ammunition, small arms, ordnance and accessories
349   Fabricated metal products not specified elsewhere

350   *Machinery manufacture, excluding electrical machinery*
351   Steam, gas and hydraulic turbines and turbine generator set units; internal combustion engines not specified elsewhere
352   Farm and garden machinery and equipment
353   Other industrial and commercial machinery and equipment

354   Machine tools and accessories; special dies, industrial moulds and jigs; power driven hand tools; metalworking machinery not specified elsewhere

355   Special industrial machinery not specified elsewhere

356   General industrial machinery and equipment not specified elsewhere

357   Office machines including electronic computing equipment

358   Air conditioning, warm air heating, commercial and industrial refrigeration equipment; service industry machines not specified elsewhere

359   Carburettors, pistons, piston rings, valves, non-electrical machinery not specified elsewhere

360   Electrical, electronic machinery, equipment and supplies

361   Power, distribution and speciality transformers, switchgear and switchboard apparatus

362   Electrical industrial apparatus not specified elsewhere

363   Household appliances not specified elsewhere

364   Lighting equipment and fixtures

365   Radio and television receivers (excluding communication types); pre-recorded records and magnetic tapes

366   Telephone and telegraphic apparatus; radio and television transmitting, signalling and detection equipment and apparatus

367   Radio and television (receiving types) electronic tubes; electronic components not specified elsewhere

369   Batteries, electrical machinery, equipment and supplies not specified elsewhere

370   Transportation equipment manufacture

371   Road transport bodies, parts and accessories; truck trailers

372   Aircraft and aircraft engines, parts and auxiliary equipment not specified elsewhere

373   Ship and boat building and repairing

374   Railway equipment

375   Motorcycles, bicycles, and parts

376   Guided missile and space vehicles, propulsion units, parts and auxiliary equipment not specified elsewhere

379   Transportation equipment not specified elsewhere

380   Measuring, photographic, medical instruments, watches and clocks

381   Engineering, laboratory, scientific and research instruments and associated equipment

382   Measuring and controlling devices

383   Optical instruments and lenses

384	Surgical, medical and dental equipment, appliances and supplies
385	Ophthalmic goods
386	Photographic equipment and supplies
387	Watches, clocks, clockwork operated devices and parts

390	*Miscellaneous manufacturing industries*
391	Jewellery and precious metal products
393	Musical instruments
394	Dolls, children's games and toys (excluding cycles); sporting and athletic goods not specified elsewhere
395	Pens, pencils, crayons, artists' materials, marking devices, carbon paper and inked ribbons
396	Costume jewellery and novelties (excluding precious metals); feathers, plumes, artificial trees and flowers; buttons and sewing notions
399	Manufacturing industries not specified elsewhere

400	**Transportation and Communications**
400	*Railway transportation*
401	Railways; switching and terminal establishments
404	Railway express service

410	*Local public transport and intercity buses*
411	Local and suburban passenger transportation not specified elsewhere
412	Taxicabs
413	Intercity and rural road passenger transportation
414	Passenger transportation charter service
415	School buses
417	Bus terminal operations; maintenance facilities for motor vehicle passenger transportation

420	*Road freight transportation and warehousing*
421	Road haulage and local storage
422	Warehousing and storage
423	Freight trucking terminal operation

430	*Postal services*
431	Postal service

440	*Transportation by water*
441	Deep sea foreign transportation
442	Transportation to and between non-contiguous territories; coastal and domestic transportation
444	Inland water transport

445 Ferries, lighterage, towing and tugboat services; local water
     transportation services not specified elsewhere
446 Marine cargo handling; canal operation; water transportation
     services not specified elsewhere

450 *Air transport*
451 Air transportation, certified carriers
452 Air transportation, non-certified carriers
458 Airports, airfields and terminal services

460 *Pipe lines, excluding natural gas*
461 Petroleum pipe lines; pipe lines not specified elsewhere

470 *Transportation services*
471 Freight forwarding
472 Arrangement of passenger, freight and cargo transportation
474 Rental of railway carriages
478 Services incidental to transportation not specified elsewhere

480 *Communication*
481 Telephone communication (wire or radio)
482 Telegraph communication (wire or radio)
483 Radio and television broadcasting
489 Communication services not specified elsewhere

490 *Electrical, gas and sanitary services*
491 Electric companies and systems
492 Natural gas transmission and distribution; mixed, manufactured
     or liquified gas production and distribution
493 Combined utilities
494 Water supply
495 Sewerage, refuse and other sanitary services
496 Steam supply
497 Irrigation systems

500 **Wholesale**
500 *Wholesale trade – durable goods*
501 Motor vehicles; automotive parts and supplies
502 Furniture and home furnishings
503 Construction materials
504 Sports, recreational, toys, hobby goods and supplies;
     photographic equipment and supplies
505 Metal service centres and offices; coal and other minerals and ores
506 Electrical apparatus, appliances and equipment, wiring supplies
     and construction material; electronic parts and equipment

507   Hardware; equipment and supplies for plumbing, heating air conditioning and refrigeration
508   Machines and equipment – commercial, construction, mining, farm, garden, industrial; equipment and supplies – industrial, professional, service establishment, transportation (except motor vehicles)
509   Scrap and waste materials; jewellery, watches, diamonds and other precious stones; durable goods not specified elsewhere

510   *Wholesale trade – non-durable goods*
511   Paper and other stationery supplies
512   Drugs, drug proprietaries and pharmaceutical sundries
513   Piece goods, notions, footwear, clothing and accessories
514   Groceries, meat, dairy, poultry products, fish and seafoods; confectionery
515   Cotton, grain, livestock; farm-product raw materials not specified elsewhere
516   Chemicals and allied products
517   Petroleum and petroleum products
518   Beer, ale, wine and distilled alcoholic beverages
519   Non-durable goods not specified elsewhere

520   **Retail**
520   *Building materials, garden supply, mobile home dealers*
521   Timber and other building materials dealers
523   Paint, glass and wallpaper shops
525   Hardware shops
526   Retail nurseries, lawn and garden supply shops
527   Mobile home dealers

530   *General merchandise retailers*
531   Department stores
533   Cash and carry stores
539   Miscellaneous general merchandise shops

540   *Food retailers*
541   Grocers
542   Frozen meat stores; meat, fish and seafood markets
543   Fruit and vegetable shops and markets
544   Nut and sugar confectionery shops
545   Dairy products shops
546   Retail bakeries, baking and/or selling
549   Miscellaneous food shops

550 *Motor vehicle dealers and petrol stations*
551 Motor vehicle dealers (new and used)
552 Motor vehicle dealers (used only)
553 Auto and home supply shops
554 Petrol service stations
555 Boat dealers
556 Recreational, utility trailer and caravan dealer
557 Motorcycle dealers
559 Automotive dealers not specified elsewhere

560 *Clothing and accessory retailers*
561 Men's and boys' clothing and furnishings shops
562 Women's ready-to-wear shops
563 Women's accessory and speciality shops
564 Children's and babies' wear shops
565 Family clothing shops
566 Shoe shops
568 Furriers and fur shops
569 Miscellaneous apparel and accessory shops

570 *Furniture, home furnishings and equipment retailers*
571 Furniture, floor covering and home furnishing shops
572 Household appliance shops
573 Radio, television and music shops

580 *Eating and drinking places*
581 Eating and drinking places (alcoholic beverages)

590 *Miscellaneous retail trade*
591 Pharmacies and proprietary shops
592 Off-licences
593 Used merchandise shops
594 Specialty retail shops not specified elsewhere
596 Mail order houses; automatic merchandising machine operators;
    direct selling establishments
598 Fuel, fuel oil, liquified petroleum gas (bottled gas) and ice dealers
599 Florists, tobacconists, newsagents and news stands; miscellaneous
    retail shops not specified elsewhere

600 Finance, Insurance and Real Estate
600 Banking
601 Banks, discount houses and licensed deposit takers
602 State banks and national banks
605 Foreign exchange establishments, foreign banks; savings banks

610	*Credit agencies other than banks*
611	Financial institutions
615	Short-term and miscellaneous business credit institutions
616	Mortgage bankers, loan correspondents and loan brokers
620	*Security, commodity brokers, dealers, exchanges and allied services*
621	Stock brokers, dealers and flotation companies
622	Commodity contracts brokers and dealers
623	Security and commodity exchanges
628	Services allied with the exchange of securities or commodities
630	*Insurance*
631	Life insurance
632	Accident and health insurance; hospital and medical service plans
633	Fire, marine and casualty insurance
635	Surety companies
636	Title insurance
637	Pension, health and welfare funds
639	Insurance carriers not specified elsewhere
640	*Insurance agents, brokers and service*
641	Insurance agents, brokers and service
650	*Real estate*
651	Operators of non-residential buildings, dwellings and residential mobile home sites; lessors of railway property and real property not specified elsewhere
653	Property agents, brokers and managers
654	House and estate agents
655	Real estate (including cemetery) subdividers and developers
660	*Combination of real estate, insurance, loans, law offices*
661	Combination of real estate, insurance, loans, law offices
670	*Holding and other investment offices*
671	Holding companies
672	Management investment companies, unit investment trusts, face-amount certificate companies
673	Trusts
679	Oil royalty companies; commodity trading companies; patent owners and lessors; investors not specified elsewhere
700	**Services**
700	*Hotels, guest houses, camps and other lodgings*
701	Hotels, motels and tourist courts
702	Guest houses and boarding houses

703 Sporting and recreational camps; trailer parks, camp and caravan sites

704 Organisation hotels and lodging houses on membership basis

720 *Personal services*
721 Laundry, dry cleaning and garment services
722 Photographic studios, portrait
723 Beauty shops
724 Hairdressers
725 Shoe repair shops
726 Funeral service and crematoria
729 Miscellaneous personal services

730 *Business services*
731 Advertising and advertising representatives
732 Consumer credit reporting agencies, and adjustment and collection agencies
733 Direct mail; reproduction and stenographic services; commercial photography, art and graphics
734 Window and building cleaning; disinfecting, exterminating and maintenance services
735 News syndicates
736 Personnel supply services
737 Computer software services; data processing services; computer related services not specified elsewhere
739 Research and development, and commercial testing laboratories; detective agencies and protective services; business services not specified elsewhere

750 *Automotive repair, services and garages*
751 Car, truck, utility trailer and recreational vehicle rental; car and truck leasing
752 Car parks
753 Automotive repair and paint shops
754 Car washes and automotive services, except repair

760 *Miscellaneous repair services*
762 Electrical and electronic repair and service shops
763 Watch, clock and jewellery repair
764 Reupholstery and furniture repair
769 Repair shops and related services not specified elsewhere

780 *Motion pictures*
781 Motion picture and tape production, and allied services

782   Motion picture film and tape distribution, and allied services
783   Cinemas and theatres

790   Amusement and recreation services, excluding cinemas
791   Dance halls, studios and schools
792   Theatrical producers and miscellaneous theatrical services; bands, orchestras, actors and other entertainers
793   Billiard and pool establishments; bowling alleys
794   Professional sports clubs and promoters; racing and track operation
799   Amusement and recreational services and clubs not specified elsewhere

800   Health services
801   Doctors
802   Dentists
803   Osteopaths
804   Chiropodists, opticians and health practitioners not specified elsewhere
805   Nursing and personal care facilities not specified elsewhere
806   Hospitals
807   Medical and dental laboratories
808   Outpatient care facilities
809   Health and allied services not specified elsewhere

810   Legal services
811   Legal services

820   Educational services
821   Elementary and secondary schools
822   Colleges, universities, professional schools, junior colleges and technical institutes
823   Libraries and information centres
824   Correspondence and vocational schools (except vocational high schools) not specified elsewhere
829   Schools and educational services not specified elsewhere

830   Social services
832   Individual and family social services
833   Job training and vocational rehabilitation services
835   Child day care services
836   Residential care
839   Social services, not specified elsewhere

840	*Museums, art galleries, botanical and zoological gardens*
841	Museums and art galleries
842	Arboreta, botanical, and zoological gardens
860	*Membership organisations*
861	Business associations
862	Professional membership organisations
863	Trade unions and similar trade organisations
864	Civic, social and fraternal associations
865	Political organisations
866	Religious organisations
869	Non-profit membership organisations not specified elsewhere
880	*Private households*
881	Private households
890	*Miscellaneous services*
891	Engineering, architectural and surveying services
892	Non-commercial educational, scientific and research organisations
893	Accounting, auditing and book-keeping services
899	Services, not specified elsewhere
910	**Public Administration**
910	*Executive, legislative, general government, excluding finance*
911	Executive offices
912	Legislative bodies
920	*Justice, public order and safety*
921	Courts
922	Police, enforcement, correctional institutions and fire protection
930	*Public finance, taxation, and monetary policy*
931	Public finance, taxation, and monetary policy
950	*Administration of environmental quality and housing programmes*
951	Air, water resource and solid waste management
970	*National security and international affairs*
971	National security
972	International affairs
990	*Unclassified establishments*
999	Unclassified establishments

Appendix III: Postcode Areas of Great Britain

Source: Royal Mail

AB	Aberdeen	DY	Dudley, West Midlands
AL	St Albans, Hertfordshire	E	London E
B	Birmingham	EC	London EC
BA	Bath	EH	Edinburgh
BB	Blackburn	EN	Enfield, Middlesex
BD	Bradford, West Yorkshire	EX	Exeter
BH	Bournemouth	FK	Falkirk
BL	Bolton	FY	Blackpool
BN	Brighton	G	Glasgow
BR	Bromley	GL	Gloucester
BS	Bristol	GU	Guildford, Surrey
BT	Belfast	GY	Guernsey, Channel Islands
CA	Carlisle	HA	Harrow
CB	Cambridge	HD	Huddersfield
CF	Cardiff	HG	Harrogate, North Yorkshire
CH	Chester	HP	Hemel Hempstead, Herts.
CM	Chelmsford	HR	Hereford
CO	Colchester	HS	Hebrides
CR	Croydon	HU	Hull
CT	Canterbury, Kent	HX	Halifax, West Yorkshire
CV	Coventry	IG	Ilford, Essex
CW	Crewe	IM	Isle of Man
DA	Dartford	IP	Ipswich
DD	Dundee	IV	Inverness
DE	Derby	JE	Jersey, Channel Islands
DG	Dumfries	KA	Kilmarnock, Ayrshire
DH	Durham	KT	Kingston-upon-Thames, Surrey
DL	Darlington		
DN	Doncaster, South Yorkshire	KW	Kirkwall, Orkney
DT	Dorchester, Dorset	KY	Kirkcaldy, Fife

L	Liverpool	SO	Southampton
LA	Lancaster	SP	Salisbury
LD	Llandrindod Wells, Powys	SR	Sunderland
LE	Leicester	SS	Southend-on-Sea
LL	Llandudno, Gwynedd	ST	Stoke-on-Trent
LN	Lincoln	SW	London SW
LS	Leeds	SY	Shrewsbury
LU	Luton	TA	Taunton
M	Manchester	TD	Galashiels, Selkirkshire
ME	Medway	TF	Telford, Shropshire
MK	Milton Keynes	TN	Tonbridge, Kent
ML	Motherwell, Lanarkshire	TQ	Torquay
N	London N	TR	Truro, Cornwall
NE	Newcastle-upon-Tyne	TS	Cleveland
NG	Nottingham	TW	Twickenham
NN	Northampton	UB	Southall, Middlesex
NP	Newport, Gwent	W	London W
NR	Norwich	WA	Warrington
NW	London NW	WC	London WC
OL	Oldham	WD	Watford
OX	Oxford	WF	Wakefield, West Yorkshire
PA	Paisley, Renfrewshire	WN	Wigan, Lancashire
PE	Peterborough	WR	Worcester
PH	Perth	WS	Walsall
PL	Plymouth	WV	Wolverhampton
PO	Portsmouth	YO	York
PR	Preston	ZE	Lerwick, Shetland
RG	Reading		
RH	Redhill		
RM	Romford		
S	Sheffield		
SA	Swansea		
SE	London SE		
SG	Stevenage, Hertfordshire		
SK	Stockport, Cheshire		
SL	Slough		
SM	Sutton, Surrey		
SN	Swindon		

There are 124 postcode areas.

Index